Kings and Queens
of
Early Britain

Tribal migrations leading to the dismemberment of Roman Britain.

Faeroe Is

Shetland Is

Orkney Is

Hebrides

Picts

ARGYLL

Votadini

Scotti

Isle of Man

LLEYN

Deisi and Ui Liathain

Scilly Is

ARMORICA (BRITTANY)

Jutes, Angles, and Saxons

N

0   100 m/s
0   160 kms

·—·▷ Jutes
□—□▷ Southern British
○○○○▷ Votadini
+++++▷ Picts
▪▪▪▪▷ Angles and Saxons
━━▶ Irish tribes

Kings and Queens
of
Early Britain

GEOFFREY ASHE

Academy Chicago Publishers

Published in 1990, 1998 by
Academy Chicago Publishers
363 West Erie Street
Chicago, Illinois 60610

Printed and bound in the U.S.A.

Maps by Julia Anderson-Miller

Library of Congress Cataloging-in-Publication data

Ashe, Geoffrey
    Kings and Queens of early Britain / Geoffrey Ashe.
        p.   cm.
    Originally published: London: Methuen, 1982.
    Contents: Includes bibliographical references.
    ISBN 0-89733-347-0 (cloth)
    ISBN 0-89733-469-8
    1. Great Britain—Kings and rulers. 2. Great Britain—
History—To 1066. 3. Anglo-Saxons—Kings and rulers.
4. Britons—Kings and rulers. I. Title.
DA28.1.A84   1990
942.01'092'2—dc20   90-32536
                                                          CIP

Contents

ILLUSTRATIONS

Following page 102:

1. Stonehenge from an early 20th-century photograph
2. Bronze Age barrow, Norfolk
3. Stone barrow at Stoney Littleton, Somerset
4. Neolithic spear-head
5. Bronze Age burial urn
6. Statue of Boudicca
7. Bust of Emperor Hadrian
8. Hadrian's Wall
9. Stone relief of the *Cucullati*
10. Two drawings of Roman pottery
11. Galla Placidia, 'Regent of the West'
12. Roman boat remains
13. Mosaic of Europa and the Bull
14. Roman pavement, Somerset
15. Runic Stone with ogam alphabet

Following page 188:

16. Tomb of the Venerable Bede
17. Bede's *Ecclesiastical History of the English People*
18. Coins from British history
19. Early Christian drinking glass
20. Anglo-Saxon wood lyre
21. Anglo-Saxon bronze bucket
22. Anglo-Saxon bronze bowl
23. St Patrick's Bell
24. St Cuthbert's Cross
25. St Cuthbert's Coffin
26. St Laurence Church, Bradford-on-Avon
27. Restenneth Priory, Angus, Scotland
28. 'Anglo-Saxon king' from an early psalter
29. Old English huntsman
30. 9th-century gold ring
31. The Alfred Jewel
32. Statue of King Alfred

Preface and Acknowledgements

THIS BOOK IS EXACTLY WHAT ITS TITLE IMPLIES. It is not a social or economic history, and does not aspire to be. It is about individuals who ruled in Britain, or are said to have done so, from the time of the earliest legendary names (Brutus the Trojan and King Lear, for instance) to the time of Alfred the Great in the ninth century A.D. The words 'king' and 'queen' must be understood in a broad sense. Not all these rulers had the precise royal title, or a hereditary claim, or even legitimate power. But all held sovereignty of some sort, in fact or fiction or the borderland that lies between.

A word about selection. In the centuries when Britain was divided into small kingdoms, it would be wearisome to list every known sovereign in every fraction of the island. I have chosen those who seem to me to emerge, however dimly, as personalities, or to have done things of importance. The resultant allocation of space may not always please. It may be felt, for instance, that there is too little about Scotland. The reason is not that I undervalue Scotland. The reason — a regretted one — is that Scotland's earliest history furnishes few rulers about whom it is possible to say very much. When clear-cut characters do begin to come forward, they have their place in the story.

Geographical terms, I am afraid, are sometimes anachronistic. Thus, the only simple way of defining parts of England in Roman times is by county names which did not come into use till long afterwards. There are problems with personal names as well, because the spellings vary, and with dates, because authorities often disagree by a year or two even in periods when the records look accurate. Here I can only make a choice, with a general warning that such hazards exist.

I shall not apologize for the attention given to legends. Quite apart from their own interest, they are a reflex and a reminder of the state of Britain throughout the period. Today we are accustomed to a country with a large population, densely packed together, documented in countless files and data-banks; a country of mass-media, detailed records, habitual travel and intercommunication. But in the whole stretch of time from misty antiquity to Alfred, Britain never had as much as a tenth of its present population. That alone, even apart from all additional factors, gives its society a profound 'otherness'. Communities clustered differently in different periods, but always there were wide seldom-traversed spaces, always there were separations by dialect and by forest and swamp and wilderness. Few went far from home except minorities engaged in war, trade or other special business. And only a small percentage of the small population could read or write.

Even the rule of Rome did not fundamentally change this state of affairs. It did foster a sense of British unity, but after its withdrawal the recording of information continued to be meagre and its transfer over distances uncertain and sketchy. Where hard knowledge was mainly local, the art of the poets and story-tellers was a major factor in any more-than-local consciousness. They reflected the nature of the British world and, in a sense, created and re-created it. They passed on some authentic facts; but they also passed on legends. With those inhabitants of the island whose forbears had been there longest, some of the legends reached back for many centuries. Furthermore, the corpus continued to develop, inspiring extraordinary new growths even hundreds of years later. Early Britain is not only a reality but a retrospective work of art. Many of the rulers presented to us are creatures of the imagination, partly or even wholly.

This is outstandingly true of a phase for which the legend-making rose to rare heights, the 'Arthurian' age. Here a special note is required. I have written on this topic before, and now believe that I hit on the key to the mystery a long while ago and put it in *From Caesar to Arthur* (1960), without grasping its significance. A belated pursuit of my own suggestion has led me to revise my ideas. Passages in chapters 6 and 7 of the present book contain matter which will not be found in standard works in this field, or my own previous writings. The argument was published first in *Speculum*, the journal of the Medieval Academy of America (April 1981, pages 301-323). That article substantiates various statements made here, and includes a number of points which are omitted, though, on the other hand, I also develop a few points made only briefly in the article.

I have presented the main case in a lecture at Keele University, and in a paper read at the Thirteenth International Arthurian Congress, held at the University of Glasgow in August 1981. All comments made to me by professional scholars have been taken into account. I would like to thank Professor A. O. H. Jarman and Professor Léon Fleuriot for help and advice, while making it clear that they are not to be held responsible for the proposed reinterpretation of Arthurian origins.

The translation of Geoffrey of Monmouth's *The History of the Kings of Britain* (Penguin) is by Lewis Thorpe; the translation of Bede's *A History of the English Church and People* (Penguin), by Leo Sherley-Price; the translation from Nennius's *History of the Britons*, by Leslie Alcock; the translation of *Gododdin*, from *A Celtic Miscellany* (Routledge, and Penguin, paperback), by Kenneth Jackson; and the translations of a Welsh poem and from Alcuin, both from *The Age of Arthur* (Weidenfeld and Nicolson), by John Morris.

NOTE TO THE 1990 EDITION:

Since this book was first published in Britain in 1982, archaeologists have become less inclined to interpret Britain's prehistory in terms of clear-cut invasions (cf. pages 20-21). The picture is not radically changed but it may have become less clear than is presented here.

On the other hand, what I suggest about the origin of the Arthurian legend has been more widely aired since 1982 and presented in books, articles and academic courses in which it has found corroboration by other scholars. Professor Barbara Moorman has supported this theory with valuable data from medieval chronicles, revealing a neglected Arthur tradition in close agreement with it. And this wider acceptance has led to its inclusion in the standard reference book on this subject, *The Arthurian Encyclopedia*, edited by Norris J. Lacy. As far as I know, no effective criticisms have been offered.

CHAPTER ONE

Kings and Queens of Legend

1

IN 55 B.C., JULIUS CAESAR CROSSED THE CHANNEL. In the thousand years or so before that, seventy-six monarchs are reputed to have reigned over Britain. We know the names of most of them. They are all imaginary.

Britain owes her pre-Roman dynasties to a book which was widely supposed, through the Middle Ages and after, to be true. Even in modern times it still has the power to influence historical writing, however often historians may say otherwise. As for its impact on literature, that can never be undone. Malory's story of King Arthur has its ancestry in this book. Spenser wove a summary of it into *The Faerie Queene*. Shakespeare, directly or indirectly, took the plot of *King Lear* from it. Milton planned to base an epic on it, before he embarked on *Paradise Lost* instead.

It is called *The History of the Kings of Britain*. Out of scanty materials it created a complete legendary scheme for the island's past. Its author was Geoffrey of Monmouth. He was a cleric, probably a Welshman, perhaps a Breton born in Wales. His date of birth is unknown, but from 1129 to 1151 he was living in Oxford and seemingly teaching there. He died in 1155. When still fairly young he had begun collecting, and embellishing, ancient British traditions. Over the years he wrote much about Merlin, the prophet and enchanter. Some of the Merlin matter went into his masterpiece on the British kings, and helped to give it its fascination.

He finished it in 1136 or thereabouts, writing in Latin, then the international medium of scholarship. It is a work of genius, and a puzzle. In the preface he asserts that he translated it from 'a certain very ancient book written in the British language' which was given him by Walter, Archdeacon of Oxford. Walter existed, and his signature appears with Geoffrey's on one or two docu-

11

ments. The question is whether the book existed. The 'British language' could mean Welsh or Breton, but there is no trace of any work in either which could have been Geoffrey's original. He shows himself to be a person of wide reading. He certainly draws on passages in earlier authors, such as a Welsh monk at Bangor named Nennius, who, early in the ninth century, compiled a *History of the Britons* (in Latin, not Welsh) containing a little history and a great deal of legend. There are indications also that Geoffrey used a Breton history which has been lost sight of. However, this can hardly have covered all the ground he covers himself. The main credit for the immense imposture — if 'credit' is the right word — is never likely to be taken away from him.

Nor does he confine himself to royal phantoms in an undocumented epoch B.C. After the seventy-sixth of them he has to face the reality of Caesar. But he plunges boldly on into centuries where he can be checked. The intertwining of his imagination with history has bizarre results. These too belong to the story of British kingship, because they help to show how even rulers who did exist could take on legendary aspects, and pass into poetry and romance. Geoffrey of Monmouth is an entertaining and memorable companion, so long as one never believes anything he says. His fictitious Ancient Britain claims our attention first, and even after it fades away we shall not be parting company with him — not altogether. At the outset he must be allowed to hold the stage almost alone.

2

Britain (Geoffrey informs us) is named after its first king, Brutus, who was a great-grandson of the Trojan prince Aeneas. Surprisingly perhaps, while almost everything he says about Brutus is his own invention, the bare original notion is not. It is found with a few family details in the earlier book by Nennius. The inspiration behind it is patriotic, a wish to give the Britons a pedigree linking them with aristocratic antiquity. In Homer's *Iliad*, the god Poseidon foretells that Aeneas will save the royal house of Troy from extinction after the city falls. The Romans took up that prophecy. They claimed that Aeneas had sailed to Italy with a party of Trojan refugees, that their own early kings were his descendants, and that the basic Roman stock was Trojan. Virgil turned the belief into poetry in his national epic the *Aeneid*, interweaving it with ideas about divine providence in the genesis of Rome and the glories of the Empire.

The Welsh fable of Brutus the Trojan, built up by Geoffrey into a full-blown pseudo-history, becomes in his hands a postscript to Virgil. He makes out that the ancient Britons shared in an august destiny and had a cousinly relationship to the Romans themselves. By 'Britons' he means the ancestors of the Welsh, not those of the English who came later; one purpose of his book is to exalt the forbears of his own fellow-countrymen. In Virgil's epic, Aeneas has a son named Ascanius who settles in Italy with the rest of the Trojan party. Geoffrey takes the line a step further, to Ascanius's son Silvius.

When Silvius's wife was pregnant, he says, soothsayers foretold that the child would be a boy who would cause the deaths of both his parents, wander in exile, but finally rise to high honour. This was Brutus. His mother died giving birth to him, and when he grew up, he accidentally shot Silvius with an arrow while hunting. Driven to leave home, he went to Greece and discovered that the Greek king, Pandrasus, had several thousand slaves descended from Trojans carried off when the Greeks captured Troy. He organized a revolt and took Pandrasus prisoner. The king agreed to let Brutus marry his daughter Ignoge and lead the Trojans away to a land of their own.

After sailing for two days the expedition put ashore on an island. It was deserted, but had once been inhabited, and had a temple of Diana. Brutus prayed to her to tell him where the migrants should go. He lay down to sleep in front of her altar, and she appeared to him in a dream and spoke:

> 'Brutus, beyond the setting of the sun, past the realms of Gaul, there lies an island in the sea, once occupied by giants. Now it is empty and ready for your folk. Down the years this will prove an abode suited to you and to your people; and for your descendants it will be a second Troy. A race of kings will be born there from your stock and the round circle of the whole earth will be subject to them.'

Greatly heartened, they sailed on. In the neighborhood of

Gibraltar they picked up more Trojans, whose leader was Corineus. Having spent some time in Gaul, where they founded the city of Tours, they disembarked in the promised land at Totnes. (For some reason Geoffrey is much interested in Totnes. In the course of the *History* a whole series of people land there.)

Britain was then called Albion. Brutus re-named it after himself, and called his companions Britons. Corineus was allotted the south-west promontory for his domain, and called it Cornwall. Diana had not been quite accurate about the giants. They were still some way from total extinction, and the number surviving in Cornwall was appreciable. The Britons suffered heavily when giants attacked their base at Totnes. At last they killed all the marauding band but one, Gogmagog, whom Corineus wrestled and threw over a cliff.

Brutus then explored the whole country looking for the best site for a capital. He founded a city beside the Thames and named it Troia Nova, New Troy. In later ages this was corrupted into 'Trinovantum'. Thus Geoffrey accounts for the Trinovantes, whom Caesar mentions as living in the Essex area. Brutus's capital was completed when Eli was judge in Israel, that is, between 1100 and 1050 B.C. He died after reigning over his fast-multiplying immigrants for twenty-three years, and was buried within the walls of his new city. It was to be re-named London, but that development was far off.

Having disposed of Brutus, Geoffrey goes on to the rest of his pre-Roman sovereigns. Some of them he dwells on, some he passes over at breakneck speed. His scheme is plainly artificial, since direct unbroken succession from father to son — or at any rate, succession within a single family line — goes on too long to be plausible. Yet although he is making it up to suit himself, the average length of reign works out at less than fourteen years, so he has no need for such a large cast of characters. Furthermore he adds princes and princesses, some of whom have no part to play at all.

The reason for this overcrowding is known, and it sheds light on his methods and the way Britain's legendary history grew. Many of his royal names are taken from a collection of old Welsh genealogies. The persons listed in these belong not to the distant past but to the sixth century A.D. and later. In copying the names Geoffrey disguises them, often turning them from Welsh into a sort of Latin, but his guiding principle is simply to work plenty of them in: rather — it has been remarked — as if he were using a page torn from a directory.

He also has characters who are pure fiction. He invents a few as explanations, on the same lines as Corineus the founder of Cornwall. A prince called Kamber, for instance, is made to account for 'Kambria' or Cambria, i.e. Wales. Others come from myths and folk-tales. One name, Brennius, is slightly altered from that of a real person, but he was not a king of Britain.

Given a clear understanding that these early monarchs are creatures of fancy, it is still worth seeing what Geoffrey makes of some of them. The next after Brutus is his son Locrinus. Locrinus's successor is his widow Gwendolen. When her son Maddan is grown up, she hands over to him, retaining Cornwall for herself for the rest of her life. Then for several generations the crown of Britain passes from father to son. After Maddan the next six kings are Mempricius, Ebraucus (who has twenty sons and thirty daughters, all listed), a second Brutus nicknamed Greenshield, Leil, Rud Hud Hudibras, and Bladud, the last of these being contemporary with the prophet Elijah. Bladud, we are told, founded Bath, and it was he and not the Romans who built the baths there, with Minerva as tutelary goddess. He also experimented with magic, and made himself a pair of wings with which he flew over Trinovantum. However, he fell on the temple of Apollo and was 'dashed into countless fragments'. Bladud is one of the kings in Geoffrey's *History* who have passed into legend outside it. The story at Bath is that he discovered its virtues as a spa through being cured of leprosy by the hot spring-water and impregnated mud.

Bladud's son Leir is the Lear of Shakespeare. If one were to ask 'What relation was King Lear to Aeneas?' it would sound like a nonsense question, but the *History* answers it: he was Aeneas's great-great-great-great-great-great-great-great-great-great-grandson. Geoffrey says he founded Leicester. His reign lasted sixty years, longer than any other for which a duration is given. Leir had no son, but he had three daughters, Gonorilla, Regan and Cordeilla. He was very fond of all three, but especially of Cordeilla, the youngest. When he felt old age coming on he resolved to divide his kingdom among them, and marry them to husbands who could help with the government. To decide which should have the largest share, he tried to find out which loved him most. Gonorilla and Regan made extravagant protestations. Cordeilla, who wanted to test her father just as he was testing her, replied less flatteringly. She loved him with all the love due from a daughter to a father, but no more. To make matters worse she told him that his value in others' eyes depended, in practice, on his possessions. Leir was furious and refused to give her a share in the kingdom. Gonorilla married the Duke of Albany (an old name for Scotland which Geoffrey uses). Regan married the Duke of Cornwall. Cordeilla married Aganippus, king of the Franks, who was willing to take her without a dowry. She went away to live in Gaul.

For a time Leir kept part of Britain as a domain of his own and divided the residue between Gonorilla and Regan, but when he was too old to resist, their husbands forced him to relinquish his share to them. The Duke of Albany, however, agreed to maintain him in his own ducal household, with a hundred and forty knights as his personal attendants. This arrangement lasted for two years. Then Gonorilla said it must end. The attendants wanted too much, and quarrelled with her own servants. Thirty would be enough, the rest could consider themselves dismissed. Leir went off in a rage to Regan, and her husband accepted him with his thirty attendants. In less than a year Regan complained to her father as her sister had done, and wanted his retinue reduced to five. He went back to Gonorilla hoping that she would allow him thirty, but now she told him that as an old man with no possessions he had no right to a train of followers, and she would not have him in the house unless he sent all of them away but one.

Leir had to accept her terms, but the misery of living with her in such an atmosphere was too much for him. He set off for Gaul hoping to make his peace with Cordeilla. On the ship he found that he was not given the place of honour, and realized the truth of his youngest daughter's saying — that he was valued and loved according to his possessions. She received him kindly, allotted forty knights to his service, and conducted him to her husband. Aganippus raised an army to support Leir. Father and daughter returned to Britain and defeated both sons-in-law. Leir, restored, reigned for three years and died. Aganippus died also, and Cordeilla stayed in Britain ruling in her own right. She buried her father in a vault under the River Soar below Leicester. After she had reigned peaceably for five years, her sisters' sons rose against her and captured her. She took her own life in prison.

There was an Elizabethan *Leir* play before Shakespeare's. Tolstoy thought it was better, but that remains a minority view. The differences in Shakespeare's version hardly need pointing out, but one fact is not so obvious — that an adapted happy-ending *King Lear* by Nahum Tate, which long excluded the genuine article from performance, is closer to the original. As far as the king is concerned, Geoffrey's story does have a happy ending. The death of the youngest daughter, though caused indirectly by the family split, is a separate tragedy happening long afterwards. No pre-Geoffrey version is known. One would suspect a folk-tale which he heard somewhere. Not necessarily a British folk-tale: he was quite capable of giving it a British setting, wherever it came from.

Cordeilla's nephews, he continues, tried to share the kingdom. But they quarrelled, and Regan's son Cunedagius emerged as sole ruler. He reigned for another thirty-three years. About this time Isaiah was prophesying and Rome was founded (the traditional date for Rome is 753 B.C.). Sixth after Cunedagius was Gorboduc, another king mentioned by Shakespeare — in *Twelfth Night* — but not dramatized by him. The dramatization, however, had already been effected by Thomas Sackville and Thomas Norton in the first of all tragedies in English, performed in the Queen's presence in January 1562.

Gorboduc had two sons by his wife Judon. Their names were Ferrex and Porrex. When Gorboduc became senile and could not reign any more, the brothers disputed over the succession. Porrex was the more ambitious and ruthless. He plotted to murder Ferrex, who, however, escaped to Gaul and returned with an army supplied by the Frankish king. This invasion was not as successful as Leir's had been, and Ferrex fell in battle. His mother Judon had always preferred him to Porrex. His death unbalanced her, and when Porrex was asleep she crept in with her maid-servants and hacked him to pieces.

The line of Brutus was now extinct. A long period of anarchy followed. Eventually five contending rulers were holding different areas and making war on each other. The most astute and audacious of them, a Cornishman named Dunvallo Molmutius, beat the others and became king of Britain. Maintaining that the monarchy had been restored for a fresh start, he wore a golden crown as a new emblem. He suppressed banditry and published a code of laws. The Molmutine Laws, confirmed and clarified by his son Belinus, endured for centuries. In the Christian era, Geoffrey assures us, they were translated into Latin, and King Alfred re-published them in English. Tudor historians adopted this bit of information. Shakespeare took note, and he refers to Molmutius's laws in *Cymbeline*.

Belinus did not inherit without trouble. He had a brother, Brennius, and fought two civil wars against him. Again a division of the kingdom was tried and broke down. At last Brennius went abroad and Belinus ruled alone. His major achievement was a programme of road-building. The first of his paved highways ran from Cornwall to Caithness, linking up cities on the way. The second ran from Menevia, later St David's, to Southampton. Two more crossed Britain diagonally. His brother Brennius meanwhile had found allies abroad, and returned harbouring schemes of vengeance against him, but their mother reconciled them.

They ruled by agreement as joint sovereigns and led a great expedition to the continent, capturing and sacking Rome. Brennius remained overseas, Belinus went home. Britain under his rule rose to a high level of prosperity. He founded a city beside the Usk, which in Roman times was to become Caerleon, a legionary base. He also gave the city of Trinovantum a magnificent new gateway, with a tower above, and a water-gate below for access to shipping on the Thames. It was called Billingsgate, after Belinus. When he died he was cremated, and the urn with his ashes in it was put on top of the tower.

This double reign gives Geoffrey's narrative a brief contact with reality and a genuine date, though it does not fit too well with his previous dates, unless the interregnum after Ferrex and Porrex was very long indeed. Brennius is a fictionalized version of a Gaulish chief who did take Rome about 390 B.C. Roman history gives the chief's name as Brennus and Geoffrey turns him into a Briton.

With Gurguit Barbtruc, Belinus's successor, the pre-Roman monarchy drifts towards a gradual decline. So does Geoffrey's interest in it. Gurguit Barbtruc, it appears, was a good king but no more than an imitator of his father, and the reign was less prosperous. He did make one momentous decision. When he was at sea off the Orkneys, he encountered a fleet of thirty ships full of men and women. Their leader's name was Partholoim. He explained that they were wandering exiles from Spain, and were called Basclenses — Basques. The king helped them to settle in Ireland, which was then uninhabited. This account of the origin of the Irish is based, like the Brutus tale, on a passage in Nennius.

Gurguit's successor Guithelin was eclipsed by his learned wife Marcia, who reigned alone after his death. She added a supplement to the Molmutine code which was known as the Law of Marcia. This also was translated and adopted by Alfred the Great, who called it the Mercian Law. Of course, as a mere Saxon, he got the spelling wrong. What Geoffrey has done here is to invent a British source for laws which Alfred actually did adopt from Mercia — Mercia being not a lady but the English kingdom of the Midlands. Fourth after Marcia was Morvidus, a sadist who was fortunately devoured by a sea-monster, and whose death brought confusion into the realm, because he left five sons. They all managed to rule at varous times, but not by any lasting agreement. With the eldest the kingdom was at peace, with the others it went through various shifts and changes, and the reign of one of them, Elidurus, was in three instalments.

After Elidurus Geoffrey rushes headlong through thirty-four more reigns, with few details of any of them. Figures such as Edadus, Cledaucus, Cap, Archmail, Pir, shoot past without a word of comment. He even has repetitions. His determination to bring in so many names gives a poor impression of the state of the kingdom, because most of the reigns must have been very brief, hinting at wars, murders and dethronements. The thirty-fourth is Heli, who is stated to have had three sons, Lud, Cassivellaunus and Nennius (not the Nennius who wrote the pseudo-history). Geoffrey pauses at last on Lud, who rebuilt and refortified Trinovantum. It was given the new name Kaer-Lud, Lud's City. The 'Lud' part became 'Lundein' and finally 'London'. This king was buried near the city gate which was called after him, Ludgate. His successor was his brother Cassivellaunus . . . but here reality enters and does not go away again, and everything alters. Cassivellaunus existed. He fought Julius Caesar.

3

The truth about the era spanned by these monarchs has to be pieced together from archaeology, and passages in classical authors. Geoffrey's Britons, ancestors of the Welsh (and the Cornish and Bretons too), were not Trojans but Iron Age Celts, who arrived in three widely differing waves, and never blended into full homogeneity. Celts of other kinds overran Central Europe, Gaul and Ireland. They had a footing for a while in northern Italy. Gaul acquired its name from the dominant Celtic nation that took possession of it. Branches of the same nation moved into Macedonia and Asia Minor.

In Britain, the settlers did not find the simple situation imagined by Geoffrey. They had various prehistoric precursors. Among these, notably, were the megalith-builders. When discussing Stonehenge later in his book, Geoffrey shows that he associates megaliths with giants. His giants of ancient Albion are — in a hazy sense — the pre-Celtic people responsible for many stone monuments in parts of the country known to him. The frequency of the stones in Cornwall accounts for his statement that the Cornish giants were still fairly numerous when the Britons arrived. Actually they were not. A Bronze Age of a thousand years or more stretched between the age of the megaliths and the advent of the first migrants who can be counted as Britons. These Celts are unlikely to have entered the island before the late seventh century. But they were spreading across it from the sixth onwards, building immense earthwork fortifications, such as Maiden Castle in Dorset, to protect communities living on hills. They brought what is known as the Hallstatt culture wherever they settled.

The Celts were energetic folk who ate heartily, feeding on pork boiled in enormous cauldrons, and drinking beer and mead. Their houses were of wood or wattle; they used stone chiefly to strengthen fortifications. A second wave arrived around 250 B.C. from Armorica, that is, roughly, Brittany and a part of Normandy. They imported the 'La Tène' culture. It was distinguished by widespread trade, skilful metal-working, fine decorative art, and efficient transport, including the first of the famous British chariots. With the La Tène immigrants came new developments in hill-fort construction, and perhaps also the growth of a warrior-aristocracy with heroic ideals and heroic saga. After them came a third Celtic strain, the Belgae, from about 100 B.C. onwards. These were more advanced technologically. They made pottery on the wheel, increased the use of native metals, and farmed the heavy soil in the valleys instead of clinging to high ground. They also had a coinage.

At some stage Britain seems to have become the educational headquarters of Druidism. To judge from traces of it in Anglesey, its establishment among the Britons was pre-Belgic: Anglesey lay outside the Belgic range. The Druids were the Celtic intelligentsia — priests, magicians, scholars, bards, royal counsellors. Over a good deal of Europe they formed an organized order wielding great influence. Women as well as men could belong to it. Druidism, so far as can be made out, was a mixture of the barbaric and the sophisticated. Human sacrifice was a feature of it. So was a doctrine of immortality which interested Greeks and Romans. The Druids were probably heirs of an oral 'wisdom' tradition, rooted far back in Asian shamanism, and borne westwards and elaborated through many generations of folk-wandering.

Out of these ethnic, cultural and religious elements the British composite was formed, plus, of course, whatever was absorbed from insular stocks existing before. If we compare Geoffrey of Monmouth with the facts, his basic error is plain at once, and so is the reason. For the British kings to be meaningfully Trojans (never mind the problems raised by their subjects), they had to be installed in the island quite soon after the fall of Troy. This was assigned to the early twelfth century B.C. and could not be shifted. The founder Brutus, therefore, comes out unavoidably wrong on two counts. He is in the middle of the time-gap between the megalith-builders and the Celts, too late to have met even the last of the 'giants', too early to fit in with the real beginning of the Britons.

Yet Geoffrey scores, after a fashion, in another way. That real beginning, the influx of the first Celtic wave, synchronizes quite well with his phase of transition after the end of Brutus's dynasty which leads up to a sort of 'Mark II' kingdom under Molmutius and Belinus. The Celts gave Britain the hill-forts; the Molmutine monarchy gives Britain a more advanced organization, and mighty public works. Could it be that Geoffrey had some method of reckoning backwards to the true foundation of Celtic Britain, in the sixth century B.C., and then reconciled this with the Brutus legend by making it out to be a re-foundation and inventing a previous dynasty? The Romans did much the same to fill the period between Aeneas and the founding of Rome.

It could be so. However, no evidence exists for any relevant folk-memories reaching back far enough. Some have detected an even longer folk-memory in the legend of Merlin bringing Stonehenge over the sea from the west, since the bluestone circle really was brought over the sea from the west. But megaliths have nothing to do with Iron Age Celtic migrations. The utmost that can be produced is a statement by Bede, the English churchman and historian, who wrote at Jarrow in the eighth century A.D. and had Celtic sources of information. He says that the Britons, 'according to tradition, crossed into Britain from Armorica'. This might be a reminiscence of the La Tène people coming over, about 250 B.C. But it would not apply to their predecessors.

In any case it is pretty certain that Geoffrey's story collapses as soon as we try to pin it down to anything more specific than a vague dating. It is not only the individual kings that are fictitious, it is the monarchy itself. No actual Molmutius-figure arose out of the first process of settlement, or indeed the later ones. Nothing suggests that the Celts ever had a single king or paramount chief. In the final phase of immigration and partial fusion, various tribal groupings took shape. Each of these — the Atrebates, the Catuvellauni and others — had a territory of its own and a ruler of its own. Until Caesar writes about them, moreover, the rulers are all anonymous.

We do have indications that just as women could be Druids, women could rule. That fact would allow Geoffrey a minor touch of credit, since he has queens in his *History*. Female rule was far from being a norm in his own time, far from being an institution which he would have thought of naturally. He wrote when the barons of England were fiercely rejecting Henry I's daughter Matilda. The reigns of Gwendolen, Cordeilla and Marcia may reflect a dim consciousness of different customs long ago.

If genuine history lacks names, religion and myth are another matter. Celtic Britain had countless deities and sub-deities. Some are portrayed in art. Some are named in inscriptions, not as early as the pre-Roman period, but early enough to be of value. Some appear in the mythology of the Celts' descendants, mostly in Wales. Though Christianity ended their divine status, they survive in story-telling, transformed into larger-than-life humans. Alongside them are heroes and heroines whose names and deeds have been handed down through many centuries, even through millennia.

Reliance on oral transmission by the bards, without writing, doomed most of this matter to oblivion. Medieval texts, however, such as the collection of Welsh tales called the *Mabinogion*, have preserved a fair amount; and among the characters whose roots are in the pre-Christian age are several legendary monarchs of Britain. The atmosphere is utterly unlike Geoffrey's, yet sometimes we can see where he got a hint for a king whom he has made pseudo-historical, and assigned to the epoch before the Romans.

Welsh legend, for instance, introduces Beli son of Manogan, a reputed ancestor of several royal families. Beli has no real relationship to chronology. He appears as king of Britain in the fourth century A.D., as a brother-in-law of the Virgin Mary, as the grandfather of another hero — Bran — who must be earlier than that. But his name recalls Geoffrey's Belinus, and there is solid evidence for a Celtic god called Belenus who is the common original. He was worshipped in northern Italy and southern Gaul, and had a temple at Bordeaux. Relics of his cult are uncommon in Britain, but forms of the name have been made out in an inscription at Binchester in Co. Durham and on a tile at Maryport in Cumbria. The spring festival Beltain may have marked a sacred day of this god-who-became-a-king.

Another case is Lludd. His evolution can be traced in more detail, though it shows how devious the path from divinity to humanity could be. Geoffrey's version of him, the Lud who is connected with London, lives just before Caesar's invasion, but some Welsh legends place his reign farther back. Ultimately Lludd is the god Nodons. As late as the 360s A.D., a new temple was built for this god at Lydney in the Forest of Dean. He was a complex being with a character of his own — a god of water, a god of dogs, a huntsman, a fisherman, a healer, a finder of lost objects (like St Anthony). Nodons was humanized in Irish mythology as Nuadu Airgetlam, Nuadu of the Silver Hand, and in Welsh as Nudd and as Lludd, who also has a silver hand. A mythical maiden Creiddylad is spoken of as the daughter of Lludd and also as the beloved of Nudd's son Gwyn. Story-tellers had lost sight of the fact that Lludd and Nudd were the same. Because of her former relationship, it has been argued that Lludd underlies another of Geoffrey's kings, Leir, and that Creiddylad became Cordeilla and thence Cordelia.

The *Mabinogion* has a story entitled *Lludd and Llefelys*. It makes Lludd a son of Beli, with Caswallawn and Nyniaw as his brothers. This is the same family which in Geoffrey's *History* comprises 'Heli' with his three sons Lud, Cassivellaunus and Nennius. The opening paragraph, telling how Lludd reigned in Britain and reconstructed its capital, is much the same as the Lud passage in the *History*. The question who copied whom is of no great interest. *Lludd and Llefelys* as a whole is a folk-tale, timeless in its setting.

It adds a fourth brother, Llefelys, who was very wise. During Lludd's reign, the Island of Britain was afflicted by three plagues. The first was an invasion by wizards called the Coranieid, who could hear everything that was spoken and borne on the wind, and were therefore invincible because they knew any opponents' plans. The second plague was a horrible shriek which was heard every May-eve and drove people mad, and no one knew where it came from. The third was that no food could be kept in the royal stores beyond a day, because, after that, it vanished.

Lludd went to Llefelys and sought his advice. To thwart the eavesdropping of the Coranieid, Llefelys made a bronze tube through which they could talk without the wind catching the sound. At first this did not work, because a demon in the tube acted like a scrambler. Llefelys got rid of him by pouring wine through it. Then he gave Lludd some insects which he was to mash in water. The liquid, as a spray, would kill the Coranieid but do no harm to Britons. He went on to explain the second plague. The shriek came from a dragon when it fought against a foreign dragon. The remedy was to dig a pit at the centre of

Britain and place a tub of mead in it with a silken cover. When the dragons next grew tired of fighting, they would change into piglets and fall on the silk cover. It would give way and immerse them in the mead. They would drink the mead and fall asleep. Then Lludd could wrap the covering round the tub, and bury it in a stone coffer in some safe place. As for the third plague, Llefelys revealed that the royal provisions were being carried off by a giant magician who put everyone to sleep while he did it. Lludd should keep watch in person with a bath full of cold water handy, so that when he felt drowsy, he could get into it and stay awake.

Lludd did as his brother advised. With the infusion of insects he exterminated the Coranieid. By careful measurement he ascertained that the centre of Britain was at Oxford, and there he trapped the dragons. They fell into a trance and he hid the tub in a stone coffer on a hill in Snowdonia. Finally he prepared a feast, and waited through the night with the bath beside him. When he grew sleepy he got into the cold water. A gigantic armoured man came in with a hamper and began packing all the food into it. Lludd challenged him to fight and won, and the giant agreed to serve him. Thus all the plagues were removed and Lludd reigned in peace and prosperity for the rest of his days. In Geoffrey's *History* there is no hint of this tale. However, as we shall see, it has a sequel which he does give, telling how the dragons returned to their proper shapes and renewed their battle. In the sequel they become symbolic, and *Lludd and Llefelys*, which, as it stands, is a medieval re-telling, may have been adapted to suit the symbolism. But there is very ancient matter embedded in it.

Another monarch who drifts into view out of the realm of myth is Bran, 'Bran the blessed' as the Welsh call him. He too was a god first. His name means 'the Raven', and is found in various forms and in other Celtic contexts. The Gauls said that their invasion of Macedonia in the third century B.C. was led by Brennos and Bolgios, and these were probably divine beings rather than mortal chieftains. 'Brennus', the name Livy gives to the Gaulish chief who sacked Rome, may be a case of the divine presence in a human representative. If so, Geoffrey's Brennius, brother and co-king of Belinus, is a Bran at two removes.

We may have a British glimpse of the god in a chapter of

Plutarch, reporting what he had heard from a Greek who went to Britain on an official mission in the year A.D. 82. Britons told this traveller about a god banished to an island over the western ocean, where he lay asleep. Plutarch says more about this god in another passage. The reasons for thinking he was Bran need not be gone into here, and the identification may not be correct. It is a fact, however, that when the legends come fully into view and Bran is more or less humanized, the motif of a westward voyage recurs.

Bran splits into two distinct characters. One is an Irish hero, assigned vaguely to the time before Christ, who goes to a magical island in the Atlantic. The other Bran is the Welsh one, the blessed, once-upon-a-time king of Britain. He is a grandson of the undatable Beli. The *Mabinogion* makes him reign in a remote past, when only a narrow channel of deep water divided Britain from Ireland, but characters and places belonging to later times are dotted through the story. Bran also figures in Celtic local lore. Near Llangollen and Land's End are prehistoric hill-forts called Dinas Bran and Caer Bran respectively. At Dinas Bran a golden harp is said to be hidden inside the hill, to be found only by a boy who has a white dog with a silver eye. In the West Country, a former custom of tipping one's hat to ravens may be a last vestige of homage to Bran the Raven.

The *Mabinogion* tale makes him a giant. No house can hold him. He reigns as king in London, but has another court, which he seems to prefer, at Harlech. On an expedition to Ireland he wades across the aforesaid narrow channel. His army crosses in ships, but he carries the minstrels on his back — a hint, perhaps, at some sort of patronage of the arts in his former divine nature; the Dinas Bran harp may be another. In his Irish war he is mortally wounded in the foot by a poisoned spear. He tells the seven survivors of the army to cut off his head and bear it back to Harlech. They do so, and it lives for seven years and keeps them in a state of enchanted happiness. Then they take it to Gwales in Penfro. There it lives on likewise for eighty years, never decaying, and their bliss continues. After that the spell is snapped and they carry the head to London, where they bury it on Tower Hill, and it protects Britain against all evils from abroad.

Bran's head with its wonder-working powers is the most intriguing thing in the story. It fits so well with what is known of Celtic ideas as to put his antiquity beyond doubt. It also sheds light on his label 'blessed'. In Welsh this is *bendigeit*, and has a Christian meaning which brings him into Christian legends. But *bendigeit* is probably a corruption of a pagan epithet which began *pen*, 'head'. The belief that the British monarchy will survive as long as the Tower ravens do may be derived from the legend of the protective Raven-hero. The head itself, however, is no longer there. Like the affair of the fighting dragons, this tale of concealment has a sequel.

4

In all the reigns and relationships, a process can be discerned at work which worked in other countries also. Some of them attained literary articulateness more rapidly, and we get a clearer picture which is helpful in appraising the British one. It is in fact normal for a nation's early poets, story-tellers and historians to create a synthetic past out of an assortment of traditions and popular fables, seeking to give coherence and continuity. Thus Greek cities were linked with Greek hero-myths by claims that this or that hero was a city's founder. The heroes themselves were linked with immemorial cults by stories making them out to have been the sons of gods or goddesses. Similarly in ancient Israel, despite much de-mythologizing in the interests of a God who allowed no rivals, the deluge-hero of Mesopotamian legend was fitted into the sacred history as Noah, with a complex branching-out of descendants; while Israel's twelve tribes were accounted for by twelve eponymous ancestors (Reuben, Simeon and the rest) who were all supposedly sons of one father, Jacob, chosen by the Lord and re-named Israel.

Such exercises often had obvious motives. They glorified a people, they supported the claims of its kings or priests, by asserting a more-than-ordinary origin. Advancing sophistication and changing habits of belief were apt to raise queries, especially where gods were involved. Who were these gods? Did they ever exist at all? The Greek author Euhemerus offered a theory which could be made to hold everything together: that the gods were real, but were exceptional human beings, often rulers, deified only afterwards. Christians solved the problem in several ways, and the way favoured by the Welsh was Euhemerus's.

Britain's legendary history is not unique or strange. It is simply the British form of a widespread phenomenon. Its unusual features are the lateness of its organization and the dominance of one man, Geoffrey of Monmouth. The first, most legendary part of his *History* shows him treading recognized paths. He wants to glorify the Britons by substantiating the tale which traced their origin to Troy, and to Aeneas's divinely-ordained migration. To contrive the royal succession from Aeneas to the coming of Caesar, he strings together characters of several kinds. Brutus, Corineus, Kamber, who 'explain' the names Britain, Cornwall, Cambria, belong to the eponymous class. He has a number of other figures of the same type. Belinus and Lud are something else: they are gods 'euhemerized' into kings. Other monarchs again bear noble names belonging to Welsh dynastic tradition, pressed into service here to supply links. And so on. Having put together the whole series, Geoffrey hitches it on to history by including a real British chief of Caesar's time in the last of his fictitious family groups.

One thing which he never does is to connect his Britons with characters in the Bible. Some Welshmen did, like those who alleged that Beli was related by marriage to the mother of Christ. A little after Geoffrey, romancers of the Holy Grail carry the pedigrees of Arthurian knights back to the Gospels. By adopting notions of this type, modern advocates of what is called the "British-Israel Theory" have tried to prove the descent of the House of Windsor from King David.

CHAPTER TWO

Island and Empire

1

WITH LUD'S BROTHER CASSIVELLAUNUS, GEOFFREY OF MONMOUTH AT LAST INTRODUCES A REAL PERSON. His *History* goes on, and we shall have reason to look at it again. But henceforth, most of the time, authentic history supplants it.

By the middle of the first century B.C. a large part of Britain had come under the dominance of the Belgae. Cassivellaunus was a Belgic chief. He was not king of Britain or even king of the Belgic-dominated portion. He ruled over the Catuvellauni, whose domain covered an ill-defined stretch of country between the Thames and Cambridgeshire. The Trinovantes on his eastern border feared him, understandably, because he had killed their own chief and seemed likely to try to conquer them. But in spite of the enemies he made, Cassivellaunus became the architect of British resistance to Julius Caesar.

In 55 B.C. Caesar was not yet dictator. He was governor and commander in Gaul, busy subjecting that part of the Celtic world to Rome. Gaul to the north of the Seine and Marne was the Belgic homeland, and opposition in that quarter was stiffened by aid from compatriots across the Channel. Migration to Britain had not severed the links. In fact, a Belgic chief named Divitiacus was remembered as having had subjects in Britain too (thus supplying one royal name, though not very enlighteningly, before Cassivellaunus). Caesar's prime object in going to Britain himself was to overawe rather than to annex. He was encouraged by envoys from British tribes offering their submission.

A coastal reconnaissance by one of his officers failed to reveal a good place to land. The officer did not go quite far enough and missed the natural harbour at Richborough north of Sandwich, a failure with costly consequences. When Caesar sailed with his main force on 26 August, he skirted the cliffs of Dover and beached his transports near Deal. He had two legions, about

10,000 men. Britons from the local tribe, the Cantii, contested the landing but were repulsed. In the next few days more peace-envoys arrived. However, the expedition was already in trouble. The moon happened to be full, and the tide, which dwellers by the Mediterranean tended to underrate, caused havoc among the ships. A second fleet which was meant to be bringing cavalry had to retreat because of bad weather. Romans who pushed a little way inland were ambushed by Britons in chariots. After an inconclusive success, which could not be followed up owing to the absence of cavalry, Caesar returned to Gaul.

The Senate in Rome approved his action. However anti-climactic, it had a psychological value which is now easy to overlook. All civilized nations of antiquity pictured their world as a land-mass with the Ocean encircling it, and while myth and legend spoke of something beyond, the feeling that the outer coasts formed a limit for those who lived within them was very strong. Before Caesar's time, geographers and traders had become aware of the British Isles, yet they seemed strange, mysterious, 'other'. To take an army to Britain at all was a bolder, more radical step than taking one to Africa or the Middle East. It put the Romans in a class by themselves.

Caesar made a second, more serious attempt the following year, with eight hundred ships, better adapted to landing on the beaches. He sailed from Boulogne early in July with five legions and 2,000 cavalry, and disembarked between Deal and Sandwich. This time he left the ships at anchor and headed for a ford on the Stour, at the future site of Canterbury. Just beyond this he captured a hill-fort, Bigbury. However, he was called back by a message reporting a violent storm which had driven most of the ships ashore and damaged them. It was necessary to haul them up for repairs and build a fortification to defend them. The ten days' delay brought Cassivellaunus on the scene, leading a mixed army recruited both by himself and by other chiefs who accepted his leadership. Caesar found this force waiting when he returned to the Stour crossing.

Cassivellaunus did not risk a battle, but harassed the Romans with chariots and cavalry. The British war-chariot carried a warrior and a driver. There is no firm evidence for scythes projecting from the axles. The warrior fought by charging all over the battlefield in his war-paint, throwing javelins, dismount-

ing when he could achieve anything on foot, then jumping back
aboard and escaping. Roman infantry could not catch up. Roman horsemen could, but when they did the Britons dismounted
and brought them down (ancient cavalry, lacking stirrups, was
not very effective). Caesar, however, had already seen that by
keeping his cavalry and infantry in close contact he could nullify
both British advantages. As his army learned to apply his anti-
chariot tactics, it became clear that the Romans were not to be
stopped, and most of Cassivellaunus's allies deserted him.

Caesar pushed on to the Thames and crossed it at a ford,
despite rows of sharp stakes planted in the banks and the river-
bed. The crossing was probably near the future site of London,
which, despite Lud, did not yet exist. Cassivellaunus fell back
into his own country, keeping up guerrilla action. At first Caesar
did not know where to find him, but the grievances of Cassivellaunus's victims supplied the invader's need. The Trinovantes
asked for Roman protection, and invited their slain chief's son
Mandubracius, who had taken refuge with Caesar, to return and
reign over them. Then several minor tribes surrendered. From
these British friends Caesar learned the whereabouts of Cassivellaunus's main stronghold. It was apparently Wheathampstead in
Hertfordshire, not a hill-fort but an enclosure on the west of the
River Lea, defended by woods, marshes and a rampart and
ditch.

The British leader was still resourceful. As Caesar approached,
he sent a message to his remaining allies in Kent, ordering them
to attack the naval camp on the coast. The attack, however,
failed, and when Caesar broke into his stronghold, he agreed to
open negotiations. Another pro-Roman Briton, Commius, acted
as mediator. Caesar was willing to come to terms, because news
had reached him of trouble in Gaul and it would be too risky to
winter in Britain. Cassivellaunus undertook to hand over hostages, pay an annual tribute and respect Trinovantian independence. The Romans left in September. Caesar's account of these
events implies that he did in the end have notions of converting
part of Britain into a Roman province. His successor Augustus
kept this plan on the agenda without pursuing it, and finally
allowed it to lapse.

2

For several decades Britain remained outside the Empire. From the viewpoint of history, however, there is no retreat back into anonymity, because some of the Belgic chiefs — men whose power, stability in office, extent of domain and external diplomacy now made them kings in foreign eyes — started putting their names on coins. The fashion was set by Caesar's friend Commius, after a series of adventures. He had returned to Gaul in high favour, but he changed sides when the Gauls rebelled. Two Roman assassination attempts failed. When he did surrender, he stipulated that he should never have to meet a Roman again. About 50 B.C. he escaped and slipped away to his own people, the Atrebates, whose main territory lay south of the middle Thames. There he became king and gradually extended his power, with that of his Belgic aristocracy, over a population with large pre-Belgic elements in parts of Berkshire, Hampshire, Sussex and neighbouring counties.

Commius died about 25-20 B.C. and was succeeded by his son Tincommius. The capital of the southern Belgic kingdom was now Calleva, later known as Silchester. (The word 'capital' is something of an anachronism, but a kingdom could have a principal centre.) Tincommius was ousted by his brother Eppillus. Towards A.D. 7 he was in Rome as a political exile, looking for support from Augustus. By that time the Atrebates had some sort of treaty with Rome, and their coinage imitated Roman designs. Augustus, however, did not see that he had any obligation to intervene, and recognized Eppillus as *rex*, a Latin title which soon appeared on his coins. Eppillus in turn was ousted by a third brother, Verica, and went away to govern a principality in Kent. Verica survived into old age and was still living in A.D. 43. A vine-leaf on some of his Roman-imitative coins witnesses to Roman trade connections, and the import of wine.

The southern kingdom was increasingly overshadowed by the northern one, the kingdom of the Catuvellauni. Despite Cassivellaunus's setback at the hands of Caesar, and despite the peace terms, his forward policy was resumed. Next after him — at least, there is no proof of anyone else between — was Tasciovanus, who reigned from about 20 B.C. with Verulamium (St Albans), as his capital. He pushed east into the country of the

Trinovantes and took their principal centre, Camulodunum (Colchester). 'Camulodunum' means 'Fort of Camulos', the Belgic war-god. The town was an inner enclosure inside a much bigger outer one, both demarcated by dykes. Its nucleus was probably a shrine of Camulos at Gosbeck's Farm south-west of Sheepen. The site had been chosen because it had good communications, yet was easily defended — against chariots, that is; Roman methods of war were not foreseen. Tasciovanus's attack shows that he did not consider himself bound by the agreement with Caesar. He withdrew, perhaps because of a warning from Augustus, who was in Gaul in 16 B.C. However, he may also have pushed across the Thames into Kent and hung on to his gains.

Next after him, between A.D. 5 and 10, came his son Cunobelinus, last and greatest of these pre-Roman kings. He was to reign for over thirty years. His name means 'hound of Belinus' — here is the Celtic god again — and in legend and Shakespeare it becomes Cymbeline. So pre-eminent was he in the portion of Britain closest to the continent that a Roman historian calls him *Britannorum rex,* king of the Britons. He conquered the much-beset Trinovantes and shifted his capital to Camulodunum. He also encroached on the Atrebates till Verica's domain was reduced to a part of Sussex. The advance was accompanied by propaganda. On some of his coins he put an ear of barley as a retort to Verica's vine-leaf, opposing British beer to imported wine. Fragments of many wine jars in his own country suggest that his nobles did not live up to this sturdy patriotism.

His reign, in fact, saw a big increase of foreign trade. From Britain the continent obtained wheat, cattle, gold, silver, iron, pearls, hides, slaves and hunting dogs. The conspicuous absentee from this list is tin. Cornish tin had formerly been much in demand, but competition from Spanish mines had ruined the industry. As for trade in the other directions, Britons imported not only wine but amber, glass, ivory ornaments, bracelets and necklaces. These are all expensive luxury goods, and most of them presumably went to the nobles. For necessities Britain was as self-sufficient as ever, both inside and outside the major kingdom. Shakespeare is justified in the words with which he makes Cymbeline's imagined stepson, Cloten, reject a Roman demand for arrears of tribute:

> Britain is
> A world by itself, and we will nothing pay
> For wearing our own noses.

These three Catuvellaunian rulers — Cassivellaunus, Tasciovanus and Cunobelinus — have a curious accidental interest. We know the first from the writings of Caesar, the third from other Roman authors and from his coins. Between the two, documentation vanishes. We know Tasciovanus from his coins only. Yet his name appears centuries afterwards in Welsh genealogies. It has become 'Teuhant', an extreme-looking but explicable corruption. The king is listed as an ancestor of Cunedda, who ruled Wales in the fifth century A.D. Geoffrey of Monmouth adopts him from the genealogists with a further change through scribal error, as Tenuantius. He makes him the nephew and successor of Cassivellaunus, and says he was followed as king by his son Cymbeline, here at least being correct. Is this a case of oral transmission through an amazingly long time? Or is it evidence for a lost history, perhaps the 'ancient book' which Geoffrey claims to have read? In either event, Tasciovanus is intriguing.

Outside Cunobelinus's domain were several other important groupings, some dominated by Belgic elements, some not. The Iceni occupied Norfolk, the Durotriges were in Dorset. Across the centre of what is now England were the Dobunni and the Coritani. Belgic settlement, Belgic culture, Belgic government extended to all in varying degrees, but scarcely beyond. The Dumnonii, whose country began in Somerset and comprised Devon and Cornwall, were Celts of an earlier breed. Two of their villages near Glastonbury — lake-villages, built on artificial islands in swamps and watery shallows — had long been centres of the pre-Belgic La Tène culture. Most of Wales was divided among the Silures, Demetae and Ordovices, with the Cornovii lying east of them. Almost the entire north of England, up to the Carlisle area and the Tyne, was held by the Brigantes. They were a largely pastoral nation, more primitive than most of their fellow-Britons, and took their name from their goddess Brigantia, the 'high one' or 'queen'. Beyond the Brigantes were four or five tribal conglomerations extending to the Clyde and Forth. Beyond those again were the Caledonians, who were people of a different stock.

In Rome, meanwhile, a fresh invasion had been discussed from time to time and deferred. The Emperor Tiberius was not interested. Caligula revived the project and even made preparations, but an army mutiny swayed his unbalanced mind against it. After his murder in A.D. 41 it was finally launched by his uncle Claudius, an unexpected conqueror — but as readers of Robert Graves know, he was an unexpected emperor in other ways. The impulse came from a political crisis. Cunobelinus had died at about the same time as Caligula. His sons Togodumnus and Caratacus shared their heritage and began new aggressions, attacking the Dobunni across their western border, and overrunning the last scrap of the Atrebatic kingdom. Its king Verica, now an old man, fled to Rome. Cunobelinus's heirs demanded his extradition. When Claudius refused, anti-Roman demonstrations broke out. It would be interesting to know what form they took: perhaps piratical raids across the Channel, perhaps mob violence against Roman merchants in Britain.

Action was called for, and Claudius had further motives for it. One was a simple need for prestige, after the morale-shattering reign of his predecessor. Another was the prospect of exploiting British resources, especially mineral wealth, and manpower for the Roman army. Another, probably, was a wish to stamp out Druidism. That had been attempted in Gaul, partly because of the practice of human sacrifice, partly because the Druids were regarded as anti-Roman. Whether or not they were originally so, the measures taken against them drove them into enmity. The continuance of their British colleges meant that the island was a haven for Druid malcontents, and a source of sedition in Gaul. Rome's invasion was not a religious war, but it did include action against the Druids, and it was therefore the nearest thing to a religious war which Rome had ever undertaken.

In the spring of 43, under the generalship of Aulus Plautius, an army of 40,000 (four legions plus auxiliaries) assembled at Boulogne. Sailing was held up by another mutiny. Its ringleaders re-asserted the old belief that the ocean was the proper boundary of the human world. Admittedly human beings lived beyond it, but that was their own business, and dwellers on the mainland ought not to go there. Claudius sent one of his ministers, a freed slave, to address the troops, with the unforeseen result that they roared with laughter, and a general outbreak of rag-ging released the tension. Embarkation proceeded.

This time the Romans knew about Richborough. Their landing in the harbour was unopposed, because the Britons had had reports of the mutiny but not its ending, and thought Caligula's fiasco would be repeated. Belatedly, Togodumnus and Caratacus appeared with their forces. After a couple of skirmishes they retired to the Medway. Peace-envoys from the distant Dobunni, whom they had been trying to conquer, now arrived at the Roman camp. As in Julius Caesar's day, victims of the overbear-ing Catuvellauni were seeking protection. Plautius welcomed their overtures and moved on to the Medway. The fiercest battle of this campaign was fought near Rochester, where the Britons contested the crossing. Plautius sent over German auxiliaries who could swim fully equipped. While these were spreading confusion by disabling chariot-horses, the main body of troops got across. The Britons stood their ground for two days and then withdrew to the Thames, near the site of London. Again the auxiliaries swam over, and the rest followed, either finding a bridge or making one with pontoons. In scattered fighting on the far side Togodumnus was killed. It is uncertain whether anything that could be called London existed even yet, but there may have been a trading post.

Camulodunum was within grasp, but Claudius wanted to enter the capital in person. Plautius sent back a report on the position. In mid-August the emperor arrived with an additional legion and some elephants, the latter, probably, more for show and morale effect than for combat. He stayed only sixteen days in Britain. Most of the time was taken up with the occupation of Camulodunum, and the reception of embassies from tribes anx-ious to make their peace with the Empire. It was resolved that some of Britain at least should be annexed as a Roman province, but the decision as to how much was postponed till the situation should become clearer as a whole. For one thing, Caratacus himself had not been brought to terms; he had escaped. The immediate victory, however, was evident, and when Claudius returned to Rome the Senate voted him a triumph. The Senate also agreed that treaties made by his representatives in Britain did not have to be referred back for ratification.

As the legions pressed on, several regional sovereigns entered into such treaties. The example of the Dobunni was followed by King Prasutagus of the Iceni, and more whole-heartedly by Cogidubnus, who was, or became, ruler of a restored Atrebatic state in the south. He may have taken charge of it under direct Roman sponsorship, when the aged king-in-exile Verica died. Certainly he went to pro-Roman extremes, assuming the names Tiberius Claudius. He did well out of the connection and built himself an opulent house at Fishbourne near Chichester. In the north, Queen Cartimandua of the Brigantes accepted Roman suzerainty before the legions got close. One historian adds, amazingly, that Claudius received the submission of the Orkneys. Meanwhile London — Londinium — had its authentic birth as a port and commercial centre. Over the next few years it grew swiftly till it covered the whole area around the modern sites of St Paul's and Leadenhall Street. Camulodunum was transformed into Colchester, a 'colony' of time-expired soldiers settled on grants of land near the abandoned heart of the old capital. Verulamium too was Romanized.

The advance of the army met with opposition, though not everywhere. Vespasian, who took command in the south-west, had to fight to subdue the Durotriges and Dumnonii. They had numerous hill-forts, and in more than twenty of these the inhabitants did not surrender without a struggle. At least one, South Cadbury Castle in Somerset, was simply by-passed but did not therefore capitulate. It had to be separately stormed long after.

3

Plautius, who was made governor of Claudius's new province, seems to have planned a frontier across the Midlands. Roman power beyond was to depend on arrangements with client rulers such as Cartimandua. However, this limitation did not work. Caratacus had gone to Wales and was holding out, supported by the Silures in the south-east and the Ordovices in the north. When Plautius returned to Rome and was succeeded as governor by Ostorius Scapula, the British leader launched a bold counter-offensive. Ostorius repulsed it, but the victory was defensive only, and he was keenly aware of the danger of pro-Caratacus risings. To prevent these he imposed a law of Julius

Caesar forbidding provincial subjects to possess weapons, except for hunting and self-defence on journeys. Then he pushed into Cheshire, and sent help to Cartimandua, who was threatened by an anti-Roman faction among the Brigantes. This may have been stirred up by Druids based on Anglesey.

Caratacus was still active. Over the next few years, however, his field of action slowly contracted. In 51 he moved into the mountainous north of Wales but was defeated at last. The Romans captured his wife, children and brothers. He escaped himself, and rode away to look for allies among the Brigantes. Cartimandua, loyal to her undertakings, arrested him and handed him over into honourable captivity. Claudius had him brought to Rome, where his courageous bearing won respect. The splendours of the city prompted him to ask a memorable question: 'When you have so much, why do you covet our poor huts?' He lived three years longer.

The Silures fought on without him, and even won a battle against a legion, but we get no more names. By 60, the south of Wales was pacified and the governor then in office, Suetonius Paullinus, marched to the Menai Straits to invade Anglesey. The island was important for a number of reasons — because of its copper ores, because of its grain (which sustained the turbulent Ordovices), but above all because it was a Druid centre, inspiring resistance and harbouring potential rebels. Paullinus built a fleet of flat-bottomed boats and prepared to ship his soldiers across. On the farther shore, Druids of both sexes were out in force — the men chanting hostile incantations with lifted arms, the women, black-clad and long-haired, brandishing torches. For a moment the Romans actually faltered. Then they advanced, massacred the Druids, and cut down the sacred groves where, it was said, Roman prisoners had been sacrificed. This was not the end of the cult. Druids were to survive as soothsayers and teachers in Britain and Gaul, and on a larger scale in Ireland. But their united power as an order, already practically extinct on the continent, was broken.

While Paullinus was in Anglesey he received alarming news. The Iceni and Trinovantes were in revolt. Roman rule had generated a crisis. At Colchester it had become clear that the new possessors were by no means liberators. The veterans seized land which they had not been allotted, and evicted the owners. Moreover, a Roman town, the Britons discovered, was much more than an enclosure containing huts and barns. It meant solid houses, large public buildings. Labourers were forced to quarry stone and make tiles under crude conditions. Also at Colchester, the Romans launched what was to be a momentous experiment in official religion — a cult of the emperor. This was not strictly worship of the emperor as a human being, but worship of his *numen,* the divine power he was supposed to embody. That distinction was tricky. The most obvious fact to the Trinovantes was that emperor-worship required an expensive temple.

For local administration, Roman provinces were largely divided into *civitates* or cantons, presided over by councils of prominent men. In Britain the system was only beginning to take shape. The prominent Britons who were cooperating thus far found that their status was a burden as well as a privilege. They had to make contributions themselves, and the new order meant a huge outlay on things they had not foreseen, an outlay shared among too few. Roman money-lenders were glad to help, at high rates of interest. One of them was the philosopher Seneca. This affair casts an odd light on his high-minded teaching. So does the fact that his most famous pupil was Nero (now emperor; he had just murdered his mother). Having lent large amounts to Britons struggling with the cost of civilization, and done well by doing so, Seneca demanded repayment in full. A similar blow was struck from another angle by Catus Decianus, the Roman treasury officer in Britain. Claudius had disbursed money to various Britons in recognition of their pro-Roman conduct. Decianus now claimed that the sums involved were not subsidies but loans, and tried to recover them.

These attempts to call in loans, real or alleged, may have been prompted by nervousness about the Iceni in Norfolk. Their king Prasutagus had honoured his treaty, but Roman policy did not regard such treaties as permanent. Sooner or later the sub-kingdoms in occupied territory were to be brought under direct rule. Prasutagus died leaving no son, and officials closed in, confiscated his property, and arrested some of his nobles. But although he had left no son he had left a widow, Boudicca (otherwise Boadicea), and two daughters. These counted as part of the confiscated property. The queen was flogged, the princesses raped. However, by a fatal miscalculation they were not actually imprisoned . . . or not imprisoned securely enough. Boudicca was free to appeal to her husband's subjects. The desperation of both Iceni and Trinovantes now had a leader to turn it into rebellion.

Suetonius Paullinus was still in Anglesey and the Romans were taken by surprise. At Colchester the colonists had been put off guard by a pretence of friendliness. A horde of Britons poured down on the settlement from the north and destroyed it. They ambushed and massacred a Roman force, part of the Ninth Legion. Apparently the law forbidding Britons to carry arms had not been enforced. When Paullinus heard, he set out for London. He also sent orders to the Second Legion, which was in the south-west, to march against the rebels. Its commander was away, and the acting commander, Poenius Postumus, ignored the governor's message and did not stir. Paullinus's force, composed of the Fourteenth Legion and part of the Twentieth, was too small to defend London, and he drew back. Boudicca captured both London and Verulamium. Both were burnt to the ground. The total killed in the three towns is said to have been seventy thousand. If so, the rising was not, properly speaking, national. It was against British collaborators as well as Romans.

The triple devastation was a grim triumph, and there were not to be any more. Some time during the year 61 Paullinus assembled about ten thousand men and awaited Boudicca in a carefully chosen spot, partly enclosed by hills and woods, with an open level to the front. No one knows where it was — perhaps near Towcester in Northamptonshire. The Britons vastly outnumbered him, but Roman discipline won, and the queen took poison. She was not the only suicide. Postumus knew that he would be called to account for disobeying orders, and fell on his sword. Paullinus followed up the victory with ruthless reprisals. But the province now had a new treasury officer, Classicianus, who was of Gaulish family and knew how the Romanization of a non-Roman people should be effected. He stood up to the governor and reported to Rome on the Britons' grievances. Paullinus was recalled on a face-saving pretext and the regime grew milder.

Though Roman historians mention no other rising, there may have been a related outbreak in Somerset. At the South Cadbury hill-fort, archaeology has shown that the village on the summit plateau survived untouched till Boudicca's time and somewhat later, but was then assaulted. The Romans slaughtered many of the inhabitants, and moved the rest to a new, non-defensible site below. It may be that some defiant chief had held out for a while, Hereward-the-Wake fashion, in an enclave comprising the hill-fort itself and the stretch of marshes, lakes and islands or near-islands such as Glastonbury, which then lay between Cadbury and the Bristol Channel.

4

Henceforth most of Britain formed the imperial province of Britannia, variously organized and subdivided at different times, but firmly Roman. The puppet kingdoms faded out. Cartimandua of the Brigantes might have survived, but she provoked a revolt by divorcing her husband Venutius and marrying a favourite. The upheaval made Venutius supreme and, owing to his queen's conduct, implacably hostile to her Roman friends. The Brigantian kingdom had to be subdued and annexed. After that Agricola, who was governor from 78 to 84, pushed on far into Scotland, defeating the Caledonians at 'Mons Graupius', which was probably east of Inverness. He sent a fleet round the north of the island to check its insularity, but he did not complete its conquest. The frontier was never beyond the Clyde-Forth line, and for most of the Roman period it ran across the north of England, though garrisons were maintained in the zone between.

Meanwhile Romanization proceeded. The destroyed towns were rebuilt, and London became the capital. Other towns arose all over the country with roads linking them. As trust slowly increased, Britons were recruited as soldiers. More and more of the chiefs, the rich and the favoured were drawn into low-level government via the *civitates.* Their sons were given a classical education. Latin became the upper-class and official language. The Celtic British language survived and was spoken by most of the population, but it was probably not written.

For two hundred years there were no more British kings or queens, and no rulers who made Britain an effectual power-base or independent domain. The governors were non-Britons, appointed by the emperor and responsible to him. Few emperors even visited the island. An exception was Hadrian, who, responding to troubles in the north, came over in 122 and ordered the building of his wall from the Solway Firth to the Tyne. Its main function was to establish the frontier and to house garrisons and patrols. It also prevented the restless Brigantes from plotting with tribesmen on the other side of it. For a long time the tribesmen posed no serious threat, but sedition persisted among the Brigantes.

Under Hadrian's successor, Antoninus Pius, an attempt was made to strengthen Roman authority beyond. A new rampart was built across the Clyde-Forth isthmus. It was made of turf, with a wooden breastwork, and forts at intervals of about two miles. Towards 183 this caved in when the Caledonians moved south. The raiders were repelled after fierce fighting, but the Antonine wall was abandoned. A few years later, tribesmen from the Lowlands raided over Hadrian's wall and destroyed military installations. After an arduous restoration of the *status quo*, another emperor, Severus, led a punitive expedition against the northern barbarians. He died at York in 211. A spell of peace followed.

The Britons, then, were reduced to passivity, deprived of their monarchs and ruled over by foreigners. What account of this period did they hand on to their descendants? What does Welsh legend make of it? What does Geoffrey of Monmouth make of it?

The farthest back we can get in British testimony is a book by a sixth-century monk named Gildas. Writing very cantankerously, over a hundred years after Britain's severance from the Empire, he is well aware that his ancestors were conquered. Indeed he overdoes the Romans' triumph and the Britons' base near-nullity. He shows no signs of knowing any tradition of resistance leaders, except Boudicca, whom he regards as brave but deceitful — a reference to the beguiling of the Colchester colonists. In his eyes the conquest was an alien imposition, and it remained so. While he shows some enduring effects of Romanization himself — for instance, he writes Latin correctly if obscurely, and calls it 'our language' — his view seems to be that it did not really 'take'. After the regime ended, the Britons carried on much as before, except that, for a while, military leadership came from a 'Roman' remnant.

When we turn to the Welshman Nennius, two and a half centuries later, we find some of the same features. This time there is a sketch of Julius Caesar's activities and restricted success. However, Nennius names no Britons opposing the main invasion. Even Boudicca has gone. (Early legend, in fact, never makes her the heroine we might expect, though antiquarian fancy gives her a grave under platform 10 at King's Cross station.) Nennius mentions Claudius and other emperors who came to Britain, actually or allegedly. In the end, he says, the Britons 'despised the authority of the Romans and refused to pay them tribute', and the connection ended. Here again is the odd absence of any personalized resistance legend, even though ample material existed. Here again is the feeling of separateness: the Romans were one nation, the Britons another, and no effective Romanization is admitted. Nennius's main difference from Gildas is that he does not stress the Britons' subjection. The lapse of time has made the conquest, in retrospect, much less of a conquest.

Geoffrey himself is well-read, and quite equal to exploiting Roman history as well as Welsh tradition. Yet his story has the same gaps, and shows the same attitude. His method of building a patriotic legend is surprising. We would expect a tremendous, inflated tale of Britons battling against Rome and going down gloriously. We get this in his account of Cassivellaunus, but not afterwards. Caratacus never appears, neither does Boudicca. 'Cymbeline' has two sons, but they are not Caratacus and Togodumnus, they are Guiderius and Arviragus. The latter is taken from the Roman satirist Juvenal, who mentions a British leader of this name as causing trouble for Rome during the reign of Domitian (81-96). Through careless reading, Geoffrey thinks that the emperor was Nero. Hence, he can move Arviragus back and make him Cymbeline's son with more plausibility.

In his *History* the invasion by Claudius leads to a brief war from which Arviragus emerges as a client ruler. He marries the emperor's daughter, reigning formidably over Britain for a long time. There is never any Roman government. The kingdom is a tribute-paying dependency, generally friendly to Rome, but autonomous; and the line of kings simply goes on. A break comes in the late second century, and Severus arrives to re-impose the

Empire's supremacy. But even after that, Geoffrey keeps his kingdom going by an ingenious device. He brings in several historical persons who did rule Britain, and were at least temporarily on the spot, and he makes them all out to have been Britons or half-Britons or Britons-by-marriage, so that all of them, even emperors, count as British kings. In this way he carries on the line till Britain ceases to be attached to the Empire and the problem dissolves.

Geoffrey takes patriotic legend-making to a point where heroic last stands and bids for freedom are unnecessary, because the conquest itself has vanished. Behind all the invention, he is reiterating the old belief that British identity survived and assimilation never went deep. This does seem to have been handed down, or rather taken for granted. When we dismiss Geoffrey's fantasies and look again at Gildas, who has no illusions about the reality of the conquest, his conviction that Britons did not become Romans is just as clear.

Much the same attitude shows itself in a batch of legends and speculations about the first Britons who adopted, or favoured, Christianity. So far as is known, the new religion spread to Britain because the Romans opened up the country to Mediterranean influences. Its early penetration was on a small scale, and there are no reliable dates for it. The Christian author Tertullian implies a Christian presence by the close of the second century. Gildas claims that there was a mission in the first. Immediately after speaking of Boudicca's rising, and the intensification of Roman rule that followed, he has a long tangled sentence in which the significant words are 'Meanwhile these islands received the holy precepts of Christ'. But the stories that name names are differently biased. They introduce British royalty and speak of British initiatives, with no Romans involved, and no missionaries in the usual sense.

Those which echo Gildas by going back to the apostolic era cannot be proved genuinely traditional. Yet they show signs of having taken shape — whenever they did take shape — in the same sort of patriotic atmosphere as Geoffrey's *History*. One Welsh tale brings in the mythic hero Bran, and invokes his epithet 'blessed' to make him live in the first century A.D. and preach the Gospel in Britain. It says further (sweeping aside Cunobelinus) that Bran was Caratacus's father, went to Rome with him, was baptized there by St Paul, and returned to his country as its apostle. Since Paul came to Rome in 62, the date at least would fit in with Gildas.

So would the date of another story connecting the first British convert with Caratacus. Paul's second epistle to Timothy (4:21) mentions two Christian friends of his in Rome named Pudens and Claudia. The Roman poet Martial addresses verses to a married couple named Pudens and Claudia, and the wife, it appears, is British. To equate Paul's Claudia with Martial's was a natural step, and the equation produced a fully-fledged legend when it was asserted that this British lady was Caratacus's daughter and, perhaps, had something to do with an early plantation of Christianity in Britain.

Finally, another real Briton, Arviragus, figures in the famous legend of Glastonbury's foundation by Joseph of Arimathea. In 63 he is said to have been reigning in Britain and to have granted a piece of land, the site of the future monastery, to the wandering Joseph and his companions. Arviragus's grant was confirmed by two successors. The names in the account suggest that its author drew on Geoffrey. What is piquant is that whoever started the tale should have hit so neatly on a time when a British chief may actually have been holding central Somerset, and able to give the wanderers a haven. Until the Cadbury hill-fort was excavated, there was no evidence for unconquered Britons in that area so long after the invasion. A linkage of legends may be hinted at in the fact that Bran appears, as Bron or Brons, accompanying Joseph in romances of the Holy Grail.

These stories, and the passage in Gildas, all seem to be hovering round a notion that there were Christians in Britain — very few, with no serious impact — in the immediate post-Boudicca phase. If a tradition to that effect really was handed down, it is unlikely ever to be recovered. Nennius and Geoffrey have no trace of it. They prefer a story which can be traced back further than those about Caratacus and the rest, very much further, yet is more and not less fantastic. It declares that the Britons were largely converted at a stroke when their king Lucius was received into the Church by envoys sent at his request from Eleutherius, pope from about 174 to 189. In another version of it, Lucius is made out to be a descendant of the ubiquitous Bran.

The story is not of British origin. It is found in a sixth-century

Roman record, where it may be due to a misunderstanding about another royal conversion. In any case the record refers only to 'Lucius, a British king'; the mass Christianization of Britons is a later improvement. The convert might have been a chief, or a man of regal descent holding some official post, but he is more likely to be a figment.

Nennius gives the date as 167, a little too early for Eleutherius, but not beyond the bounds of a reasonable uncertainty. Geoffrey, however, makes Lucius die in 156. As he has only three precise dates throughout the *History,* his choosing to give one at this point, and its plainly erroneous divergence, is a minor puzzle. Bede mentions the same year at the beginning of a chapter in which he mentions Lucius, but he makes it clear that it is not Lucius's own date, which he gives, like Nennius, as 167 in another part of his book.

An explanation for the date given by Geoffrey does exist. It is far-fetched yet interesting, and if it does happen to be right, this may be another case like that of Tasciovanus, pointing to his having drawn on actual history in a form now unknown. We sometimes find that early Christian historical writings have a twenty-eight-year error. The reason lies in a change of chronological starting-point. Our *Anno Domini* dating reckons from Christ's birth, the Incarnation, or rather from the year inaccurately assigned to it by a sixth-century monk. An earlier system, however, dated events from Christ's death, the Passion, and put it in the year which we now call A.D. 28. Sometimes a writer, copying a manuscript, would transcribe a date counted from the Passion without making it clear that it was. Readers unaware of the fact might then assume that the date was counted from Christ's birth and be twenty-eight years wrong.

That might have occurred in some document used by Geoffrey. If so, his date for Lucius, A.D. 156, results from the shortcomings of an earlier scribe, and to get it right we must add twenty-eight, making it really A.D. 184 — 156 from the Passion. In that very year an actual Lucius was momentarily prominent in Britain. He was a general, Lucius Artorius Castus, and he led British troops across the Channel to put down a revolt in Armorica. For Britons this was an unprecedented action, which could well have made an impression on them, and on any author interested in their affairs.

An early chronicle reckoning from the Passion, and including some such phrase as 'year 156, Lucius Artorius Castus *dux Britonum*' (leader of the Britons), might have reached Geoffrey by way of a copy in which he supposed that the 156 was *Anno Domini* and that he was reading a reference to the legendary king — *dux* meaning 'ruler', as it could. As we shall see, a chronological error of the same type may underlie Geoffrey's second date as well, so the guess at a Passion-dated document in the background is worth considering. And so perhaps is a further possibility, that he took 'Castus' not as a name but as an adjective; regular capitalization of initials was not an early practice. *Castus* could mean 'pious', 'holy'. Geoffrey could have read *Lucius Artorius Castus dux Britonum* as 'Lucius Artorius the pious ruler of the Britons', a further reason to mistake him for the Lucius of Christian legend.

5

The view of the Roman age which Geoffrey fictionalizes is not wholly absurd. Until a few years ago, his concept of a distinctive Britain surviving throughout would have been dismissed. In historians' eyes the 'pre-Roman Iron Age' ended with the conquest, 'Roman Britain' followed, and after that came 'sub-Roman Britain'. Today, chiefly because of archaeology, there is more willingness to see Celtic society as going on, with the Roman regime as an intrusion after which Celtic society re-surfaced. The intrusion was vast, powerful, creative; yet it did not destroy everything that was there before, or wholly break continuity, and most of its effects faded or altered when active rule was withdrawn.

Superficially at least, however, the Britannia of the third century was strongly Roman. From 212 onwards (or perhaps 214) all its male inhabitants other than slaves, in common with all free men throughout the Empire, were Roman citizens. Some of the more fortunate lived in well-appointed villas, with farmlands and workshops supplying most of their needs. Such upper-class Britons found considerable scope in a system which gave them local power through the network of cantonal and municipal councils. Delegates from these attended an all-British provincial council which could advise the governor. The higher officials and commanders, though non-British, might come from anywhere in the Empire. Exclusive control by a 'master race' from Italy was a thing of the past. *Romanitas,* Roman-ness, denoted not so much nationality as civilization; for the better-off, a way of life; for the majority, hard work and taxes and conscription, yet still a certain stability, and, for one sex, a hope of escape through promotion in the army.

Britannia was fairly prosperous. The population was probably about two million. Light industry and mining flourished. Agriculture was inefficient, but it produced surpluses of grain which could be exported (though sometimes compulsorily, a source of complaint). Wheat, rye, barley and oats were all regularly grown. Before the conquest, oats may have been ignored as a weed, but under Rome an oat crop was highly valued as fodder for the cavalry mounts. Turnips and cabbages, peas and parsnips, were raised in vegetable plots. All the familiar fruits were already known — cherries, apples, pears, plums, raspberries, blackberries, sloes, medlars. The Britons had figs and mulberries and, in the sunnier places, vines. Their farm animals included all that might be expected: cattle, pigs, horses, chickens, geese, pigeons.

Meanwhile the country was more or less at peace, if with a wary consciousness of the tribes of Caledonia. It was towards the close of this century that their main grouping began to be spoken of as 'the Picts'. Most of the Picts lived north and northeast of the Clyde-Forth isthmus, though there may have been a few scattered communities south of it, overlapping Britons. Another source of disquiet was piracy by barbarians from across the North Sea. But that, at first, was minimal.

Through most of the third century, the Empire beyond the Channel was not nearly so well off. The lack of any fixed rule of succession caused repeated civil wars between would-be emperors, and the troops had a vested interest in these, because the pretenders paid for their support. Population declined, cities declined, morale declined. At last the Empire was gradually pulled together, first by Aurelian, then by Diocletian, a Balkan peasant who rose in the army by his own abilities and attained the purple in 284. He tried to regulate the economy and stabilize the currency. Judging the system to be too complex and widely extended for a single head, he divided it at the summit, sharing power with a colleague, Maximian, whom he made co-emperor. Both had the supreme title Augustus. Diocletian ruled in the east, Maximian in the west.

An important feature of the restored Empire was an attempted religious unification. This was meant to complete a process which had been gathering momentum for several decades. Through Diocletian, *Romanitas* became a mystique. The Empire was a divine Cosmopolis. All its peoples' gods formed a single hierarchy maintaining it. At the top was the 'Unconquered Sun', a Godhead symbolized by the sun in the sky, and embodied below in the earthly ruler. In the growing mystique Diocletian still stood alone. The emperor-worship which had first been tested at Colchester was vastly expanded and taken much more seriously. The emperor surrounded himself with oriental ritual, and wore a diadem and sumptuous robes. Diocletian had ended the imperial crisis, but the Empire was altered. Politically, it was no longer even centred on Rome. Power was at the headquarters of its overlords, wherever they might happen to be.

CHAPTER THREE

A Dawning of Possibilities

1

DIOCLETIAN HAD NOT BEEN EMPEROR LONG WHEN BRITAIN SUDDENLY BECAME INDEPENDENT UNDER A SINGLE SOVEREIGN. For the first time, Geoffrey of Monmouth's monarchy was a fact. The upstart's name was Carausius. We cannot be certain where he came from. A Roman writer speaks of him as *Menapiae civis*, a citizen of Menapia. The Menapii were a coastal tribe living in the Low Countries, and Carausius is often assumed to have been one of them. However, they do not seem to have had an actual town called Menapia. Furthermore, he is also called *Bataviae alumnus*, a foster-son of the Low Countries, the implication being that although he lived there, he was born somewhere else. Other candidates for his birthplace are Monapia, the Isle of Man; Menevia, afterwards St David's in Wales; and a possible Irish Menapia near Wexford. Whether he was a continental Menapian or a native of the British Isles, Carausius, like Diocletian, was a self-made man with no advantages of birth. In the words of one Roman historian, he was 'quick in thought and action'. The mementoes of his startling career hint at a bold character and a lively, literate mind.

It would be interesting to know how he rose to power. He comes into view only during a late phase of that process. There are indications that troops in Britain were in action about 285, perhaps repelling raiders from Ireland, and Carausius may have commanded them, thus gaining credit with the Britannic legions. In 286 he played a leading part in a campaign by Diocletian's colleague Maximian against the Bagaudae — bands of rebellious peasants, deserters and terrorists who infested northern Gaul. Later in the same year Maximian put him in charge of the Classis Britannica, the fleet which patrolled the Channel.

Here we confront another portentous name, the name of a people, not a person. The reason why the fleet needed a first-rate admiral was that the coasts of Gaul and Britain were being harassed by Saxons. Thus these forefathers of the English, with a language which was the ancestor of the English language, emerge fully from obscurity. The Saxons and their kinsfolk the Angles had long been drifting towards imperial territory from a homeland in Schleswig-Holstein. They were skilled seafarers and ruthless pirates, darting about elusively in long crazy boats, with crews who rowed and bailed by turns. From crowded coastal settlements west of the Elbe they were venturing out to raid richer countries. Eventually they would pass from raiding to land-seizure, with painful results for Gaul and worse for Britain. In Carausius's time that had not yet started. But raids had been troubling south-east Britain, on and off, for some decades, and now the problem was becoming acute.

Carausius tackled it with energy, overtaking the Saxons' boats and recapturing their plunder. Soon, however, the very people he was protecting began to complain. They asserted that the stolen goods which he recovered did not always find their way back to the owners. He was accused of keeping a portion for himself and his sailors. Then the charges grew graver. The admiral was deliberately not stopping the Saxons on their out-ward voyage when he could; he was waiting till they had done their thieving, so that he could pounce on them returning with booty and find something to take. Under his command the Roman fleet was a piratical force preying on the pirates them-selves, with the pirates' victims as the net losers.

Whether or not the accusations were true, Maximian believed them. Diocletian sensed a threatening crisis. His appointment of Maximian as full co-emperor, about this time, was prompted in part by the need to give him full powers to deal with it. Max-imian unwisely condemned Carausius to death without first taking him into custody. Hearing of the sentence, Carausius took evasive action on a scale his employers can hardly have fore-seen. Late in 286, or early in 287, he withdrew most of his fleet to British ports and declared himself emperor in the island. The troops supported him. So did one of the legions in Gaul. He deployed it to hold Boulogne, together with a long coastal strip and some country inland including Rouen.

The civilians of Britain acquiesced in his coup. They had major grievances arising out of the recent imperial reforms, such as the introduction of a new coinage replacing the old at a highly adverse exchange rate. Carausius put himself forward as a deliverer, and one of his early moves was to create a currency of his own. New coins began to appear with his bearded, bullnecked head on them. On one he was called *Restitutor Britanniae*, Restorer of Britain. On another, a trident-bearing symbolic figure greeted him with the Virgilian words *Expectate veni*, meaning 'Come, O awaited one'. No coin of the official Empire had ever carried a quotation from Rome's greatest poet. While the islanders may not have felt quite the warmth implied, Carausius at least had the merit of keeping taxes at home. Britons did not have to contribute to the upkeep of a bureaucracy and army in distant countries which many had never heard of.

During the first year or so of Carausius's reign, Maximian was too busy to attempt any action. He was marching up and down the Rhine fighting Frankish barbarians, with whom Carausius may have had an agreement. In the autumn of 288 Maximian at last began assembling a new Channel fleet, and in the following April it sailed for Britain. Carausius met it near his own shores and defeated it. In 290 he offered the emperors a negotiated peace, which they accepted. Their main object was to gain time. They had no further hope of getting rid of him quickly. While they waited for the right moment, he could be trusted, in his own interest, to defend Britain against the Irish, Picts or anyone else. Carausius himself did not see the treaty in that light. He claimed it as a *de facto* recognition achieved by success, giving him a place in the imperial scheme of things. In that spirit he celebrated a triumph and insisted that he was a true Roman, protected by Jupiter, Mars, Minerva and Neptune.

A continued propaganda by coinage reflected his claims. It is clear that this was an aspect of his rule which he cared very much about, and he, or his designers, showed resourcefulness and originality. Even at the start of his reign, he had taken care to mark the change promptly by overstriking existing issues. Then came the *Restitutor Britanniae* coin and others, out of Carausian mints. One of these was in London; one was at a place beginning with C, which may have been Clausentum (Bitterne by Southampton); and the third was in the Gallic enclave, perhaps at Rouen. These injected Carausius's special motifs into a coinage following standard patterns, but of higher quality. For the first time in forty or fifty years, citizens of a Roman land had good silver denarii. After the agreement of 290 the emphasis shifted. Some of Carausius's coins referred to 'the three Augusti' — himself, Diocletian and Maximian. One portrayed all three as *Carausius et fratres sui*, Carausius and his brothers. Later, Diocletian was to imitate these excellent issues. At the time neither he nor Maximian responded. Their own currency took no notice of their impudent brother.

Britain's emperor held the whole territory intact. A milestone near Carlisle shows that his power extended to the frontier, and there is every reason to think that the barbarians beyond stood in awe of him. He founded a chain of fortifications along what came to be known, ominously, as the Saxon Shore. Two or three small forts already existed, but he built stronger ones at Richborough, Portchester and probably several other places, and seemingly remodelled the fort at Burgh Castle near Yarmouth. The Classis Britannica was given new bases, while the troops in the forts were ready to trap any raiders who might effect a landing.

In this respect, and in others, Carausius's conduct during his brief undisputed reign was non-aggressive. He did not try to advance his frontier in Gaul, or to attack or subvert the official emperors. As for them, they still denied him recognition, yet they still left him alone. In fact they never did conquer him. But presently they began a second attempt.

It was launched, slowly and deliberately, in 293. The imperial commander was Constantius Chlorus, who had risen to power through an expansion of the new system of government. Early in the same year Diocletian had attached junior emperors to the senior ones. He and Maximian remained the only Augusti, but now each had a 'Caesar' as his assistant. Diocletian's was Galerius, Maximian's was Constantius. Part of the arrangement was that the Caesars had to divorce their wives and marry daughters of their respective Augusti. While the sovereign power was thus vested in a closely-knit tetrarchy, each of its members had regional responsibilities. Constantius was in charge of Gaul, and therefore had the task of recovering Britain.

His first move was to disable Carausius on the continent. He besieged Boulogne, closing the harbour with a mole, which bottled up part of the British fleet and cut off relief from across the Channel. After stubborn resistance the defenders had to give up. It was bad luck: the next high tide opened a gap in the mole. Successful, but in sobering circumstances, Constantius remained cautious. The offensive against Carausius could not be allowed to fail. And then, during autumn of the same year, news reached Gaul that the Emperor of Britain was dead. His finance minister Allectus had murdered him and taken control.

There was no sign of a British surrender. On the other hand, there was no sign that the position was any more urgent. Methodically Constantius prepared a new fleet, meanwhile subduing tribes in Gaul and the Low Countries which had shown sympathy for Carausius. Maximian strengthened the forces along the Rhine to prevent a diversion by barbarians on the German side. In September 296 Constantius was ready. His troops boarded the transports.

Allectus had turned out to be a dismal successor to his victim. Even that remarkable coinage had become uninteresting, with the assassin's profile crudely portrayed on one side, and lifeless little pictures of ships on the other. Britain awaited the blow passively. When it came it was double. Undeterred by a sidewind and menacing weather, Constantius's second-in-command, Asclepiodotus, put to sea from the mouth of the Seine with a portion of the fleet . . . but only a portion. Constantius himself had the rest of it at Boulogne. Allectus's reply was to mobilize his naval forces against one opponent, his land forces against the other. He sent ships to stop Asclepiodotus off the Isle of Wight. He tried to block Constantius by stationing an army near London, composed of troops withdrawn from the north (including Hadrian's Wall) and Frankish mercenaries.

His strategy fell to pieces. The British fleet never fought. The enemy slipped past in a fog and landed near Southampton Water. There Asclepiodotus disembarked the invasion force and burned his ships. Allectus rushed his army westwards and made a stand in Hampshire, near Silchester, the old capital of the Atrebates. But the soldiers were exhausted, morale was low, and the loyalty of the regular troops was doubtful. Only the mercenaries were fully engaged, and they suffered heavy losses. The battle ended in a rout. Allectus was killed trying to escape. A remnant of the army got back to London in a state of total indiscipline. The city was in danger of looting by the mercenaries. At this juncture, however, Constantius managed to appear in his turn as a deliverer. After a false start, frustrated by the weather, several of his troopships had succeeded in getting into the Thames. Imperial order was restored in the capital. When he arrived himself the citizens welcomed him. Whatever their retrospective feelings about Carausius, any zeal they might have felt for the traitor Allectus was long since defunct.

Constantius responded. After all, he was receiving the rebels back into civilized society. He marked the occasion by issuing a gold medallion. A specimen found at Arras weighs 53gm. On one side is a fine profile of Constantius, looking more like a portrait than most such images; he is rather heavily handsome, with a Roman nose. On the other he is seen again, seated on horseback with a spear in his hand. Before him a female figure, the guardian spirit of London, kneels submissively at the gate of her city. So that there can be no mistake, the letters LON fill a space below her. Above Constantius are the words *Redditor lucis aeternae*, Restorer of the Eternal Light. Yet in spite of the fanfare, and the ease and relief with which Britain returned to the imperial fold, Carausius was remembered. His name was given to Britons long after his death. Coins issued by an ephemeral fourth-century pretender show that he either bore it or adopted it. The name appears on a Christian memorial stone near Penmachno in Caernarvonshire.

As we might expect, Geoffrey of Monmouth makes an eventful story out of all this. By a curious irony, having at last got a genuine 'king of Britain' to talk about, he treats him as a usurper whose reign does not count. The end is wild confusion, with Asclepiodotus figuring as a Briton, the Duke of Cornwall. He becomes king and slaughters the Romans in London. Yet the fantasy has one point of interest. Geoffrey says a number of Romans were beheaded beside the Walbrook, a stream running through the City, long since hidden underground. In the 1860s the archaeologist Pitt-Rivers explored its bed and unearthed about thirty-six human skulls, with few other bones. These have been invoked as confirming Geoffrey, to the extent, at least, that he knew some tradition of a massacre with decapitations beside the Walbrook during the final disorder. The objection is that Roman coins were lying near, and none was later than Marcus Aurelius, who died in 180. A plausible explanation is that the stream-bed was a dumping-ground for the heads of executed criminals, and a few of the skulls were found in Geoffrey's time, whereupon he invented the massacre — or borrowed it from some other inventive person.

To revert to history, Constantius made a wise break with precedent. After his victory he stayed in Britain for a while and attended to its needs in person. One of these, he judged, was a partition into smaller administrative units. For some decades Britain had been divided into two provinces, Britannia Superior and Inferior. The first comprised the south, the Midlands and Wales. The second covered the east and north. Constantius effected, perhaps in stages, a double split. Britannia Superior was broken up into Maxima Caesariensis, with London as its capital, and Britannia Prima embracing Wales and the west, probably governed from Cirencester. Britannia Inferior became Flavia Caesariensis, capital Lincoln, and Britannia Secunda, capital York.

Constantius extended the Saxon Shore fortifications. The outcome of his programme was a chain of eleven coastal forts from the Wash to the Isle of Wight, with high and thick walls, and sockets for artillery. From adjoining harbours new scout-ships presently went out on patrol. These were fast and light, painted sea-green as camouflage, and manned by twenty rowers in sea-green uniforms. They were nicknamed *Pictae* because they were supposed to look like the curraghs of the Picts. Britain had become more Pict-conscious. Allectus's withdrawal of Wall garrisons had encouraged raiding from the north. Constantius returned the garrisons to their quarters and led punitive expeditions beyond, one during his first stay in Britain in 296-7, the other when he was there again in 306. The second took him into the far north of Scotland; he believed in being thorough. He also ordered a general rebuilding of northern forts, including outposts beyond the Wall, such as High Rochester in Northumberland. At some stage he may also have fortified Cardiff and Holyhead, against the Irish.

On the civilian side, less is known. However, he began a new building programme at Verulamium, and paid a much-appreciated tribute to British craftsmen by recruiting a team to help in the restoration of Autun in Gaul, which had suffered from attacks by Bagaudae. He also took an unusual interest in education. A feeling of stability and security returned.

He made his second visit to Britain after a reshuffle of the tetrarchy which turned him into a full Augustus. On 1 May 305 Diocletian abdicated. So, under protest, did Maximian. Their two Caesars were promoted. Galerius became emperor of the east, Constantius of the west, with his capital at Trier (Trèves) on the Moselle. For each of them Galerius appointed a new Caesar as junior colleague. But Constantius's health was failing. After his overawing of the Picts he died at York on 25 July 306.

2

Long before that, he had done something for British posterity which was even more memorable than his works of peace and defence. Or at least he had brought more memorable characters on to the stage. As already mentioned, he divorced his first wife in 293 for reasons of state. The lady thus turned away was named Helena. She takes us into a different world — into several different worlds. More people have heard of her reputed father than have ever heard of Constantius himself, or his colleagues in empire.

We confront this personage face to face if we follow Geoffrey's legendary story a little further. He builds up to an unexpected entrance. The apocryphal 'king' Asclepiodotus reigns in peace for some years. Then he is overthrown by Coel, Duke of Colchester, who assumes the crown. Constantius comes to Britain and agrees to a treaty confirming Coel as a tributary sovereign. Helena is Coel's beautiful and talented daughter, whom he has groomed for government. He dies soon after signing the treaty and Constantius marries her, becoming king of Britain.

Coel of course is recognizable at once.

> Old King Cole was a merry old soul
> And a merry old soul was he;
> He called for his pipe and he called for his bowl
> And he called for his fiddlers three.

Like several Britons of renown, Old King Cole is said to have been buried in the monastic graveyard at Glastonbury. Wherever Geoffrey found him, he represents somebody's attempt to explain the name 'Colchester'. It means in reality 'the Roman station on the Colne'. 'Clun' in Shropshire is a variant of the same river-name, which was originally 'Colun'. That is as far as etymology goes. Certainly the name is British, not Anglo-Saxon. But to admit Old King Cole we would have to suppose that the river was called after a person, or else that a person was called after the river, and there is no reason to suppose either.

Coel, therefore, is phantasmal, and it is not likely that the Helena whom Constantius married was his daughter. It is not even likely that she was the daughter of some British noble living at Colchester, because their wedlock began and ended before Constantius was in Britain. The truth seems to be that she was born about 255 at Drepanum in Bithynia, now northern Turkey. There she is said to have been a barmaid. If so, it was no handicap. All the emperors in the last part of the fourth century were, like Diocletian, soldiers of peasant origin who rose from the ranks. Constantius married her when he was simply a young army officer, with useful connections but no social or political standing. Their son Constantine was born at Naissus (Niš, in Yugoslavia) about 280.

When Constantius took office as Caesar in 293, it broke up the family twice over. Besides divorcing Helena and marrying the daughter, or rather step-daughter, of Maximian, he had to send Constantine to Diocletian's eastern court, with a tacit understanding that he would be a hostage for his father's good conduct. Helena herself was provided for, but retired from public life. Her departure was to prove temporary.

In 305, promoted to Augustus, her ex-husband wanted to have Constantine with him. He asked his co-emperor Galerius for his son's release. Afraid of a family coup, Galerius demurred and wavered, signed a travel warrant, and then changed his mind, but too late. Constantine had gone. After the swiftest possible passage through Europe, he joined his father at Boulogne. They crossed to Britain together and he took part in the expedition to Pictland.

When Constantius died at York in 306, his son had made a name for himself. He was a tall, imposing young man, brave, intelligent, self-controlled. The troops proclaimed him Augustus. Many of them were British. The action showed a growing awareness that things could happen in Britain, decisions could be taken there. Britons had no wish for another Carausian secession, but they realized that they were not bound to be passive within the Empire. In that realization was a seed of future events.

At first Constantine remained in the island. He carried on his father's work, improving the highways and building new ones, both in the north to link up the refurbished defences, and in Wales. The measures taken by father and son helped to give the Britons another spell of tranquil prosperity, which lasted till the 340s. Constantine, however, soon had external problems to grapple with. Galerius grudgingly recognized him as Caesar but not Augustus, and tried to set up a favourite as Augustus over him. The sequel was a chain-reaction. In October 306 the unauthorized proclamation in Britain was echoed and countered by another in Italy. The citizens of Rome itself had become restive at being ruled by emperors who no longer lived there, and were stripping away their privileges and exemptions in such matters as taxation. They set up a son of Maximian named Maxentius as a rival Caesar. A tangled civil war followed. Maximian himself emerged from his enforced retirement, supported his son, then quarrelled with him and negotiated an agreement with Constantine, who was now in Gaul. Again the agreement had a marital clause. Constantine divorced his wife and married Maximian's daughter Fausta.

This renewed struggle took a different course from those which had torn the Empire in the third century. It acquired a religious dimension. The reason lay in a feature of imperial policy which had begun to cause rifts shortly before it broke out. Every ruler in Diocletian's system had endorsed the mystique of the Unconquered Sun as the Empire's God and patron, with all other deities as his subordinates. But this cult had raised a problem about the Christians. As the only major body refusing to conform to it, they stood convicted of a sort of supernatural treason, which endangered the Empire by offending God and his earthly viceroys. Also the Church was disturbingly well organized and effective. It was a state within the State, and therefore a menace.

Feelings of this kind had inspired persecutions in the past, but most of them were less than whole-hearted. With the rise of the imperial cult, and a more totalitarian spirit in government, the issue had grown acute. Moreover the Christians were no longer a petty sect, they were numerous. Diocletian had dismissed his Christian civil servants and soldiers, and in 303, with Galerius, had launched a new and would-be-annihilating persecution. The Augusti ordered that all copies of the scriptures should be confiscated, churches should be torn down, and Christians should be compelled to sacrifice at pagan altars. Where these edicts were fully enforced, many Christians who resisted were put to death, or condemned to forced labour, which was death a little deferred. But the rulers themselves were never in full agreement on the anti-Christian policy. Galerius pursued it ardently, out of conviction. Constantius did not. He had some churches destroyed, but he exerted little pressure on individuals. In Britain only three martyrs are recorded — Alban at Verulamium, Julius and Aaron at Caerleon — and although they are stated to have been victims of this persecution, it was probably an earlier one.

Constantine was even less zealous than his father. A Spanish bishop came to live at his court and insinuated a different point of view. As the civil strife grew more bitter and complex — in 308 there were six emperors at once — his thoughts moved towards an inversion of the official theory. Doubtless the Empire's troubles were due to divine anger. But could it be that the cause of the anger was the persecution itself? The troubles had increased since it began. Perhaps God, whoever he might be, approved of the Christians and was confounding their oppressors.

In 312 Constantine marched against Maxentius, who was still holding out in Italy, but whose behaviour had reduced Italian enthusiasm for him. Constantine is said to have been convinced of God's true will when he saw a cross in the sky (probably a halo phenomenon, caused by ice crystals in the sunbeams) and heard a celestial message, 'In this conquer'. He defeated Maxentius at the Milvian Bridge near Rome, and emerged as sole emperor of the west. His colleague in the east was Licinius. In 313 they published the Edict of Milan guaranteeing the Christians toleration and full civil rights. Ten years later he marched against Licinius and defeated him too. Thus a man invested with power in Britain, and at first a ruler of Britain only, had risen to the topmost pinnacle of the world.

Despite the glare of historical limelight, Constantine remains enigmatic. He reached his conclusion about the Church, he even thought he had been divinely guided to it, yet he hovered outside. He favoured Christianity, yet chiefly as a state cult with more conviction and talent behind it than the paganism which Diocletian had tried to reorganize. It was to be a new religious embodiment of *Romanitas*, the imperial mystique, the Eternal Light which his father had restored to Britain. The upper classes began drifting into the fold as he wished. He found, however, that Christians were not as firmly united in triumph as they had been under persecution. The heretic Arius, who denied the equal divinity of Christ, had a vocal following. Since a split in the Church would stultify his reason for favouring it, Constantine summoned the Council of Nicaea in 325 to draw it together, but failed to heal the breach.

Another of his actions was the planting of the central apparatus of government at Byzantium, re-founded as Constantinople, and today called Istanbul. This left the Bishop of Rome less overshadowed by the civil power, and placed him and his successors on the road leading to a political papacy. That was not the intention, although a forged document called the 'Donation of Constantine' would eventually make out that it was. In the populous east, Constantine governed the Church himself. The atmosphere of emperor-worship lingered on at his pompous, autocratic court, where several relatives found that the slightest hint of disaffection was fatal. He did finally receive baptism, but only in 337 when he was dying. Posterity knows him as Constantine the Great.

For his mother Helena, the non-daughter of Old King Cole, he felt a deep respect. Drawing her into court life, he gave her the title *Venerabilis et Piissima Augusta*, the Most Honourable and Religious Empress. *Venerabilis*, which might appear less than tactful, then meant simply 'deserving of reverence' and implied nothing about her age. He also re-named her birthplace 'Helenopolis'. She became a Christian about the time of the Edict of Milan, not waiting till she was on her deathbed. In her case there was no public motive. It was a genuine conversion. She attended church among the populace, plainly dressed, and gave generously to charity.

When she was in her seventies she made one of the most famous of pilgrimages. In the Holy Land, her son was busy building ornate holy places for the new state religion. The sites of Calvary and the nearby Holy Sepulchre had been blotted out two centuries earlier by a temple of Venus and an adjacent terrace, which, ironically, marked where they had been and so made it possible to bring them out into the light again. The Emperor told Macarius, the Bishop of Jerusalem, to dismantle the edifices of paganism and restore the old configuration. He must then put up a church enclosing both sacred sites, a church 'worthy of the most marvelous place in the world'. That, in the current climate of taste, meant a lavish use of gold, mosaic and expensive marble. Helena went to Jerusalem to keep a family eye on the work in progress, and visit the scenes of the Gospels.

As it turned out, her journey made her a heroine of Christian legend. Constantine, it seems, cherished a hope that the cross of Christ might still exist. He suggested to Macarius that a search should be made for it during the work on Mount Calvary. In due course it was found, and according to the story, or rather stories, Helena played a leading part. She had a dream which guided the search; or she met a Jew who knew a secret tradition, and extracted it by a fairly ruthless interrogation. At any rate, so it is said, she told the excavators to clear out an old rock-cistern used long before as a dumping place for rubbish. In it they discovered three crosses, and the panel of wood mentioned in *Matthew 27:37* with the title 'King of the Jews'. To settle which was the right cross, Macarius brought a sick woman to the spot and made her touch all three, and one of them cured her.

Whatever the extent of Helena's role, the cross, or an object accepted as the cross, was undoubtedly found. Its dismemberment began very soon. As early as 346 another bishop of Jerusalem, St Cyril, speaks of its being spread 'fragment by fragment' throughout most of the Empire. An early reference to King Arthur has been read as a hint that he carried one of the fragments into battle. Today such relics are notoriously widespread. However, sceptics who gibe that there are enough of them to build a ship, and so forth, have overreached themselves. Measurement has proved that if they were all collected and stuck together, they would not come anywhere near to making a cross large enough for a crucifixion. Strictly as far as cubic capacity goes, they could all be genuine.

Helena made a long stay in the Holy Land, but died somewhere else in 330. She may have returned to her Bithynian birthplace. Her body was taken to Rome for burial. In the Orthodox Church she and her son came to be honoured as 'the holy, illustrious and great emperors, crowned by God and equal to the Apostles'. She was enrolled among Catholic saints in a less Byzantine style. St Helen's day is 18 August.

In medieval legend Britain was not the only country to claim her. She was also said to have been born at Trier or Trèves, and to have presented its cathedral with another precious relic, the Holy Coat. However, the Roman basilica which was the nucleus of the cathedral was not built till after her death, and while we have fairly early evidence — of a sort — for the Cross story, we have none for the Coat story. Only the Britons made anything interesting of her beyond the main legend. They and their Welsh descendants did a surprising thing. They turned her into a demi-goddess.

Her husband and son had left their mark on the British landscape in the shape of the improved road system linking centres in Wales and the Border country. To these roads, popular belief allotted a tutelary spirit. Much the same happened in Brittany, where folklore used to speak of a long-lived enchantress named Ahès by whom the roads were made. In Britain her counterpart was a more splendid figure, Elen Luyddog, Helen-of-the-Hosts, ordainer and patroness of the highways where the troops marched. Whether or not she had a prior existence as a deity, she emerges into view as a mythification of the Empress Helena. The southward road from Caernarvon in particular was known as Sarn Helen (Helen's Causeway), and her name survives in Moel Hilyn (Helen's Hill) and other items of Welsh topography. A tenth-century genealogy of the princes of Dyfed, mixing fact and myth, trace their line back to 'Constantine the son of Constantius and Helen Luicdauc who went out of Britain to seek the Cross'.

3

Helen-of-the-Hosts evolved further, as we shall see, into a legendary British Helen who even had touches of the Greek one. But her later, more romantic image was a consequence of events half a century after the passing of Helena. For Britain it was a half-century of gathering clouds. Barbarian enemies were threatening again on three sides. The Picts, deterred through a long lull, were again growing bold enough to raid over Hadrian's Wall: little, bearded, tattooed men armed with spears and slings. Raiders from Ireland, hitherto only an occasional source of trouble, began after a while to cross over repeatedly in fleets of curraghs. Some were to conquer parts of Wales and hold it for decades. Most were called Scots; the Scottish colonization of Caledonia, which gave it the name we know, was still far off. Their curraghs were big, seaworthy craft, made with many hides stretched over wooden frames. Each carried a band of warriors with swords, spears and round bull-hide shields. When they were ashore their leaders summoned them with frightening blasts on enormous curled war-horns.

And after a while, also, the Saxons reappeared. No longer merely piratical, they were more and more ready to beach their boats and venture inland. Britons came to know how they looked at close quarters — fierce, fair-haired, drably clothed in loose tunics, cloaks and trousers. Their characteristic weapon was the short-sword, *seax*, from which they took their name. They also felled the inhabitants with eight-foot lances and immense bows, shooting arrows tipped with bone or iron.

The crumbling of the peace had its origin in 342 when Pictish raiding parties poured over the Wall. They accepted terms and withdrew. But the Britons, alarmed and anxious, grew increasingly unhappy with the sons of Constantine who had shared out the Empire. The burden of maintaining the huge state-mechanism was heavy, the benefits were becoming less evident. In 350 many Britons supported a pretender, Magnentius, who won temporary control of most of the Roman west. He may have been half British himself. After three years he succumbed to the attacks of the emperor he had challenged, a second Constantius, less magnanimous than the first. Constantius II was aware of the Britons' discontent. Despite a promise of amnesty, he sent a special envoy named Paul to seek out traitors. Martinus, the governor, defended some citizens whom he knew to be innocent. Having made many arrests, Paul tried to arrest Martinus himself. Martinus drew his sword to kill him, failed, and turned the sword on himself before he could be seized. The suicide of the just governor aroused an indignation which Paul did nothing to appease. He put his prisoners in chains and shipped them off to Constantius to be tortured.

In 360 the Picts broke the peace terms and ravaged the Wall area, aided by Scots from Ireland. This was the first major invasion, and it inflicted lasting harm on the north. The Caesar Julian (afterwards dubbed Julian the Apostate because of his desertion of Christianity) sent over a general, Lupicinus, with four regiments of German and Balkan auxiliaries. The invasion was repulsed, but the Britons were not reconciled. Their supposed protector Lupicinus treated them with cruelty, rapacity and contempt. Julian, who had an outstanding capacity for misjudgment, thought the danger was over and cut British military expenditure. Five years later the Picts were busy yet again; so were the Irish, including, it seems, a tribe of 'Attacotti' reputed to be cannibals; and so were the Saxons.

Thus far the three marauding nations had never acted in concert. But imperial neglect inspired an alliance. In 367, organized, it would seem, by some unrecorded genius who kept in the background, all the barbarians swooped on Britain together. The Picts crossed the Wall, the Scots and Attacotti moved inland from the west coast, and a swarm of Saxons disembarked in the south-east with Frankish comrades — fellow-Teutons of theirs who were also active in northern Gaul. Britain's defence had been entrusted to two commanders, the 'Duke of the Britains' (*Dux Britanniarum*, plural as referring to the four British provinces), and the 'Count of the Saxon Shore' (*Come Litoris Saxonici*). Both came to grief. Fullofaudes, the Duke, was ambushed and taken prisoner. Nectaridus, the Count, was killed in a catastrophic battle. Among the harassed population, loyalty had declined further, to the point of outright disaffection. In the north a body of Britons called *areani*, posted beyond the frontier to spy on the Picts, betrayed information to them. As the barbarians swept across the countryside looting, they were joined by resentful peasants, and slaves abandoning the villas.

Throughout that winter Britain was in anarchy, with foreign and domestic plunderers everywhere. The army contingents were demoralized, and weakened by mass desertions. The Emperor Valentinian tried two generals who achieved nothing. In 368 he appointed a Spaniard, Theodosius, who proved to be equal to the crisis. Theodosius ferried troops over to Richborough and marched to London. The city was under virtual siege, and he could get no trustworthy information on what was happening anywhere else. He sent out reconnaissance parties and only attempted a campaign when he had formed a clear picture. Then he announced a pardon for army deserters and tackled the enemy piecemeal, pacifying first one region and then another, leaving the difficult northern zone to the last. By the end of 369 peace was restored.

Theodosius did his best to prevent a recurrence. He re-manned the Wall, disbanded the untrustworthy *areani*, extended the coastal defences, imported more troops — Germans considered to be pro-Roman. However, the old order had sustained a blow from which it would never quite recover. Rich estates had been devastated, slaves had vanished. Henceforth many of the great landowners were driven to improvise, using fewer of their buildings, or going over to light industry such as the manufacture of farming tools. Squatters moved into villas and lit cooking fires on the mosaic floors.

Britain as a whole was resilient and far from ruin. Perhaps, despite the losses of the wealthy, more of the ordinary people than ever before were tolerably well off — a higher proportion, that is, of a contracting population. Yet the signs of dissolution and insecurity were not effaced. *Romanitas* was still the only imaginable way of life, but faith in the actual imperial scheme, with its dependence on an unreliable and oppressive power outside Britain, had ebbed. Another declaration of independence was not in prospect; not yet. As a precedent, Carausius was too radical for most. The proclamation of Constantine, however, had been a brilliant success. An initiative in Britain was thinkable.

That was already plain even at the time of Theodosius's victory. He had to cope with a plot among the soldiers to set up a political exile as their own emperor. While he stamped it out, and restored order or a semblance of it, the beginning of a long transition was only fourteen years away.

CHAPTER FOUR

An Emperor Transformed

1

EARLY IN 383 THE ROMAN WORLD HAD AN ODDLY ASSORTED TRIO OF OVERLORDS. All were Christians; the last pagan reaction, under Julian, was long past. Senior in authority was Gratian, son of the Valentinian who had grappled with the British débâcle. Valentinian had made Gratian co-emperor at that time, though he was still a child. On his father's demise, Gratian had been accepted as the western Augustus, with his little half-brother, another Valentinian, as a very junior colleague. A few years later he had appointed an emperor of the east, Theodosius, who was a son of the Spanish reconqueror of Britain, and had taken part in that operation himself.

Gratian was now twenty-four, Valentinian II eleven, Theodosius about thirty-seven. Both the younger partners were giving grounds for disquiet. Gratian, in Gaul, was declining from a good beginning into widespread dislike. Religious without real virtue, he poured out money foolishly and allowed his officials to take bribes. Most of his time was spent in the company of priests who gave him bad advice, and barbarians whom he took on too-frequent hunting expeditions, snubbing people who thought themselves entitled to favour. His fondness for companions regarded as savages was losing him the loyalty of much of the army. Valentinian was sovereign of Italy, and the Illyrian province on the far side of the Adriatic. The seat of the Italian court was Milan, not Rome. Power was in the hands of a regent, Valentinian's able and comely mother Justina. Like several of the Empire's fourth-century rulers, she was an Arian heretic. Her son acquiesced in that belief, which caused friction with a mainly Catholic population.

Once again, something stirred in Britain. The most notable soldier in the island was Magnus Clemens Maximus, a Spaniard like the first Theodosius, to whom he was related, or claimed to be. He had served with him in the war of reconquest and stayed on. Maximus was a tough, audacious man, sternly Catholic and anti-heretical, a first sketch for a Conquistador. Warmly respected for his leadership in still another Pictish campaign, he now held a high command, being perhaps (it is not certain) the *Dux Britanniarum*. However, he nursed a grievance over past delays in his promotion. He was popular, both with the troops and with civilian Britons.

His proclamation as Augustus in 383 was the doing of the army, like that of Constantine. How far he was a leader of revolution, how far he was a creature of circumstance, it is hard to say. But the event was momentous, even though no one realized it at the time. In retrospect Maximus is the first ruler of Britain who faces both ways. He is a figure in Roman history, but he is also part of the island's later story, the originator of independence, the source of legitimacy for claimants to power long afterwards, a reputed ancestor of Welsh dynasties and, in Welsh romance, a sort of honorary Briton himself.

His personal reign in Britain was brief, and little is known about it. He re-opened Carausius's London mint, inactive since 326. Also there is a hint in the family history of a Welsh king, Voteporix, that he devolved authority over south-west Wales on to an amenable Irish chief. If so, this was probably the first instance of a policy destined to be crucial in Britain's development — the attempted domestication of the barbarian enemy. But Maximus had larger issues to face. The contrast between Carausius and Constantine made the logic of his position clear. Whatever his wishes he could not merely sit tight, holding Britain alone. The neighbouring continent might be in feebler hands than those of the great Diocletian's partners, but sooner or later it would defeat him. Accordingly he took the offensive. He proclaimed a righteous war against the devout but unworthy Gratian and the abuses he sanctioned. His force included thousands of British volunteers. This was more like a national expedition than anything that had happened before, or would again, until the days of the Plantagenets.

Maximus landed at the mouth of the Rhine and was welcomed by disaffected officers. From there he marched on Paris. Near the city, Gratian tried to stop him. Fighting lasted five days, but in the end Gratian's unpopularity told. His Moorish cavalry changed sides and the rest of his army disintegrated. Maximus rewarded some of the Moors and took them into his service as guards. Meanwhile the deposed emperor fled south with three hundred horsemen. The cities closed their gates to him. He arrived at Lyons and was detained there by the governor. According to an account which circulated later, the governor promised to protect him and then, when Maximus's men caught up, handed him over to be put to death. It is a fact that he was murdered at supper on 25 August, perhaps by Andragathius, one of Maximus's generals. A further allegation that Maximus rewarded the murderer is beyond proof or disproof.

Whatever the extent of his complicity, Maximus now had no opponent in Gaul. He made Trier his capital, and sent a chamberlain to Constantinople to parley with Theodosius. It was observed with interest that the chamberlain was not a eunuch. For several decades, eunuchs had been the principal courtiers and diplomats of the Eastern Empire. Maximus, in those early days, refused to employ them, though he did later. The gist of the agreement which his virile ambassador proposed was that Theodosius should recognize him as emperor of the west.

This raised the question of the boy Valentinian, who, in theory, should have succeeded his half-brother. Maximus demanded that he should leave Italy and live at Trier, with the status, in effect, of a puppet. The regent Justina replied by sending him a personal envoy. With some astuteness in view of Maximus's strong Catholicity, she chose Ambrose, Bishop of Milan, the most eminent figure in the Catholic Church of the west. The future saint urged that it was unreasonable to expect the lad and his mother to cross the Alps in winter. He persuaded Maximus to drop his demand and allow Valentinian to go on reigning in Italy with its Illyrian adjunct. The price was his exclusion from everything else. Theodosius, who was busy with problems of his own, felt obliged to consent. He put up statues of Maximus, one of the tokens of recognition. For Britain and Gaul it was only an acknowledgement of a commitment those countries had already made. Spain now followed suit, and so did the western portion of Roman Africa, with no sign of reluctance. Egypt did not then count as Africa and remained with Theodosius, but when Maximus was named in a speech in Alexandria, the Egyptians cheered.

It seems clear that he was an improvement on most of his predecessors — competent, energetic and, while sometimes devious, never corrupt. He could commit acts that were very hard to defend, but, as will appear, he could admit an error and change course. If he had come to power legally he might have done well. Since he had not, he could never rely on being left in peace, and therefore he maintained a strong army and taxed his subjects heavily to support it. Yet even in this his record was distinctive. The Gauls suffered, but paid; and unlike most emperors he extorted taxes from the Germans, 'by the mere terror of his name', as a near-contemporary put it.

His reputation as a patron of the Church and a pillar of orthodoxy was soon widespread. Bishops from all quarters gathered at his court in Trier. Servility was the norm, with a single exception — Martin, Bishop of Tours, afterwards acknowledged a saint, a former soldier remembered for the tale of his cutting his cloak in two on a cold night and giving half to a beggar. Martin at first rejected Maximus's overtures, saying he would not be the guest of a man who had killed one emperor and denied another his rights. In reply, Maximus insisted (as he did to the end) that he had not wished to reign, and had only defended the power the army thrust on him.

At last, to his delight and relief, Martin came to a banquet with some of his clergy. One of the priests was placed among officers of the highest rank, Martin himself sat on a stool next to the emperor. When a waiter brought Maximus a goblet of wine, he was told to give it to Martin first. Everyone assumed that Martin would then hand it to Maximus. Instead he passed it to his priest, saying no one had a better right. The gesture startled the company but increased Maximus's respect. Afterwards he often invited Martin to visit him, and they discussed topics of mutual interest. Maximus's wife listened intently, sat at Martin's feet, and, much to his distress, cooked for him and waited on him at table. His biographer, with a reminiscence of *Luke* 10:38-42, praises her as a combination of Mary and Martha.

Maximus's Catholic faith was sincere: sincere enough to lead him into setting a fearful precedent. He was the first Christian to put heretics to death. His victims were the Priscillianists. Priscillian, Bishop of Avila, was the founder of a sect in Maximus's native Spain. It was one of many embodying the Gnostic or

Manichaean outlook, élitist, hyper-'spiritual', with a system of life-denying rigour which included renunciation of sex. If a convert had a spouse, the marriage was broken up. That at least was the theory. In practice, it asserted, Bishop Priscillian travelled with a group of spiritual 'sisters', and showed his indifference to fleshly taboos by praying among his disciples with no clothes on.

In 384 a synod held at Bordeaux condemned his teaching. He appealed to Maximus, with disastrous results. The emperor had him arrested. During a visit to the court, Martin extracted a promise that the heretic's life would be spared. But after he had gone a trial was held, and in 385 Maximus passed a death sentence and sent tribunes to Spain to proceed against the heretics. He was urged on by the fanatical Bishop of Ossanova, Ithacius, and several of Ithacius's colleagues. The examination of suspects was less than sympathetic. Pallor suggestive of fasting, and supposedly tell-tale quirks of dress, constituted the main evidence. The leader and six followers were beheaded. A Priscillianist writer, Tiberion, was banished to *Sylina Insula,* the Isle of Scilly — not 'Isles', a point of some interest. At that time most of the present islands were joined together. It has been claimed that the submergence of the ground between is part of the basis for the legend of Lyonesse, the sunken land beyond Cornwall.

Martin indignantly hurried back to Trier, with the support of Ambrose and many other bishops. On the way he was met by some palace functionaries whom Maximus had sent at the request of Ithacius and his clique. They tried to prevent Martin from going farther till he had given them a pledge not to make trouble. He brushed them aside and went on. Rumours were spreading which made the emperor's conduct look even uglier. People said he was condemning the heretics as an excuse for seizing their property. The charge was not absurd. Some of them had decided that a total contempt for worldly goods was quite compatible with possessing plenty of them.

On Martin's arrival, Maximus kept him waiting, while Ithacius clamoured for his arrest. At last the emperor let him in and tried to appease him, but having no success, angrily told him to leave, and ordered the execution of two former adherents of Gratian for whom Martin had also been interceding. That night Martin returned to the palace offering a bargain. If the two prisoners were pardoned, and the tribunes were recalled from Spain, he would make his peace with the hostile bishops including Ithacius and join in communion with them. Maximus agreed, and the persecution was halted. Martin, however, remained unhappy, feeling that he had condoned the persecutors. For some time after this he avoided gatherings of bishops. According to his biographer, his miracle-working was less effective. The Pope censured Ithacius and his protector, but the precedent was set, the damage was done.

Meanwhile it had become plain that the uneasy equilibrium of the three emperors could not hold. To survive, Maximus would have to emulate Constantine further, and push on into the richer and more populous parts of the Empire. His heavy taxation, and the rumours about his motives in the Priscillianist affair, were due to his need to pay for war preparations out of depleted provincial treasuries. Martin predicted shrewdly that if he continued to tread in Constantine's path he would be equally successful in Italy, but not beyond. Theodosius would be too much for him.

Maximus took his next step in 386. He sent his son Victor to Milan to renew the demand for Valentinian to come to Trier. It was accompanied with an accusation that the Arian court at Milan was persecuting Catholics. This, Maximus insinuated, would justify him in marching into Italy to protect them. Here he was on dubious ground. The trouble which he referred to had been simmering for some time. Justina had asked Ambrose, as Bishop of Milan, to allow Arians the use of one of the city's churches. His refusal had been backed by mass Catholic demonstrations, which had led in turn to repressive measures by Justina and to a fine being imposed on the merchants. As a result the court was unpopular with the citizenry, but to speak of Arian persecution was a little extreme.

On receiving Maximus's demand, Justina temporized. In spite of her quarrel with Ambrose about the church, she asked him to go to Trier again, discuss the position further, and also try to recover the remains of Gratian. There was no real prospect of these negotiations leading to an agreement, but their failure, she hoped, would enable her to discredit Ambrose by a charge of collusion. The only outcome was that he excommunicated Maximus, chiefly for his conduct in the Priscillianist matter. That avoided the charge of collusion. It did not deter Maximus from exploiting his claim to be the champion of the Catholic faith.

He appointed Victor as Caesar and began to move troops towards the Alps. The following year he strengthened his army with reinforcements from Britain (not solely or chiefly from the Wall, as used to be thought), and undertook the invasion of Italy to 'restore order'. He reiterated what he had said about persecution, and added that he was protecting the Jews as well, because a synagogue had been burnt in Rome. Valentinian tried again for an agreement, with more sincerity than his mother had shown. He urged that the emperors should combine against the barbarians, who were looking ominous to the north-east of Italy.

Maximus made a show of concurrence, and got his troops through the Alpine passes unopposed, telling the vanguard to explain that they were coming to aid Valentinian. The pretence worked for long enough to achieve its object, ceasing to carry conviction only when Justina and her son fled from Milan. They sailed round Greece and took refuge with Theodosius. The eastern emperor, who was as strictly Catholic as Maximus himself, told Valentinian that the Italians would never want him back unless he were reconciled to the orthodox faith. He also married Valentinian's sister. His preparations for war with the pretender from Britain were unhurried. He drew together contingents from every part of the Roman east, together with barbarians — Goths, Alans, Huns.

His warnings about Italian public opinion were borne out. Nobody wanted to fight for Valentinian and his mother, especially when they were not even there. Almost unresisted, Maximus occupied Rome in January 388. Britons entered the ancient capital with a swarm of Goths and German auxiliaries. A few months later the conquerors advanced round the head of the Adriatic, while a fleet sailed in to support them. But in June, at last, the eastern emperor moved. His army was still not as large as his fellow-Spaniard's, but in two clashes on the bank of the Sava he was victorious. Maximus retreated to Aquileia, a city on the Italian side of the Julian Alps (it was destroyed in the following century by Attila). Theodosius followed hard behind him. A counter-attack failed, and suddenly all was over. Under pressure from the townspeople and his own soldiers, Maximus surrendered and was brought to Theodosius three miles outside the city. Theodosius was inclined to be lenient. However, some of his officers hustled Maximus away and, on 28 July 388, beheaded him.

Maximus's navy was overtaken and routed off Sicily. His son Victor was captured in Gaul and killed. His general Andragathius, the alleged murderer of Gratian, committed suicide by jumping off a ship. Some of his Moorish guards were put to death, doubtless as traitors, in view of their behaviour in Gaul. But there were no mass reprisals. Theodosius proclaimed a general pardon. Wintering in Milan, he provided for Maximus's orphaned daughters and did what he could to reimburse citizens who had lost by the war. Valentinian was restored, very much under control. His mother opportunely died and he returned to orthodoxy.

Beyond the Alps the outlook was clouded. Frankish tribes had taken advantage of Maximus's absence to press farther into Gaul. Britain, which had launched Maximus, was a virtual power-vacuum, with the Wall weakened and the garrisons elsewhere much reduced. There too the barbarians were closing in yet again, and for several years the Empire did nothing.

2

That is the Roman story of Maximus. The British story overlaps it and shades off into legend. We cannot be sure where fact ceases and fiction starts. The significant point is that a British story exists at all, not merely as pseudo-history concocted by medieval imagination, but as a traditional growth rooted in the events and woven round Maximus as an emperor so deeply involved with Britain that folk-memory adopted him as a prince of the island.

Early writers — pardonably — confuse the name with the names of other emperors, especially Maximian, Diocletian's co-Augustus. But there is never any doubt who they mean. One belief which can be traced a long way back concerns the northwest of Roman Gaul, Armorica. A large part of it became Brittany, with a language of its own related to Welsh, because a great many Britons went over and settled there. This colonization was certainly going forward in the 450s, but according to the Welsh it started a full lifetime before, under Maximus's aegis. The pioneer settlers were British soldiers who went overseas in the course of his activities. That was how Brittany, as such, began.

Here we meet Nennius again, the ninth-century Welsh monk who tells the tale of Brutus the Trojan in a brief, pre-Geoffrey form. He is quite clear about Maximus's role in Breton origins.

> Unwilling to send back his warlike companions to their wives, children and possessions in Britain, he conferred upon them numerous districts from the lake on top of Mount Jove to the city called Cant Guic, and to the western mound, that is, the West Ridge. These are the Armorican Britons, and they remain there to the present day.

The settlers are pictured here as being, at first, far more widely scattered than the eventual concentration in Armorica would suggest. Cant Guic is Quentovic, an ancient port which used to lie between Etaples and Le Touquet. Nevertheless the last sentence shows that Nennius has the origins of Brittany in mind.

He does not name any Briton as the head of these veterans. Others call him Cynan — in Breton, Conan — surnamed Meriadoc. Geoffrey of Monmouth, as we might expect, knows the facts in detail. Maximus was half British by birth, son of a brother of Coel. (Chronologically, of course, this does not work. Geoffrey betrays the aforementioned confusion over names, giving the spelling as 'Maximianus', and the dates become confused too, making Maximus alive at the time of the real Maximian.) Conan was a relation by marriage who was Maximus's rival for power in Britain. After some fighting they made peace. When Maximus crossed to Gaul, he 'went first to the kingdom of the Armorici, which is now called Brittany' and established a footing there. Then he sent for Conan and offered him the territory as a domain which he could build up into a 'second Britain'. Conan accepted the offer, and British forces overran the whole area. Maximus's campaigns against Gratian and Valentinian came after that. When he was beaten, his surviving British troops were left leaderless. Trekking back across Europe, they joined their fellow-countrymen in Armorican Gaul as subjects of Conan.

Geoffrey is aware of a query which Nennius leaves hanging. If these warriors settled in Armorica without women, how can the Bretons be descended from them? He is unsure about this. At first he says that during the conquest, the Britons killed male Armoricans but spared female ones. The implication is that they kept the women for themselves. Then he says Maximus ordered the transfer of many Britons of both sexes from the island to the new domain. Then he either forgets this or assumes that it failed to happen, and asserts that Conan rejected any 'mixture of blood with the Gauls'. His third story is that Conan tried to arrange an emigration of women only. This introduces another figure of British legend, St Ursula, though in adapting her adventures Geoffrey never mentions her name, and we only discover who is meant by looking in other places. (Strictly speaking, some copies of his book do give the name, but the copyists may have put it in as an explanatory note.)

St Ursula is a British princess who belongs somewhere about here in history if she belongs anywhere. Her legend goes back to a Latin inscription at Cologne, of the late fourth century or early fifth, in which a certain Clematius explains that he has restored a ruined church after seeing a vision of some virgins martyred on the spot. In the ensuing centuries the virgins become popular saints at Cologne. They are declared to have been British and to have been martyred under Maximian in the great persecution. When hagiographers begin putting names to them, the number is given as eleven, and Ursula is one of them.

Soon afterwards the number shoots up to eleven thousand, with Ursula as the leader. She is stated to have been a princess of Britain, sought in marriage by a heathen. To avoid this fate she went overseas with ten ladies-in-waiting, and each had a thousand companions. Their eleven ships were driven into the mouth of the Rhine. They made a pilgrimage to Rome and returned via Cologne, where they were beset by Huns. Ursula had to endure a second heathen wooing, by the chief Hun. She repelled him, and he and his followers massacred all the virgins. Then (belatedly, one would think) angels chased the barbarians away. The citizens of Cologne buried the remains.

This inflated version puts Ursula and her virgins later than Maximian's persecution, at a time when the Huns were in western Europe. It also makes them martyrs of chastity rather than religious faith. The tale was 'confirmed' in the twelfth century by the finding of an old graveyard containing thousands of bones. Unfortunately many of them belonged to men, many to children; and as a sceptic has remarked, it is hard to be sure about the virginity of a dismembered skeleton. However, it was revealed to a visionary that other Christians had suffered along with the eleven thousand. Epitaphs were set up naming some of them, including King Picmenius of England and King Papunius of Ireland.

Ursula herself is as elusive to the historian as to her suitors. The most anyone can urge in her favour is that people in Cologne would scarcely have said their martyrs were Britons unless there was a reason for doing so. As for Geoffrey's version, it is prompted, again, by his confusion of Maximus with Maximian, in whose reign the virgins were originally supposed to have lived. According to him, Conan's request for wives for his settlers in Armorica was addressed to Dionotus, the Duke of Cornwall, who ruled Britain in Maximus's absence. Dionotus had 'a daughter of extraordinary beauty, whom Conan had always wanted for his own'. This is Geoffrey's anonymous Ursula. Besides her, Dionotus collected eleven thousand daughters of nobles and sixty thousand commoners, and shipped them off down the Thames. A storm dispersed the fleet on its way to Armorica. Many of the maidens were drowned. The rest were cast ashore among savage Huns and Picts, who, to make matters worse, had been enrolled by Gratian as auxiliaries against supporters of Maximus. On being sexually rebuffed, they assailed their prisoners with weapons. One way or another, almost the whole expedition perished.

This, of course, leaves us still in doubt as to where the proto-Bretons did get their wives, since Dionotus's consignment never reached Armorica. The answer which was accepted on both sides of the Channel knows nothing of Ursula, and is the one Geoffrey implies first — that the settlers killed off Armorican men and took possession of the women. That simple and brutal answer is found in the *Mabinogion*.

It comes at the end of a story enlarging on another popular theme, the identity of Maximus's virtuous wife who treated Martin of Tours with such reverence. Insular tradition makes her a Briton, and a sister or cousin of the Armorican conqueror. As far as her nationality goes, tradition could be right. Maximus appears in Welsh royal pedigrees. He may have owed his status among the Britons partly to having married one and become, so to speak, a Briton-by-marriage. In that case princes in later ages could have had credible claims to be descended from him.

Geoffrey makes his wife a daughter of Conan's uncle Octavius, Duke of the 'Gewissei'. That name will presently raise curious issues, but here it seems to mean the people of Gwent in south-east Wales. Like Geoffrey's Ursula, she is nameless. But when discussing the marriage, someone asserts Maximus's kinship to the house of Constantine and to Helena. In the *Mabinogion* that family connection takes a further twist. The wife herself becomes Helena in her mythic guise — Elen Luyddog, patroness of the highways, shifted away from the time of the real Helena. This is a fancy of unknown date. An early Welsh genealogy, which includes both Elen and Maximus but in different generations, shows that at one time she was not thought of as married to him. In the *Mabinogion,* however, she is. Conan appears as her brother and not her cousin, under the Welsh form of his name, Cynan.

None of these background complications matter much. The tale which brings the couple together is a pure romance, interesting as well as charming. It is called *The Dream of Macsen Wledig.* 'Macsen' is an inaccurate Welsh version of 'Maximus'. 'Wledig' is a rather cryptic title which occurs as *gwledig* in early texts. Derived from the Welsh for 'land', it seems to mean an army commander who attains a more or less legitimized power — a 'land-holder'. Four or five men are styled so who flourished during the last phase of the Western Empire. All but Maximus are native to the island, so the bestowal of the title on him is another token of his adoption as a compatriot.

The theme of the story is the captivation of Roman majesty by the beauty and enchantment of Britain. In its present form it belongs to the thirteenth century, but it is clearly a re-telling with additions, and the nucleus may be much older. The events have no serious relation to history. 'Macsen' is not proclaimed emperor in Britain, he is emperor already before he comes there. The island indeed is outside the Empire, under the rule of Beli son of Manogan, in his origin, as we saw, a Celtic god.

Macsen, the story-teller begins, was lord of Rome. He was wise and handsome, the fittest to be emperor who had ever reigned.

One day he rode out hunting along the river above his city, accompanied by thirty-two vassal kings. At the hottest time of the day they rested in a valley. Macsen lay down, and his chamberlains made a screen for his head, propping shields against spears.

Thus protected from the sun, he dropped off to sleep and dreamed that he was going farther upstream. He made his way over a vast mountain, the highest in the world, and saw a plain stretching out beyond, and broad rivers. Down across the plain he was wafted without effort, to a city at a river-mouth with a splendid castle and many ships in the harbour, the tallest among them having planks of alternate silver and gold. Going aboard by a gangway of walrus-ivory, Macsen was borne over the sea to the fairest island in the world. His dream carried him across it to a far coast, with a strait lying close to rugged mountains, and another island across the strait.

There too he found a castle. He entered by the gateway and walked into a spacious hall. Its roof was of gold and its walls glittered with jewels. It was furnished with golden couches and silver tables. On a couch facing him sat two auburn-haired young men. They were dressed in black silk. Their hair was bound with golden frontlets, and on their feet they wore buskins with golden fasteners. They were playing at gwyddbwyll, a game of skill, with pieces made of gold on a silver board.

They were not alone in that hall. At the foot of a pillar was an ivory throne with images of two eagles on it. Here sat a noble-looking old man, carving pieces for the game. Facing him, in a golden chair, sat a maiden whose beauty was blinding like the sun. Her dress was of white silk, held in at the waist by a belt with golden clasps. The frontlet on her head was encrusted with pearls and rubies. As Macsen approached she rose to greet him. He threw his arms round her neck. Then they sat down together in her chair, which was wide enough for both.

At that moment the real world broke in on his dream. The huntsmen were preparing to go home. Spears and shields were clashing, horses were stamping and neighing. Macsen woke, and rode back to Rome with his companions. But a yearning for the unknown maiden continued to haunt him. For a week he brooded and neglected business, till a chamberlain warned him that the Romans were murmuring at his apathy. He told his dream to his wise men, and they advised him to send out messengers in search of the maiden.

For months the messengers wandered about the world in vain. Then Macsen returned to the place where he had slept during the hunt, and now it seemed to him that he knew which way he had gone. He assembled a new search party, thirteen trusted men, and told them what he could recall of his dream-journey. Setting off, they reached the mountain as he had said; they climbed over it; they traversed the plain to the seaport; they sailed across to the Island of Britain. On they went making for the farther shore, and at last they came to Snowdonia, and then to Caernarvon, and looked across the narrow waters to Anglesey. 'This,' they said to one another, 'is the place our emperor saw.' They entered the castle, and there, sure enough, the two young men were playing gwyddbwyll, the old man was carving pieces, the maiden was in her chair. The old man's name was Eudaf. The youths were his sons Cynan and Gadeon. The maiden was his daughter Elen. The messengers knelt down at her feet and saluted her as empress of Rome.

She was cautiously willing to believe their story, and to accept Macsen's proposal of marriage, but said they must go back to him and tell him to come and fetch her. They hurried home with relays of horses. Macsen heard her message, led an army to Britain, and defeated its ruler Beli. On arrival at Caernarvon he recognized the place at once. Elen was true to her word and the pair were married. Despite what she had told his envoys, he did not exactly 'fetch' her, but stayed in Britain. At her request he made her father its overlord and converted three towns into strongholds for her, Caernarvon itself, Caerleon and Carmarthen. Elen took personal charge of the building of roads to link them together. It was because she had such a multitude of workmen at her command that the roads were called the Roads of Elen Luyddog, Helen-of-the-Hosts.

Macsen's lingering in Britain was not an outright dereliction of duty, because it counted as conquering. However, the Romans had a custom that if an emperor remained abroad in this way for seven years, he must forfeit his diadem and never return. The seven years slipped away. When Macsen was at Caerleon he received a letter from a new emperor who had replaced him. It took the form of a curt warning, addressed to him as to one well aware of the custom: 'If thou come, and if ever thou come to Rome . . . ' Macsen had no intention of acquiescing in banishment. He replied: 'And if I go to Rome, and if I go. . . .'

He gathered as many as he could of the troops he had brought to Britain, and marched homewards taking Elen with him. The countries on the way submitted, but the City itself held out. A further year passed in a siege which made no headway. Then reinforcements came. In the distance Elen recognized the standards of her two brothers, Cynan and Gadeon. They had brought an army of Britons. It was small, but more than equal to twice the number of Romans. Macsen welcomed his brothers-in-law and took them to watch an assault on the city rampart. They said they could do better. Going to the rampart at night, they measured it carefully and ordered carpenters to make new scaling-ladders, one for every four of their men. The secret of their plan, however, lay not so much in equipment as in timing. Romans broke off fighting at noon to eat; Britons ate earlier, and then drank till they were in high spirits. During one of the lunch-hour lulls, the Britons (in high spirits) clambered over the wall and took the pretender by surprise. After a fierce battle they had Macsen's capital in their hands. So he received it back from the Britons alone.

There, properly speaking, this patriotic romance ends. But the text as we have it in the *Mabinogion* adds an appendix, where the tradition of the beginnings of Brittany reappears, with the solution to that query about the colonists' wives. Macsen, we are told, rewarded Elen's brothers by giving them permission to win a province for their own people. They went off into Armorica and, after many years of campaigning, conquered it. Gadeon decided to return to Britain, Cynan remained as ruler with a portion of the British army. During the war they had slain all Armorican men but left the women alive for themselves. Afraid that the British language would be corrupted in semi-alien households, they cut out the women's tongues. Hence, in the first Breton generation, one sex talked and the other was mute. This gruesome touch, so unlike the rest, is due to a fanciful etymology which the author gives for the Welsh name of Brittany, 'Llydaw'. The notion is that it comes from *lled*, 'half', and *taw*, 'silent'. Its currency can be traced in older writings than *The Dream of Macsen Wledig*.

Some of this is found on the Breton side of the Channel too, in the *Legend of Saint Goeznovius* (Goueznou, a Breton saint). The dedication of this work gives the author's name as William, the date of composition as 1019. Those details have been challenged as spurious, but the main argument for their being so is now known to be invalid, and in any case it does not signify for the present purpose. 'William', or whoever he is, opens with a preface about the British settlement in Armorica and various sequels to it, which he claims to be basing on an earlier 'Ystoria Britanica'. Again the leader is Cynan, or Conan, though as we might expect, the Breton writer knows geographical details which Welshmen do not. Again the Britons exterminate Armorican males, take over the women, and cut their tongues out. But the etymological basis of the 'tongue' legend has gone. The author lacks the clue, being out of touch with the Welsh and their ideas, and gives the legend alone. More surprisingly, he says nothing about Maximus. The Britons simply arrive as colonists and carve out their mini-empire. Over the Channel, Maximus's fame seems to have waned.

In Britain it has one or two offshoots. 'King Massen' figures in a medieval Cornish miracle-play called *Breunans Meriasek,* the *Life of Meriasek*. The name of its saintly hero is more correctly Meriadoc, which is also Conan's second name, though no link is apparent. In the play, which is long and rambling with several disjointed episodes, 'Massen' is a righteous and devout king who has been twenty years on the throne. It is not clear where, but certainly he is less than a Roman emperor. One of his courtiers falls into the hands of a heathen tyrant and is freed by a miracle. The story may dimly recall the orthodoxy and piety of Maximus's court, resulting, presumably, in divine favour.

Finally, a strange Welsh folk-tale has planted itself near Dinas Emrys, a Snowdonian hill-fort, rich both in archaeology and in legend. It concerns not Maximus himself but a son of his, Owen. The name is a Welsh form of the Roman Eugenius. He may have had a son so called, though there is no record of it. Between Dinas Emrys and a neighbouring lake, Llyn Dinas, Owen fought a giant. Taking advantage of hollows in the ground, they discharged missiles at each other from cover: arrows according to one version, or balls made of steel according to another. The combat was fatal to them both. Dinas Emrys, as we shall see, is the locale of another legend, about a man who married one of Maximus's daughters. While Owen's battle with the giant, as it stands, is an isolated oddity, it may have been part of some lost dynastic saga.

CHAPTER FIVE

Disasters and New Beginnings

1

MAXIMUS IN THE *MABINOGION* IS SEEN THROUGH A ROMANTIC HAZE. But even the Welsh were aware of another side to him. However popular he had been with their forbears, however boldly he had embodied British initiative, his career had had consequences and these were not good. When we turn back to the only Briton who wrote about him even moderately close to the facts, we find that the balance is different. His popularity is acknowledged, but is altogether outweighed by his bitter aftereffects. For this author, in retrospect, he accordingly becomes a villain.

The author is Gildas, that monk whom we have met briefly and shall unfortunately be meeting again. Probably towards the middle of the sixth century, he wrote the treatise already cited. It is called *De Excidio et Conquestu Britanniae* ('On the Ruin and Conquest of Britain') and is described, with uncommon candour, as a *liber querulus* or Complaining Book. Gildas counts as a saint — mainly, perhaps, because the Church in the British Isles was generous in its bestowal of sainthood — but he is a maddening historian. When he might tell us much, he tells us little, because he is not really writing history. Even the historical section of the book, reviewing events from the Roman invasion to the sixth century, takes the form of a tirade against most of his fellow-countrymen; and the much longer remainder is a denunciation of some of the rulers in his own time, which soon leaves facts behind and wanders off into biblical rhetoric.

Here, however, is what he says about Maximus.

The island retained the Roman name, but not the morals and law: nay rather, casting forth a shoot of its own planting, it sends out Maximus to Gaul, accompanied by a great crowd of followers, with an emperor's ensigns in addition, which he never worthily bore nor legitimately, but as one elected after the manner of a tyrant and amid a turbulent soldiery. This man ... first attaches to his guilty rule certain neighbouring countries or provinces against the Roman power, by nets of perjury and falsehood. He then extends one wing to Spain, the other to Italy, fixing the throne of his iniquitous empire at Trier.

He raged with such madness against his lords that he drove two legitimate emperors, the one [Valentinian] from Rome, the other [Gratian] from a most pious life. Though fortified by hazardous deeds of so dangerous a character, it was not long ere he lost his accursed head at Aquileia . . . .

After this, Britain is robbed of all her armed soldiery, of her military supplies, of her rulers . . . and of her vigorous youth who followed the footsteps of the tyrant and never returned.

Gildas's point is in the last sentence. His judgment is that Maximus's adventure left the island defenceless against the barbarians. Hence the ensuing 'ruin and conquest' in his title. For him this was the real end of Roman Britain, and as the events receded into the past, his compatriots seem to have taken the same view whether or not they shared his attitude to Maximus. Traditions about the sequel are obscure and tangled, with the effect of a passage into twilight. Gildas's own account is a mixture of fairly credible statements and absurd blunders. It leaves us wondering what happened to the teaching of history between Maximus's time and his own.

According to him, the Britons after 388 were not merely without defences but incapable of building up new ones, because too few men remained who had any military knowledge. The barbarians began to encroach once more. Gildas mentions Picts and Scots but not Saxons, though later he implies that these were active as well, because he speaks of the Britons 'dreading' them. Soon a British deputation arrived at the imperial court with a request for Roman troops to return. Rome answered the call. A legion was dispatched and drove back the barbarians. On Roman advice the Britons built a wall across the island from sea to sea, which could be used as a defensive line, but as they made it of turf it was of little use. The legion went back to the continent and soon the raiders were over the border and the coasts once again, whereupon the process of appeal and response was re-enacted. This time the Romans sent cavalry and a fleet. They made it clear that this was another rescue, not a re-occupation. Before withdrawing, their officers instructed the Britons in making weapons, and built a new frontier wall of stone, and coastal watchtowers. After that, Britain was abandoned.

This is an astonishing muddle. Gildas knows about the two walls and the Saxon Shore forts — after all, they were visible when he wrote — but he shifts their construction to the very close of the Roman period. Nevertheless, Roman history and the findings of archaeology show dimly what was happening, and Gildas is not too wildly astray in his main thesis. The Maximus affair was indeed the beginning of the end. Roman Britain was in manifest decline from then on. Gildas exaggerates in saying that Britannia had no 'armed soldiery' at all, but the numbers were fatally reduced. The Picts did raid again, more or less at will. Scots and others from Ireland, with an enterprising king named Niall, not only raided but settled, occupying parts of Wales and establishing footholds in Somerset and Cornwall.

The emperor Theodosius died in 395 without having taken any measures about Britain. His sons shared the Empire, Honorius in the west, Arcadius in the east. Honorius was a boy of ten, and showed very little spirit or ability as he grew older. A part-Germanic regent, Stilicho, was the effective ruler of the west. The first of Gildas's 'rescues' of Britain can be equated with the arrival of an army which he sent — probably led — in 396-8. If this was a response to a British appeal, it would have come from spokesmen of the *civitates*. The imperial troops, by then, had hardly anything in common with the disciplined and homogeneous infantry of the early Caesars. The old armament of cuirass, short-sword and oblong shield had largely vanished. Most of the soldiers were barbarian mercenaries, some of whom held land in the Empire under treaty. Goths on horseback, Germans carrying long swords and pikes and circular shields, mingled with exotic slingers and archers. Still the generalship of Stilicho, with the Roman treasury to draw on, was enough. Britannia, after a fashion, was set on her feet again.

Stilicho may have taken the first steps towards a crucial development of the fifth century: the transfer of authority in the border areas to British chiefs, in theoretical continuity with the Empire. Through a belated Roman improvisation, or a move soon afterwards on the same lines, much of Wales became the domain of Cunedda. A Welsh genealogy traces his descent from a line of British office-holders with Roman names. His own name, however, is Celtic, and he began his career near Edinburgh. We do not know what arrangement brought him to Wales, but within a few decades his family and followers had suppressed or brought to heel the Irish invaders and were parcelling out the country themselves.

In the doubtful zone between Hadrian's Wall and the Firth of Clyde, Roman officials made belated attempts to checkmate the Picts by sponsoring settlements of pro-Roman Britons. These moved towards autonomy and cohesion. About the middle of the fifth century we hear of a certain Ceredig or Coroticus, who ruled an incipient Strathclyde from Dumbarton, the 'Fort of the Britons'.

Writers in later centuries refer to Cunedda, Ceredig and one or two others as *gwledigs*. This is the title which was bestowed retroactively, and fantastically, on Maximus. Like him they are portrayed as dynastic founders, and so they were in the outcome, but their power had its origin in a makeshift system of regional commands and native militia. The cryptic records of the fifth century hint at a tension, perhaps a conflict, between Roman-sponsored border chiefs and the surviving cantonal councils of lowland Britain.

2

Gildas, then, is more or less right about the first rescue, apart from his misdating of the northern wall. He is also right about its being temporary. Stilicho withdrew most of his troops from Britain in 401 to help defend Italy against the Gothic king Alaric. However, there is no good evidence for the second rescue; and the final convulsion which led to independence took a shape of which Gildas knows nothing.

In 406 three Teutonic tribes, the Vandals, Alans and Suevi, poured across the Rhine and overwhelmed the defences. They swept all the way to the Pyrenees. Turned back by Spanish militia guarding the passes, they wandered about Gaul plundering. Britain was virtually cut off. A response came, not from the councils, but from the residual army. The sequence of events is not wholly clear; the soldiers may have embarked on their new course a little earlier; but the crisis ensured that they would persist in it. They copied their predecessors of 306 and 383, proclaiming an emperor of their own. However, they seem to have been thinking of Carausius as well as Constantine and Maximus. The apparent intention was not to bid for the Empire, or for any part of it outside Britain, but to set up a ruler having plenary powers, so that the island's safety would no longer be in the hands of an overlord who was not merely feeble but fast becoming inaccessible. What the soldiers wanted, in fact, was a controlled emperor on the spot. Probably many civilians did too. But the soldiers were to do the controlling, and their sagacity was not of the highest.

They gave Britain an emperor named Marcus. We know nothing about him except that he failed to please them and was killed. Late in 406 they tried again, giving Britain an emperor named Gratian, a civic official and a Briton himself. His nationality gives him a fleeting interest, but curiosity is unsatisfied. We know nothing else about Gratian either, except that he too failed to please and, after a four-month reign, was killed. The third attempt was in 407. The soldiers chose a comrade of low rank, whose only recommendation was that his name was Constantine, and therefore auspicious.

This one lasted long enough to go down in history as Constantine III (the second had been a son of the great Constantine). He too may have been British. His reign was not a popular upsurge as Maximus's had been — nothing is said about volunteers flocking to his standard — but several of his chief officers belonged to the island. One was Edobic, a Frank, but born in Britain. Another was Gerontius, who was British-born. 'Gerontius' is a name that looks Roman but is Celtic.

A son of Constantine named Constans emerged from a monastery to join him. That too is interesting because, apart from legend and guess-work, it is the earliest indication that Britain had monasteries. As a Christian mode of life, monasticism had begun in the east a century earlier. Climate and custom delayed its spread beyond Italy, but Martin of Tours, Maximus's saintly friend, founded communities in Gaul. Disciples of his may have done likewise across the Channel. If Constans's monastery was in Britain, it cannot be located. The records of Glastonbury claim a very early foundation, but they are not trustworthy as far back as this.

Constantine III survived. Yet even in a weakening Empire, he was in the grip of the same logic as Maximus. The notion of a purely insular emperor was not viable. To stand a chance of holding Britain securely, he had to hold more than Britain. If the legitimate Empire did not destroy him, the barbarians would. It may be that the army had removed its previous nominees because, after this issue was grasped, they had failed to face it. Having reorganized the administration to suit himself, Constantine took virtually all the troops to Gaul, putting them under the command of two generals, Justinian and Nevigastes. Several Gallic contingents declared in his favour and added to his strength. While trying to contain the Vandals and their allies, now mostly roaming in the south-west, he made his way along the Rhine safeguarding the frontier in his own estimation by treaties with other barbarians — Franks, Alemanni, Burgundians.

Constantine passed on down the Rhône. On behalf of Honorius, Stilicho sent a commander named Sarus to oppose him. It was one of Stilicho's last military actions; he died in 408. There was fighting near Valence. Justinian and Nevigastes were killed, Constantine promoted his Frankish lieutenant Edobic and his Briton Gerontius, who turned out to be the ablest commander in his service. Sarus had been besieging Valence itself, but he judged the pretender to be too strong and returned to Honorius in Rome, paying bands of Bagaudae guerrillas to let him through the Alpine passes unscathed, a sad comment on the Western Empire's sickness.

Setting up headquarters at Arles, Constantine gave his son Constans the title of Caesar. With his monastic background, Constans proved useful in gaining support from the clergy. St Martin was dead, but two former disciples of his rallied to Constantine. One was a Spanish ecclesiastic, Heros, whose enemies had forced him to flee to Gaul. Constantine made him Bishop of Arles. The other was Lazarus, whom Constantine made Bishop of Aix — an honour not helpful to his own good name, because it was rumoured that Lazarus knew more than he should about the death of the bishop he replaced.

Meanwhile Constans had gone to Spain himself. Most of the authorities accepted the new regime. In Spain, however, Honorius had two wealthy cousins, Didymus and Verinian. Constans demanded their surrender. They retorted by arming the slaves and peasants on their estates, beating Constans's troops in Portugal, and advancing towards the Pyrenees. Constans summoned reinforcements in the shape of a body of auxiliaries, ironically dubbed the Honoriaci because they had been recruited under the emperor's auspices. They included Moors and Scots. With this motley and turncoat crew the ex-monk was more successful, capturing the two cousins with their wives. He returned to Gaul, leaving Gerontius in charge in Spain (an unwise act), and posting the Honoriaci to guard the Pyrenean passes (another unwise act, because it involved displacing the reliable Spanish militia and thus affronting Spaniards in general).

Constantine proclaimed his triumphant son co-emperor. He executed Honorius's cousins and then decided, early in 409, that this was the proper and tactful moment to make overtures to Honorius. They had more fruitful results than might have been expected. The effete emperor needed all the support he could get against Alaric's Goths. He recognized Constantine and sent him a robe of office. With protestations of friendship, Constantine entered Italy at the head of a medley of Britons, Gauls and Spaniards.

Honorius's reaction, however, was not relief but alarm. He now suspected that a general of his own, Alavicus, was plotting with Constantine. After a parade in which Alavicus marched in front of Honorius, the general was assassinated on the way back. Honorius dismounted and publicly thanked God for the deliverance. Feeling that the atmosphere was not one of trust, Constantine withdrew from Italy and held court at Arles, where he celebrated imaginary victories. Constans joined him, but the retreat from Italy marked him as a sinking man.

In October 409 the break came. It was the Briton Gerontius who acted. In view of the sequel, it would be fascinating to know whether his move had a motive of dawning nationalism. Still in Spain with a major part of Constantine's forces, he declared against him. With his consent, the Honoriaci opened the Pyrenean passes, let the Vandals and their companions through and joined them in plundering. Gerontius did not wish to be a ruler himself, but a king-maker. His nominee was a friend called Maximus — another auspicious name — whom he installed as emperor at Tarragona. Then he stirred up Gaul against his late leader. Much of Gaul was ripe for stirring. It was clear by now that Constantine, in the south with a reduced army, stood little chance of restoring stability. The Armoricans revolted, forming a provisional government and taking measures for their own safety. Whether or not British settlers were already there to take part in the rising, the Britons in their homeland, momentously, did the same.

Britain's declaration of independence in 410 was prompted not only by the failure of its imperial nominee, and (perhaps) by Gerontius's incitements, but by a fresh Saxon onslaught of extreme ferocity. Whatever token garrisons Constantine had left in the island were negligible and useless. The councillors of the *civitates* decided that they had had enough. They threw out the officials Constantine had appointed. Technically they were back under the wing of their lawful emperor, Honorius, but that meant nothing and everyone knew it, including Honorius. He addressed a message to the *civitates* telling them to look after themselves. The crucial point, legally, was his recognizing the Britons' right to take up arms. Since the early Roman measures in Britain, that right had been severely restricted. Anybody forming an armed band without permission was in serious breach of the law. A Britain self-armed would be self-governed. Whatever Honorius's wishes, problems closer to home left him with no alternative. On 24 August 410 the Goths under Alaric entered Rome and sacked it. The emperor himself had gone to Ravenna, where he occupied himself with a chicken farm.

Britain's new and permitted course was unique, and remained so. The notion that the island was left defenceless by a Roman withdrawal of the legions is a total myth. The legions left because Constantine took them with him, and the subsequent change of Britain's status was active, not passive. Alone among Roman provincials, the Britons not only achieved autonomy before barbarian conquest but maintained it, fought back, and, out of that struggle, created a heroic tradition. Roman culture,

Roman Christianity, even a hazy Roman allegiance, were not cast away. But the inheritance had fallen in practice to a free Celtic people who would change even what they kept. Although they were to succumb at last, their phase of self-rule had results which no other imperial land could parallel and no conqueror could destroy.

That was for the future. On the continent, the men of 407 were nearing the end of their resources. Constantine was still holding out in Arles. He had tried to counter Gerontius by sending the loyal Edobic beyond the Rhine to recruit auxiliaries among his fellow-Franks and the Alemanni. Gerontius, however, had had more success with reinforcements. When Constans returned to Spain, the Briton defeated him, chased him back across Gaul, captured him at Vienne after a short siege and, early in 411, put him to death. Then he marched south to besiege Constantine.

He was too late. An army faithful to Honorius arrived at Arles, and most of Gerontius's troops deserted. He escaped with a Spanish unit. The Spaniards despised him for running away from the disaster, and resolved to put an end to him. One night they left their camp and tried to break into a house where he was lodging. The alarm was raised and he climbed on to the roof, accompanied by a friend, several servants and his wife Nonnichia. They had bows and arrows and shot again and again, holding back the mutineers. When the arrows ran out, Gerontius allowed his servants to let themselves down the wall in the shadows and creep away by a path the Spaniards had not blocked. For some reason Nonnichia could not follow — perhaps she was lame — and though Gerontius might have escaped himself, he would not leave her.

At dawn the soldiers tossed blazing missiles into the house and it caught alight. Gerontius's friend asked to be beheaded, and he complied. Nonnichia took the sword, turned it against herself and begged her husband to kill her too, before she fell into the mutineers' hands. Again he complied. A Christian author approves her quasi-suicide even though she was a Christian herself, because it was a choice between death and dishonour, and he speaks of her end as merciful. Gerontius tried to kill himself also. After three awkward cuts with the sword he stabbed himself with a dagger. No doubt it was because of these hurried and clumsy efforts that he lived long enough to tell the Spaniards what had happened. That burning house in Provence was the pyre of a man who, possibly, was the inspirer of British independence. We do not know enough to be sure, but we can hazard a guess from the fact that his name became royal and honourable. It reappears for centuries afterwards in the form 'Gereint' or 'Geraint', being given to princes of the West Country and to a knight of Devon in medieval romance.

Constantine remained at Arles under seige by Honorius's troops. He had no option. With him was a younger son, Julian. Edobic returned at last with recruits, but the imperial army ambushed and dispersed them. Edobic took refuge with a landowner, Ecdicius, to whom he had once done a good turn. The obligation did not restrain Ecdicius from cutting off his head and presenting it to Honorius's general in hope of a reward. The general, another Constantius, treated the betrayal with scorn and gave him nothing.

When Constantine heard of Edobic's death he felt a call to religion. He laid aside his purple robe and insignia and went to the city church. His court-bishop, Heros, who had acted with courage during the siege, ordained him as a presbyter. He then surrendered with Julian on a pledge of clemency. The intention was that they should go to Honorius at Ravenna, where Heros thought that the emperor's respect for the clergy would preserve their lives. They had not gone very far when they were waylaid. Yet another decapitation followed. Only the pretender's head completed the journey, in September 411. Gerontius's shadow-emperor Maximus dropped back into the obscurity from which he could hardly be said to have arisen. The imperial commander Constantius was rewarded with the hand of Honorius's sister Galla Placidia. They made an able couple. Constantius played an outstanding part in prolonging the Western Empire's life, and their son Valentinian became its last emperor to show any durability, though he lacked other qualities.

Constantine III left little impression in Britain as a ruler. Gildas and Nennius do not mention him. Bede does, but Bede probably found him in Roman history rather than insular tradition. However, despite the fiasco of his reign, he passed into legend of another kind. For the Welsh he became Bendigeit Custennin, Blessed Constantine. The 'blessed' is unexpected. It is not a corruption of a pre-Christian epithet as it may be with Bran. Perhaps part of the explanation is a notion that Constantine's murder, after abdication and ordination, might count as a martyrdom. Weight must also be given to hints that tradition confused him with the greater Constantine who liberated the Church. The 'Bendigeit Custennin' of legend was a composite based on both, and may have had touches of still another Constantine who came later.

3

Independent Britannia made no attempt to enthrone a new emperor. Power, for the moment, was in the hands of the councillors whom Honorius had entrusted with the island's safety. It is likely that border chiefs in Wales and the north — those from whose ranks the *gwledigs* Cunedda and Ceredig emerged — were also making their influence felt. For the first few years there is little to show what kind of government the Britons set up, or how they organized their defences, though it appears that at this stage they were holding their own against the barbarians. A less centralized, more agrarian mode of life was returning, aided by one or two solid gains of independence, such as the end of compulsory grain exports. Celtic habits were beginning to reassert themselves, notably in art.

Yet some at least of the cities survived, if in manifest decline; civilization still meant *Romanitas*, Roman-ness, as a sentiment at least; and the upper classes contrasted themselves with the Saxons, the Picts, the tribes from Ireland, and had no doubt that they were civilized and the others were not. If political *Romanitas* was fast ebbing, the new, religious *Romanitas* launched by Constantine the Great survived and flourished. Britain still had the church, in communion with the Bishop of Rome, and London and other cities had bishops of their own, officers in the hierarchy he headed. The upper classes were predominantly Christian, and no positive force resisted the conversion of the majority, though this was to take many years. A brief pagan revival in the 360s, which produced the temple of Nodons at Lydney, had succumbed to the pressure from the court and episcopate.

British Christians had never known large-scale persecution, not even under Diocletian, because of Constantius's unwillingness to enforce his edicts. That was one reason why, as a Celtic form of Christianity slowly took shape, it had subtle differences. In the Mediterranean lands, the Church had been oppressed by pagan authorities with support from pagan priesthoods. Christians, therefore, had learnt to detest the gods and dismiss them as devils who misled the human race. The old system and the new were starkly opposed. But Celtic Christianity in ex-Roman Britain had no memory of a similar ordeal and took a milder view. The same was to apply to the rest of the British Isles, where Rome's writ had never run and persecution had never been an issue. In time, much pagan mythology was domesticated in Christian folklore and legend. Clerics might object, but they did not have the same sense of evil to work upon. Old deities gradually reappeared not as malign demons, but as heroes and heroines, fairy-folk and enchanters, kings and queens, in the story-telling of a Christian culture that was creative enough to give them this renewed life. Hence Bran and Lludd and the rest.

At the time of Britain's first independence such developments still lay far ahead. However, the vigour of its young Christianity was becoming plain to the world. There is in fact more on record about Britons in religion than in politics, and it is partly through religious events that we know the little we do know about the island's fifth-century rulers.

One Briton who had already made an impact was Pelagius, founder of what came to be known as the Pelagian heresy. He was a well-read amateur of theology, perhaps a doctor, certainly not a priest, though he may for a time have been a monastic lay-brother. In 405 he was in Rome, writing books and expounding a view of human nature which was more optimistic and less guilt-laden than the general sense of the Church allowed. Pelagius stressed the freedom of moral choice and played down original sin, denying that human beings were born tainted or untrustworthy.

He was a big, genial, easy-going person, unwilling to give his thoughts the rigidity of doctrine. Unfortunately some of his followers stated them in provocative terms which caused trouble. An opponent sneered at him as 'heavy with Scots porridge' (was the British breakfast already known on the continent?). He moved to Carthage and then to Jerusalem. There the two court-bishops of the pretender Constantine make a brief historical reappearance in 415, accusing him of heresy. They had both left Gaul in an atmosphere of scandal, and now they mismanaged their case. Pelagius, however, came under more effective fire from St Augustine. In 418 Pope Zosimus declared that the Briton was indeed a heretic. Three years later Honorius approved a decree forbidding Pelagians to approach nearer to Rome than the hundredth milestone. Pelagius himself died about this time, possibly in Egypt. His ideas continued to carry weight, and it could be claimed today that he has won a belated and anony-mous victory. The thinking of many Christians is far closer to his than to Augustine's.

Pelagius's fame was international among the intelligentsia. The fame of another British Christian was to prove more popu-lar and lasting. St Patrick became the patron saint of a country not his own, and of a people destined to spread throughout the world. His name is the Roman Patricius; he also had a Celtic name, Magonus or Maun. Born to Christian parents between 380 and 390, somewhere near the long western coastline of Roman Britain, he fell a victim at sixteen to one of the Irish sea-raids. The raiders took British prisoners back to Ireland and sold them as slaves. Patrick spent six years tending sheep in Antrim, then escaped and found his way, very circuitously, home.

Since Ireland had never been part of the Roman Empire, it had not shared in the official Christianization. Patrick was convinced that he should return as a missionary. With that end in view he took holy orders. For many years no opportunity came. By the 420s, however, a few Irish had been converted through other contacts. These were probably Pelagian. An Irishman, Coeles-tius, had been one of Pelagius's most vocal and tiresome sup-porters. In 431 Pope Celestine I sent over a bishop. He soon withdrew in the face of hostility, and in 432 Patrick was ap-pointed to take his place.

Patrick had the advantage of knowing the country and the language. Also he was a man of impeccable character, very courteous and without arrogance. His mission lasted for almost thirty years, and achieved much success despite enmity from the Druids, who still flourished in Ireland. He did not, of course, effect a miraculous mass conversion, but he put the Church on a firm basis, laying the foundation of the rich Christian culture which was to make Ireland the most civilized country of western Europe in the so-called Dark Ages.

Accidentally, it is only because of Patrick that we know anything of substance about the north British *gwledig* Ceredig, or Coroticus, and his rising domain around the Clyde. Some time during the 450s Coroticus's warriors crossed the North Channel and pounced on a gathering of Irish, including freshly baptized converts. They slaughtered some and carried off others to sell as slaves, just as Irishmen had carried off Patrick long before. Since Coroticus and most of his raiders were nominal Christians, their action gave the converts a discouraging introduction to their new co-religionists. Patrick wrote a letter of protest without result, and then another. A copy of the second has been preserved.

In it Patrick mentions Picts as associates of the Britons, and denounces them as apostates — Christians who, for practical purposes, had reverted to heathenism. The fact that any Picts had become Christian enough to apostatize was due mainly to another Briton, St Ninian. Harder than Patrick to pin down, he is said to have been an older contemporary, born near the Solway Firth, who met St Martin of Tours and then went among Picts in central Scotland. The mission at any rate is a fact of history. He built a church at Whithorn in Galloway called the *Candida Casa*, the White House, because it was made of whitewashed stone. In his Pictish journey, legend claims that he wandered on through the Highlands. Inscriptions, church dedications and place-names as far afield as Caithness and the Shetlands attest to a widespread reputation if no more. He is supposed to have died in 432, just when Patrick was beginning his work in Ireland.

Patrick and Ninian both made their mark outside their native land. So indeed had Pelagius done, and farther away. However, it was the spirit of Pelagius which penetrated the Church in ex-Roman Britain, and became an issue in ruling circles.

The edict of 421, excluding Pelagians from Rome, was followed by another banishing them from Italy. These blows helped to cause a sectarian hardening which the founder himself had never intended. Some of his followers began an active campaign among his own nation. The first Pelagian leader in

Britain was Agricola, the son of a bishop (clerical celibacy was not yet enforced). Soon the heresy found support in high places. It has been conjectured that this came from a sort of Celtic Nationalist group, and that chieftains from outlying regions favoured a doctrine condemned by Rome because it weakened the Roman link.

When Pope Celestine grasped what was happening, he sent an envoy to take matters in hand. The Empire might have written off Britain, the Church had not. The envoy was Germanus, who had held civil military posts in Gaul before becoming Bishop of Auxerre. In 429 Germanus crossed to Britain accompanied by Lupus, Bishop of Troyes, and moved to strengthen the organization of the Church. He staged a public debate between orthodox bishops and Pelagian spokesmen. This was probably held at Verulamium, afterwards St Albans, still a fairly prosperous town with a Roman-style municipal government, though the theatre was derelict and used as a refuse dump for the market. The Pelagians seem to have been well-dressed, cultivated people with an air of having friends in high places, but the bishops' case was well argued and impressed the audience.

Germanus's tour was interrupted by news that a host of Saxons and Picts in alliance was pushing inland. The Britons had raised a force to oppose it and asked Germanus to help. He went to the British camp, which was in hilly country, it is not known where: possible in the Chilterns, since there are traces of deep barbarian penetration south-west of the Wash, and of a brief Pictish presence in East Anglia, which might have some connection with events in this period. Germanus, anyhow, took charge of the situation. He baptized many of the soldiers — it was Easter — and then posted the army in a valley with certain instructions. When the invaders entered the valley Germanus suddenly shouted 'Hallelujah!' All the Britons roared 'Hallelujah!' several times and the Picts and Saxons fled. Satisfied with his mission on every count, Germanus returned to Gaul. He had not succeeded altogether. Pelagianism survived, and Germanus was back in Britain in 446. After that, however, it died as a sect, though it persisted among the Irish as a point of view.

British Christians in later times cherished various traditions about the visits of the admired and canonized prelate. Nennius, in his *History of the Britons*, gives an account which brings us round again into the realm of government. He names St Germanus's chief opponent, and the name leads us right into the strange territory of fifth-century Britain. We are never told plainly, here or anywhere, who it was that sponsored the heresy at top levels. But on one point Nennius is emphatic. Whether because of this sponsorship or for some other reason, Germanus came into conflict with a British ruler called Vortigern.

1

Stonehenge, the most famous neolithic relic in England, from an early 20th century photograph. It stands on Salisbury Plain, Wiltshire, in the form of an inner and outer circle. Built in at least two stages beginning c. 2700 B.C., its interior ring of 'blue stones' was completed by 1400 B.C.

2

Bronze Age barrow, or burial mound, Norfolk.

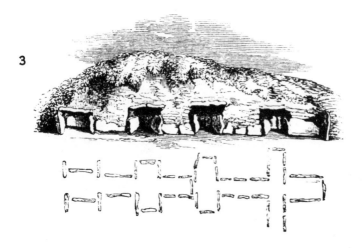

3

Stone barrow at Stoney Littleton, Somerset. When excavated in 1816, this barrow had been greatly disturbed, but an earthen burial urn containing charred bones was found intact in one recess. The barrow was 107 feet long and 13 feet high at the top point.

4

5

Neolithic spear-head or celt found near Chelmsford, Essex. (Side and front views)

Bronze Age burial urn. Cremation was popular during the early Bronze Age and ashes were interred in earthen pots.

6

STATUE OF BOUDICCA (D. A.D. 62). ERECTED BY PRINCE ALBERT ON THE THAMES EMBANKMENT NEXT TO THE HOUSES OF PARLIAMENT, THIS ROMANTICIZED RENDERING OF THE QUEEN OF THE ICENI WAS MADE BY THE CELEBRATED VICTORIAN SCULPTOR THOMAS THORNCROFT.

7 BUST OF EMPEROR HADRIAN (RULED A.D. 117-138), WHO VISITED BRITAIN IN A.D. 122.

8 HADRIAN'S WALL, LOOKING TOWARDS HOUSESTEADS, NORTHUMBRIA. BEGUN BY HADRIAN IN A.D. 120, THIS STONE WALL STRETCHED 73 MILES ACROSS NORTHERN BRITAIN CONNECTING A LINE OF 14 FORTS FROM SOLWAY FIRTH TO THE MOUTH OF THE TYNE RIVER.

9

THE *CUCULLATI*, OR HOODED ONES, A MYSTERIOUS TRIO OF DEITIES, ADORN THIS STONE RELIEF, THOUGHT TO BE ORIGINALLY FROM SHORNEGRAFTON. IT IS NOW EXHIBITED IN THE MUSEUM AT HOUSESTEADS, THE BEST PRESERVED FORT ALONG HADRIAN'S WALL.

10A

Ornate Pottery from Castor in eastern Northamptonshire from the Romano-British period.

11

Drawing of the 5th-century Roman Empress Galla Placidia (d. A.D. 450). Daughter of Theodosius I and wife of Constantius, the imperial commander, she became 'Regent of the West' ruling on behalf of her son, Valentinian III.

10B

Decorated Pottery from the Upchurch Marshes, Southeast England. This blue-black ware was a common everyday ceramic of Roman Britain.

12

REMAINS OF A ROMAN BOAT FOUND IN THE THAMES NEAR LAMBETH IN 1911 DURING CONSTRUCTION OF A PUBLIC BUILDING COMPLEX.

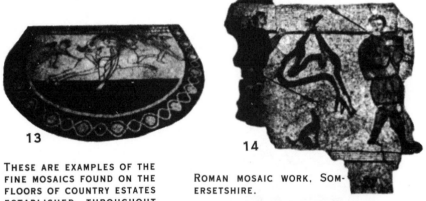

13

THESE ARE EXAMPLES OF THE FINE MOSAICS FOUND ON THE FLOORS OF COUNTRY ESTATES ESTABLISHED THROUGHOUT SOUTHERN BRITAIN BY WEALTHY ROMAN SETTLERS IN THE 3RD AND 4TH CENTURIES.

14

ROMAN MOSAIC WORK, SOMERSETSHIRE.

15

RUNIC STONE FROM KIRK MAUGHHOLD, ISLE OF MAN, CONTAINS AN INSCRIPTION 'CARVED BY IUAN THE PRIEST'. BELOW THIS IS THE ALPHABET IN BOTH RUNIC AND OGAM CHARACTERS. OGAM WAS THE NATIVE CELTIC WRITING USED IN IRELAND AND BRITAIN FROM ABOUT THE 4TH CENTURY ON, AND IS FOUND ON STONES PRIMARILY IN THE SOUTHERN AND WESTERN COASTAL REGIONS, WHERE THE IRISH FORM OF CELTIC WAS SPOKEN. RUNES HAVE THEIR ORIGINS IN SCANDINAVIA AT ABOUT THE SAME TIME, AND WERE EMPLOYED MAINLY FOR MAGICAL, TALISMANIC OR OWNERSHIP INSCRIPTIONS ABOUT THE ANGLO-SAXONS.

CHAPTER SIX

High Chief and Last Roman

1

THE NEXT THREE CENTURIES WERE TO BRING A SWEEPING CHANGE. Gradually, with many shiftings of fortune, most of Britain came under the dominance of a new people. Saxon settlers, together with kindred Angles and Jutes, created England or 'Angle-land' and left the Britons' descendants holding power only in Wales, Cornwall and part of Scotland.

To try to unravel this transformation, or at any rate the first phases, is to become aware of curious tensions. The process in outline is fairly clear, but the personalities who presided, both the Britons and their supplanters, are elusive. To this period belong the most potent and memorable legends in a thousand years, yet they are attached to precisely those names and actions which are hardest to be sure about. We confront the greatest among the early kings, permanently so in romance, long believed to have been so in reality; and the time of his reign is the obscurest of all, shrouding his career and even his existence in mystery.

On the British side, the central figure in the opening act is that Vortigern with whom Germanus is said to have clashed. The Britons' descendants long afterwards, grimly holding out in Wales, were to blame him in retrospect as the base ruler who betrayed Britain to the Saxons. Yet in the first account of these happenings his name does not occur. Admittedly the account is by Gildas in his Complaining Book, and Gildas has an aversion to naming anybody before his own time.

The context of his confused narrative is the fact (and a fact it is) that counter-attacks against the barbarians, especially the Picts, always failed to destroy their capability or deter them for long. At last the Britons — presumably, once again, spokesmen of the *civitates* — made another plea for Roman aid. Gildas says they addressed their message to a certain Agitius in despairing terms.

> To Agitius, now consul for the third time, the groans of
> the Britons . . . . The barbarians drive us to the sea; the sea
> throws us back on the barbarians; thus two modes of death
> await us, we are either slain or drowned.

'Agitius' seems to be a garbling of the name of Aëtius, who was
consul for the third time in 446. This general's labours for a
tottering world were prodigious (soon afterwards, he beat back
Attila's Huns), but no help was forthcoming for the Britons.

Nevertheless, Gildas goes on, they enjoyed a final respite and
a last spell of prosperity. Yet their major problems remained
unsolved. There were internal troubles and a plague. The fatal
step was taken by someone described as their *superbus tyrannus,* 'pre-eminent ruler'. *Tyrannus* does not imply actual tyranny. It suggests that the man's power was doubtfully legitimate,
at least in Gildas's censorious eyes. Whoever he was, he tried to
play off one set of barbarians against the others. Three shiploads
of heathen Saxon mercenaries were allowed to settle in the
eastern part of the island. These, and compatriots of theirs who
followed, made a show of willingness to fight for the Britons
against the Picts and Scots. But they soon demanded more pay,
not in cash but in kind, for their own services and the maintenance of the families they had brought over. When the Britons
failed to produce it, they mutinied and spread carnage and
pillage throughout the land, right across to the western sea. For
a time it appeared that all was lost, ruin was total. It was not; but
the protagonists of the second act were to be different.

Much the same story appears in Bede about two hundred
years later. His version is based on Gildas, but he gives further
details. He calls the *superbus tyrannus* 'King Vortigern' — here is
the execrated name — and depicts him, as Gildas also does,
acting in concert with a national council. Bede mentions and
dates the message to Aëtius, getting the name right, and thinks
the first of the mercenaries came at Vortigern's invitation somewhere about 450, the emperors being Valentinian III in the west
and Marcian in the east. He affirms, as Gildas never plainly does,
that they genuinely fought for the Britons, though with ulterior
motives.

After speaking of their advent, and the advent of many more

in their wake, he has a passage distinguishing the three peoples — Angles, Saxons, Jutes — whom Gildas and others lump together as Saxons, and explaining where each group settled. He names the first arrivals as the brother chieftains Hengist and Horsa, seemingly Jutes who came to Kent. But he also indicates an early presence of Angles farther up the east coast. This fact gives a special interest to his account of the revolt. It is so close to Gildas that Bede tends to be overlooked as an independent witness. But he has a touch of his own which is very noteworthy indeed.

> It was not long before such hordes of these alien peoples crowded into the island that the natives who had invited them began to live in terror, for the Angles suddenly made an alliance with the Picts whom they had recently repelled, and prepared to turn their arms against their allies. They began by demanding a greater supply of provisions; then, seeking to provoke a quarrel, threatened that unless larger supplies were forthcoming, they would terminate their treaty and ravage the whole island. Nor were they slow to carry out their threats. . . . These heathen conquerors devastated the surrounding cities and countryside, extended the conflagration from the eastern to the western shores without opposition, and established a stranglehold over nearly all the doomed island. Public and private buildings were razed; priests were slain at the altar; bishops and people alike, regardless of rank, were destroyed with fire and sword.

The special point is the Anglo-Pictish alliance, which suggests that the onslaught may have come largely in the midlands and north, though Kent doubtless played its part. Bede, living and writing at Jarrow, may have known a northern tradition which Gildas did not.

Nennius, in his *History of the Britons*, gives a still more detailed version which reflects the views of the ninth-century Welsh. In this, the first settlement is accidental, and the evils that ensue are wholly Vortigern's fault. His joint responsibility with a council has faded out. Hengist is an exile who arrives with a warband seeking the British king's protection. Vortigern decides to employ these warriors, and gives them land in the Isle of

Thanet. After that the account looks more and more fanciful as it goes on. Hengist is the sole aggressor, and nothing is said till much later about confederates farther north. He introduces Vortigern to his beautiful daughter, and the infatuated monarch hands over the whole of Kent as the price of marriage. Hengist honours his undertakings to some extent, campaigning in Pictland, but his aims in Britain become obvious, and Vortigern's son Vortimer fights the Kentish host with success. Vortimer dies, however, and the king tries to make peace. Three hundred British nobles attend a meeting for reconciliation. The treacherous heathens massacre nearly all of them. Hengist imprisons Vortigern and extorts more territory. The king himself dies soon after, an aged and discredited wanderer.

One purpose of this romance is to make out that the Britons in general were blameless and brave (not Gildas's view, nearer to the events) and that all the guilt can be pinned on one betrayer. What Nennius says about enmity between Vortigern and Germanus is meant to underline the king's wickedness. So is an accusation that he committed incest with his own daughter. Other Welsh writers have much the same opinion of him. They do not add much, except that they call him 'Vortigern the thin' — perhaps because he was, or perhaps in a metaphorical sense, suggesting a lack of substance in his character. The Welsh form of his name, Gwrtheyrn, is found in Caernarvonshire at Nant Gwrtheyrn, Vortigern's 'hollow' or 'water-course'. This is a secluded spot on the coast, with a stream flowing down a ravine into Caernarvon Bay. The king's grave is said to be beside it.

2

Is this royal villain a purely imaginary scapegoat, or can we count him among the rulers of Britain? If we can, what was his position, how long did he hold it, and what did he do?

Once again, the coming of the Saxons (the word being used in a broad sense, as it often is, to include Angles and Jutes as well) is a fact of history. Pressure of population had driven them to seek new lands. For some time they had been spreading through Frisia, the modern Holland. More of it was habitable then than in later years, because the inundation which formed the Zuider

Zee had not yet happened. Yet it was scarcely an endearing country. Many of the native Frisians lived on mounds along the coast, subject to flooding and sometimes between the high and low water marks, so that they were islands for a part of each day. The mound-dwellers ate fish, drank rain-water and warmed themselves with peat. When their mounds crumbled, they built them up again with mud, dung and vegetable refuse.

The migrant Saxons had mingled with the mound-dwellers. Some early writers even refer to Saxons as 'Frisians'. But, understandably, they were dissatisfied with their surroundings and disposed to move on. They now had better ships, with sails made of leather. Some went to Gaul, near Boulogne and Bayeux and along much of the lower Loire. Others headed for Britain, where archaeology shows traces of settlements well before the mid-fifth century, not only by them but by native Frisians and others from the same part of Europe. Some may have been squatters whom the Britons simply failed to evict. Others may already have been authorized immigrants. The latter would have been accepted on the same basis as other Teutonic tribes in the Roman world, who were allotted land in return for military service and called *foederati*. When the story tells how Vortigern allowed Hengist to make his home in Kent, the essential picture is in keeping with known facts. This would have been a case of a British ruler recruiting *foederati* himself. Moreover Hengist himself may quite well have existed. A geographical scribe in Ravenna, unlikely to have been influenced by British legends, speaks of the Saxons having moved into the island under the leadership of their prince 'Anschis', which could be a corruption of 'Hengist'. Also a Hengest appears in a story sketchily told in the Anglo-Saxon epic *Beowulf,* and another poem connected with it, feuding against a rival in Frisia.

However, the Nennius version is incredible. Hengist and his war-band may have settled in Kent as *foederati*. But the notion that this was the beginning of the occupation, and that the whole Anglo-Saxon horde originated from this one colony, cannot stand up. Not only do we know of those other colonies, we know that some of them were a long way from Kent. Angles were in Cambridgeshire, having probably entered via the Wash; they were in part of Lincolnshire; and kinsfolk of theirs were in astonishing places, far from the sea, including, for instance, the

Thames valley.

Bede and Gildas are closer, and better, to the extent that they recognize a settlement of a wider kind. But their dates do not work. There is not enough time between the appeal to Aëtius in 446 and a supposed Saxon advent around 450 for all the vicissitudes which Gildas puts in the interval. Worse, two Gaulish chronicles earlier than Gildas and Bede show that people on the continent thought the Saxons were ascendant in Britain about 440, before the writers in Britain say they even arrived.

A likelihood remains that Vortigern was a real ruler who entered into a deal with them. This deal, however, was only one of several — local arrangements made in different areas, over a fairly long stretch of time, bringing in bodies of Saxons as *foederati* on a footing which was at first peaceable. Possibly fellow-tribesmen of theirs were still harassing other parts of Britain in the old way, and squatting without leave. In the end the *foederati* themselves mutinied, plundered their employers, and encouraged more of their own people to come over and join the spoliation. If a group sponsored personally by Vortigern took a leading part in the revolt, tradition could easily have simplified and dramatized the whole process, making him the guilty party.

Can we give him any more substance than that? 'Vortigern', in the Celtic British language, would have meant 'high chief' or 'high king'. Applied to this fifth-century ruler it may have been a title and not a name. It did come to be used as a name, but so did the Roman title 'Augustus'. If it was a title in this case, Gildas's phrase *superbus tyrannus* may be a Latin rendering of it, or of a general notion of over-kingship which 'Vortigern' expresses in Celtic terms.

Nennius locates Vortigern's immediate forbears in Gloucestershire. It appears, also, that before Bradford-on-Avon received its English name it was called after him. However, we get a little closer to him in some notes which stand at the end of Nennius's narrative in the chief manuscript. They may really belong with a chronicle called the *Annales Cambriae* or Welsh Annals, composed of historical miscellanea from the fifth century to the tenth, which the scribe has copied out after it. At any rate these notes are straightforward-looking, with no legendary fancies to make them suspect. They put Vortigern's rise to power in 425. If he started out as a local kinglet in Gloucestershire, he undoubtedly succeeded in asserting a wider claim. We can infer that much on several grounds. In the first place, if he arranged for Saxons to settle near the North Sea, he must have reached a point sooner or later when he had jurisdiction there. In the second place, the stories of his clash with Germanus not only fit in with the saint's visit in 429, but suggest that Vortigern was the main sponsor of the heresy which Germanus came to combat; and in order to be so, he would have had to be powerful in the populous regions where Christianity counted for most. Lastly we have clues hinting that he was a recognized successor to Roman authority, a status which would have given him influence over a wide area even if it was contested.

The Roman connection is intriguing. This is one case where Geoffrey of Monmouth's fantasies may have a background of fact. In his account of Vortigern (which is largely an expansion of the one given by Nennius) he says that before Vortigern was king of Britain, he had the title of Duke of the Gewissei, the people inhabiting Gwent. Geoffrey gives that title to only one other man, Octavius, the alleged father of Maximus's British wife. How it descended to Vortigern is not explained, but Celtic custom would have sanctioned transmission in the female line. The repeated title indicates that Geoffrey may have got hold of a notion about Vortigern having a family link with Maximus, presumably through a marriage of his own.

Now there is separate evidence that he made such a marriage. A little way west of Llangollen in northern Wales, the road turns up Valle Crucis, where a Cistercian abbey formerly stood. On the right, enclosed in railings, is a pillar which once had a cross on top. After the dissolution of the monasteries it was thrown down. In 1696, when it was lying on the ground, an antiquary deciphered a Latin inscription on it. Later the broken shaft was set up again. The lettering belongs to the early ninth century. Today it is too worn to be read reliably, but the transcript shows that it gave the pedigree of a certain Eliseg, ruler of the Welsh kingdom of Powys, which included the Llangollen area. It traced the royal line back to a son of Vortigern called Britu, 'whom Germanus blessed'. This is supported by a passage in Nennius saying that one of Vortigern's sons deserted him and accompanied his saintly adversary back to Gaul.

According to this inscription, Vortigern's wife who bore Britu was Sevira, a daughter of Maximus. He did marry into the family. It is on record that one result of Maximus's downfall was that his young daughters became imperial wards. A marriage of one of them to a suitable Briton would have been in keeping with late imperial policy, as part of an arrangement handing over authority to him. Vortigern would probably have been younger than his bride, but not absurdly so. This then may be the key to his career — a treaty with a marriage clause, near the end of Roman Britain, which he exploited after independence as giving him rights over the whole country.

The rest of the picture would cohere tolerably well. Vortigern's quarrel with the Church was perhaps mainly a display of authority. His council, briefly mentioned by Gildas, would have been a successor to the provincial council of Roman times, bringing together representatives from the *civitates*. Vortigern would have governed with it but probably, in practice, reduced its powers. The futile appeal to Aëtius may have come from it as the last act of a body which still looked nostalgically across the Channel. It may also have been under Vortigern's auspices, rather than those of the dying Empire, that Cunedda took control of Wales.

The same notes which put Vortigern's rise to power in 425 also speak of Saxons coming in 428 — yet another date. All that can be said is that this agrees with the overall impression. Several settlements were authorized, one perhaps in 428, one towards 440, one about 450, possibly more. Later these all became confused, and the confusion was augmented by dim recollections of Saxon squatters in other places, and of raids, such as the one frustrated by Germanus. Whatever the extent of Vortigern's role, it was his misfortune to reign throughout the whole period. Some of the *foederati* were already domineering over their British neighbours about 440, and a broad revolt extending intermittently through the fifties and into the sixties dismissed Vortigern with ignominy in his old age.

Neither he nor any other Britons who dealt with Saxons deserved the charges of stupidity, treachery, cowardice and so forth. In the face of barbarian harassment they were carrying on a well-tried imperial policy, the enlistment of other barbarians as *foederati*. But they were doing it without the Empire's resources, and above all, without its treasury. When Saxons swarmed into

Britain in unforeseen numbers, the arrangements made for their maintenance broke down. Thereupon the Saxons turned from peaceable settlement to pillaging expeditions and eventually to landtaking, reinforced by more and more of their fellow-countrymen. The transition to 'Angle-land' had begun. It was not, however, to go undisputed.

3

Welsh legend gives another glimpse of its arch-scapegoat, bizarrely introducing the next major figure. Nennius tells how Vortigern tried to turn his back on the results of his policy. He went to Wales and began building a fortress. The walls kept collapsing. He consulted his wise men — apparently Druids, raising their heads again after long repression. They replied that the only remedy was a human sacrifice, and one with a special and peculiar victim. He must find a boy born without a father and sprinkle his blood on the foundations.

Vortigern sent out messengers. They found a boy whose mother claimed to have conceived him without male agency. When the messengers brought him to the place, he turned the tables on Vortigern's soothsayers. He pointed to a stone and asked what was concealed under it. They had no idea. He told them that if it was lifted up they would find a pool, and in the pool a folded tent and two vases. All was found as he predicted. Then he said that two serpents were hidden in the tent, one red, one white. When the tent was unfolded the serpents duly appeared. They fought, and at first the white defeated the red, but presently the red recovered and drove the white off the tent. The boy expounded the scene symbolically. The pool was the world, the tent was Britain, the red serpent stood for the Britons, the white for the Saxons. Some day the Britons, or their descendants, would reconquer their lost lands. Nennius does not explain how the serpents got there, but they were the dragons trapped in a tub of mead and reduced in size by King Lludd, as told in the *Mabinogion*.

While the prophetic youth had a word of comfort for Britain, he had none for Vortigern. The unworthy monarch should give up his abortive stronghold and go away, and he himself would take charge of the site. He disclosed that he was Prince Am-brose, *Emrys gwledig,* the son of a Roman consul. Another thing which Nennius does not explain is how that noble paternity agrees with the earlier statement that he had no paternity at all.

The locale of this tale is the hill-fort Dinas Emrys in Snowdo-nia. It overlooks the valley of Nant Gwynant, north-east of Beddgelert, and close to the scene of that other legend about Maximus's son Owen and the giant. If Vortigern married one of Maximus's daughters, Owen would have been his brother-in-law. The triple ramparts of the hill-fort enclose a fairly level plateau. Archaeologically this is a rich site. Like all the Celtic hill-forts it dates from the pre-Roman Iron Age, but it was not abandoned. In the Roman period there was a stone building here with an actual pool near it, an artificial pool, dug soon after the Roman conquest. Furthermore, someone lived in Dinas Emrys at about the right time for Nennius. Traces of a fifth-century occupation have been unearthed on a rising patch of ground. The occupant seems to have been a Christian, and to have enjoyed a degree of wealth and comfort.

We have no solid reason to believe that he actually was Emrys, the *gwledig* Ambrose, another holder of that title given to Cunedda and Ceredig and, in fanciful retrospect, to Maximus. But Emrys was a real person and an important one, even though the circumstances of his meeting with Vortigern, and their rela-tive ages, are plainly fabulous. Gildas names him, and that is saying much in view of Gildas's reluctance to name anyone.

The prelude to his entrance is the nightmare of the Saxon revolt. Gildas mentions a consequence of it which gives a rough date. He speaks of British refugees going abroad. That is his way of referring to a colonization of Armorica. The earlier one sponsored by Maximus is 'not proven', and certainly fictitious in the sense of the total conquest implied by legend. But British refugees did arrive on the continent in the 450s, coming chiefly from the south-west. It is not likely that they had been much hurt themselves by Saxon aggression, but evidently the future looked bleak to them. In 461 a bishop who had joined the migration, Mansuetus, is recorded as attending a council at Tours. The Britons seem to have spread out over an area stretch-ing beyond the borders of Brittany, but that north-western cor-ner of Gaul was the favoured objective. Their new land was by no means free from enemies. Saxons who had migrated to Gaul were living around the lower Loire and on islands in the river. A chief of theirs, whose name comes down as Corsoldus, ravaged a tract of Brittany. But here the Britons, though few, held their own.

In the homeland, Gildas continues, the Saxons pulled back from the points reached in their marauding forays and returned to their enclaves near the North Sea. The retirement may have been voluntary; it may have been hastened by British action. Certainly it meant withdrawal into an area which was still no more than a fraction of Britain, and this looked enough like a turning of the tide to encourage a counter-effort. It came under the leadership of Ambrosius Aurelianus. He it is who becomes the Ambrose or Emrys of the legend, the supposed lord of the Snowdonian hill-fort. Here we have the reality of him, flourishing fairly soon after the migrants went to Armorica.

Gildas calls him a man of discretion and moderation, the last of the Romans in Britain. His parents, who had been killed in the devastation, had 'doubtless worn the purple', that is, been of imperial family. Bede virtually copies Gildas except that he makes the name 'Ambrosius Aurelius'. Nennius of course has the Roman association also (the father of Ambrose is a consul), but he adds little more, except a hint that Ambrosius was Vortigern's enemy long before the Saxon revolt — which stultifies the tale about his first meeting Vortigern as a boy after it, yet may be correct. The chronological notes which follow Nennius in the manuscript refer to an inter-British battle between Ambrosius and someone called Vitolinus at Guoloph, probably Wallop in Hampshire. It is said to have happened 'twelve years from Vortigern's reign', but as it is not clear whether this means the beginning or the end of his reign, it is unhelpful. Nennius mentions Ambrosius again as becoming a High King over the kings of the Britons. If (as is improbable) the assertion carries any weight, it would have to correspond to a later period of political break-up, not to the time of his emergence.

Whatever the value of such oddments, Gildas himself, closer to the events, does not make Ambrosius any kind of king but simply a war-leader, the initiator of an armed counter-move against the Saxon settlements. The surviving patriots flocked to him. When did this happen? After the migration to Armorica, and after the Saxons' withdrawal to their home bases: seemingly in the 460s. Such a dating sheds light on Gildas's eccentric use of the word 'Roman' in speaking of this British leader. It has come down to him in tradition, but lost its meaning on the way, causing him to make a baseless guess about Ambrosius's origins. In north-west Europe during the 460s 'Roman' was a label which denoted a political leaning.

Gaul, or most of it, was still shakily a part of the Empire despite various barbarian inroads. About 457 the north had come under the control of a general named Aegidius, who was virtually independent, but theoretically loyal to Rome. Seven years later he was succeeded by his son Syagrius, who ruled from Soissons as a *de facto* capital, got the Franks in Gaul to accept him as sovereign and called himself 'King of the Romans'. The title had no place in the imperial scheme, yet it reaffirmed the theoretical loyalty. Shared interests, shared trouble with the Saxons, created an informal British alliance. Aegidius probably helped the Britons to settle in Armorica. A Gaulish history, describing a combined assault on the Loire Saxons a few years later, seems to include Britons among the 'Romans'. A British leader might then have counted as a Roman in Syagrius's sense, through a friendly relationship with him, a Roman-rather-than-barbarian inclination in the final confusion of the Western Empire.

So Ambrosius's counter-thrust looks as if it belongs in the 460s. That dating is supported further by clues which begin to trickle through from the other side. The invaders' own scanty traditions were written down long afterwards in the *Anglo-Saxon Chronicle*. It records no defeats — minstrels did not sing about those — but we can glean a little from the cessation of victories. The relevant early entries concern Kent. While their dates cannot be trusted, they are interesting. In 455 the revolt of the *foederati* is well under way: Hengist fights the Britons at Aegelsthrep, perhaps Aylesford, and assumes the kingship of Kent. In 457 he wins a battle at Creacanford, perhaps Crayford, and the Britons flee to London in terror. But the next battle, in 465, is not claimed as a victory, and then the *Chronicle* is silent for eight years. Once again we can fairly picture a British recovery, with Ambrosius commanding during the 460s and taking action to hem the Saxons in.

We may also have glimpses of him in the names of a few places, such as Amesbury in Wiltshire. The 'bury' part is Saxon, but the first part was originally 'Ambr'. Amesbury was the site of a British monastery which existed before the middle of the sixth century, and one guess is that Ambrosius founded it. More likely, however, he stationed troops here. In the later Empire it sometimes happened that a force would be named after its head or nominal head. So it was, for example, with the Honoriaci, Honorius's men, the auxiliary body that deserted to the pretender Constantine. There were also Theodosiani. Ambrosius's men could have been Ambrosiaci or Ambrosiani, and his name could have passed to a military base used by them. The same might apply to a few other 'Ambr' places, such as Ambrosden in Oxfordshire.

His initiative may have been part of a wider anti-Saxon drive drawing in some of the Britons who had gone to the continent. It was about this time that the Loire Saxons were overthrown near Angers by the combined 'Roman' forces of northern Gaul. Britons helped to destroy their ships. After this the surviving Saxons, or most of them, moved away. It was a moment of hope both in Britain and in the nascent Brittany.

4

When Geoffrey of Monmouth gives what he pretends is the truth about these events, he is no more writing history than he is anywhere else. Yet his way of doing it leaves an impression worth considering — that the new overseas Britain in Armorica had an early importance beyond what is now evident. Its population, in reality, was still small and scattered, but study of Geoffrey suggests that this was a high-quality, literate society, and that it handed on information which he used and which, if it could be recovered, would put this period in a fresh light. The impression is strengthened by a sentence of Gildas, who speaks of the emigrants taking away history books with them. Geoffrey draws on Nennius and other authors in the homeland, giving his own colourful embroidery of their statements. But if he had drawn on these only, it is hard to see how his story could have emerged quite as it does. An additional factor is at work in his mind, and it seems to be a Breton factor.

He takes the name of the patriotic leader from Bede and reverses it, making him Aurelius Ambrosius. Aurelius, or Ambrosius, is the rightful king of Britain who comes into his own after a usurpation by Vortigern. But the basis of his right is a fact unmentioned by previous authors.

When Maximus fell, according to Geoffrey, the next king of Britain was Gracianus. He was assassinated, and the barbarian onslaughts and Roman rescue described by Gildas (one rescue, not two) promptly followed. The only British leadership came from Guithelinus, Archbishop of London, who urged the Britons to learn to defend themselves. However, as soon as the Romans had gone, the barbarians surged in again. It was in this crisis that the Britons made their futile plea for help to Aëtius, or Agicius as Geoffrey spells it, echoing the erroneous Gildas.

As soon as its failure was manifest, Archbishop Guithelinus crossed over to Armorica. Here the kingdom founded by Conan Meriadoc was flourishing under Aldroenus, the fourth king in succession from him. The Archbishop offered him the crown of Britain if he would assume charge of the island's defence. Aldroenus declined to take on such an afflicted country, but accepted the offer on behalf of his brother Constantine. Constantine shipped an army over to Britain and cleared out the barbarians. He was crowned in Silchester. He had three sons: Constans, who became a monk, and Aurelius Ambrosius and Uther, who were much younger.

After a peaceful reign of ten years, Constantine was murdered by a treacherous Pict. During the debate over the succession, Duke Vortigern came forward as king-maker. Visiting Constans, he urged that as the two younger princes were still in their infancy, Constans should leave his cloister and become king. The enthronement of a renegade monk did not meet with public approval, but Vortigern pushed it through, knowing that Constans would be a puppet in his hands. He installed his own supporters in positions of power, and enrolled a guard of Picts. Presently the Picts decided that Vortigern should be king, and murdered Constans. Vortigern made a show of being sorry, but actually matters were working out as he had hoped. He assumed the crown. The guardians of Ambrosius and Uther took them to Brittany for safety, and they lived at the Breton court.

Now Hengist and Horsa landed in Kent with their three ships. They told Vortigern they had been banished, and offered him their services. They soon proved their usefulness in a campaign against the Picts. Vortigern rewarded Hengist with lands in Lindsey (north and central Lincolnshire). Hengist brought over many more of his fellow-countrymen, and married his daughter Renwein to Vortigern, receiving Kent in exchange.

It was at this time, says Geoffrey, that St Germanus and Bishop Lupus of Troyes came to Britain to preach against the Pelagian heresy.

The swift growth of the Saxon colony, in numbers and strength, turned the Britons against Vortigern. They transferred the crown to Vortimer, his son by a previous marriage, who attacked the Saxons in Kent and beat them. But his stepmother Renwein poisoned him, and Vortigern resumed power. He brought Britons and Saxons together for a peace conference at the Cloister of Ambrius in Wiltshire. The Saxons came to it with daggers hidden in their boots, and when Hengist gave a signal they slew four hundred and sixty British nobles, who were buried together on the spot. Vortigern gave way completely, allowing the Saxons to occupy London, York and other cities. He fled to Wales to build a fortress ... here Geoffrey tells very much the same story as Nennius does, but the red and white serpents are restored to their old magnitude as dragons (hence, in part, the Red Dragon of Wales) and the prophetic boy becomes the young Merlin, who thus enters literature. Geoffrey relates how he foretold Vortigern's downfall, warning him that Constantine's sons, now grown up, were sailing from Armorica to dispossess him and rescue Britain.

It happened as Merlin said. Aurelius Ambrosius landed with his brother Uther and was hailed as rightful king. He besieged Vortigern in the castle of Genoreu — the hill-fort of Little Doward near Ganarew, beside the Wye — and there the usurper was burnt to death. Ambrosius turned his attention to the Saxons. Hengist was defeated and slain at Conisbrough in Yorkshire. Ambrosius governed from York and then from Winchester, issuing orders for the rebuilding of Britain's cities and the restoration of order. He resolved to put up a monument over the nobles who had been murdered at the peace conference. The result was Stonehenge, which he acquired ready-made. It had been built in Ireland by giants. Merlin dismantled it by his secret arts, the stones were shipped over to Britain, and he reassembled the circle on Salisbury Plain.

Ambrosius's reign was cut short by Paschent, a surviving son of Vortigern. He incited an Irish prince to invade Britain on his behalf, which the prince was willing to do in reprisal for the theft of Stonehenge. Uther marched to oppose the Irish. Ambrosius could not accompany him, because he was lying ill at Winchester. Paschent bribed a Saxon assassin, who got access to the king disguised as a doctor and killed him with a poisonous drug.

This whole romance has a puzzling duality. Geoffrey is more or less following the Gildas-Bede-Nennius sequence of events — the barbarian attacks, the appeal to Aëtius, the coming of Hengist, the disasters under Vortigern, the revival under Ambrosius — though he invents periods of time which distort it. But he seems to be trying to combine this story with another one which is dated farther back. His king Gracianus is based on the pretender Gratian who was proclaimed in Britain in 406 and almost immediately murdered. Archbishop Guithelinus exhorts the Britons soon after Gracianus's death. The interregnum with its barbarian troubles does not last very long, yet Geoffrey passes straight to the appeal to Aëtius, dated by Bede to 446. Then he brings Guithelinus on to the stage again, alive and active, sailing to Armorica to look for a successor to Gracianus. And while his embassy is totally incompatible with the date of Aëtius, it follows on quite well from the episodes just before the appeal. It results in the accession of Constantine, and he, of course, is a romanticized version of the pretender Constantine III, who did succeed Gratian and reigned from 407 to 411 with his son Constans, a monk who left the cloister as Geoffrey says. One series of events is cutting across another. So also with the British mission of Germanus and Lupus. It occurred in 429. Geoffrey puts it in correct sequence with Constantine, but not at all with the supposed mid-century advent of the Saxons.

Not only are these two strands in his narrative, there is a contrast between them. Whenever he mentions a person or event belonging to known history, which can be checked, he takes the reader into his earlier time-scale. 'Gracianus', Constantine, Constans, Germanus, Lupus, are his only characters in this part of the *History* who can be detected and dated in records outside Britain. In his treatment of the Gildas-Bede-Nennius matter, even Aëtius would be unrecognizable if we could not identify him from Bede. Apart from that, despite all that Geoffrey adds, he never brings in anything having the same sort of authenticity, or synchronizing the story with happenings in other countries. It all takes place in a world of its own.

Moreover, Geoffrey's extra, authentic characters inject a Breton factor which the older accounts entirely lack. He takes it for granted that the Britons had settled Armorica under Conan. Nennius writes of that before him. But neither Nennius nor anyone else portrays the salvation of Britain as the work of the Breton royal house, Conan's descendants, or makes Constantine and his sons (real and alleged) belong to that house. So we might suspect Geoffrey's use of a narrative handed down by the Britons overseas: a narrative which drew in matters that were known on the continent, and which had a certain coherence, a certain relationship to fact, but improved whatever truth it contained for the Bretons' greater glory. One stray clue supports that suspicion. In an Irish version of Nennius composed in 1072 — that is, well before Geoffrey — Ambrosius is said to have been in Brittany.

5

The impression of lost British history on the continent recurs when we try to answer a simple question. Geoffrey's enthronement of 'King Aurelius Ambrosius' is not evidence as to fact. Gildas, let us recall, does not speak of Ambrosius as a king, and he is not at all likely to have been so during his military activities in the 460s. But if he was not, who was?

The Britons had accepted monarchical rule, even if it was limited, as the reference to Vortigern's council suggests. St Patrick's letter to Ceredig is trustworthy evidence for the breakaway Clyde kingdom. Excavation at Dumbarton, the 'Fort of the Britons', favours the belief that it was Ceredig's stronghold. By the mid-460s the rest of the country was in transition. The Britannia of Roman days no longer existed. Its cantonal system was probably far gone in decay. There was not even a British coinage. Though the Saxons had withdrawn from their advanced positions, large patches of the east and south-east were securely theirs, with a rising generation born in the settlements. Yet the British-held portion of the island was still by far the largest, with nine-tenths of the population, and while Ceredig is proof of secession in the north, there is no such proof anywhere else. No other regional kings are mentioned as yet.

At this stage, then, it is likely that most of the Britons still had a paramount sovereign at least in name. United Britannia was still within living memory. There could no longer, indeed, have been a king of Britain even apart from Ceredig's portion. The formation of Anglo-Saxondom in the island had ruled out the geographical title. But there could, for a few years, have been a king of the Britons or a preponderant number of them, including perhaps the ones who had moved to Armorica, just as there were kings of the Goths and Franks, with titles taken from their subjects and not from their ill-defined domains. This is more than a speculation. Continental records show that someone called the 'King of the Britons' was recognized overseas, even in Rome. The question is not whether he existed — he did — but whether his title means what it seems to mean and apparently might mean; whether we can allow him to fill the vacancy.*

The last western emperor with any staying power had been Valentinian III, son of the general who crushed the pretender Constantine. After he was murdered in 455 the reigns were ineffectual and soon over. In 467 Leo I, the eastern emperor, intervened by appointing a Greek named Anthemius as his colleague in Rome. Gaul was an immediate problem. The north was held by the 'Roman' Syagrius, and much of the east-central region by the Burgundians, who were friendly. But the uncontrolled Visigoths in the south-west were making threatening gestures. Jordanes, author of a *Gothic History* in the sixth century, tells what happened.

> Leo . . . chose as emperor [of the west] his patrician Anthemius and sent him to Rome. . . .
>
> Now Euric, King of the Visigoths, perceived the frequent changes of Roman emperors and strove to hold Gaul in his own right. The Emperor Anthemius heard of it and asked

* See Preface, pp. 7-9.

the Britons for aid. Their king Riotimus came with twelve thousand men into the state of the Bituriges by the way of Ocean, and was received as he disembarked from his ships. Euric, King of the Visigoths, came against them with an innumerable army, and after a long fight he routed Riotimus, King of the Britons, before the Romans could join him. So when he had lost a great part of his army, he fled with all the men he could gather together, and came to the Burgundians, a neighbouring tribe then allied to the Romans.

We know more about this episode. The 'state of the Bituriges' was Berry in central Gaul. After a pause somewhere on the north side of the Loire, the Britons occupied Bourges, Berry's chief city. A letter written to their king has survived. Its author is Sidonius Apollinaris, a Gallo-Roman civic official who became Bishop of Clermont about this time. He spells the name "Riothamus', which is closer to the presumed British original. His letter introduces its bearer, a landowner who complains that the Britons have been luring his slaves away, perhaps by enlisting them as mercenaries. He is very polite to the British leader: 'I am a direct witness of the conscientiousness which weighs on you so heavily, and which has always been of such delicacy as to make you blush for the wrongdoing of others.' However, he is uncertain about the reception the landowner will get: 'I fancy that this poor fellow is likely to make good his plaint, that is if amid a crowd of noisy, armed and disorderly men who are emboldened at once by their courage, their number, and their comradeship, there is any possibility for a solitary unarmed man, a humble rustic, a stranger of small means, to gain a fair and equitable hearing.'

To another correspondent, Sidonius reveals that the Britons fell victim to a betrayal amounting to treason. The Imperial Prefect of Gaul, Anthemius's deputy, was a certain Arvandus. In 468, before the Britons reached Berry, he wrote to Euric advising him not to come to terms with the 'Greek emperor', meaning Anthemius, but to attack 'the Britons posted north of the Loire' and divide up Gaul with the Burgundians. Arvandus was detected and impeached by the Senate, but Euric acted on his advice. By then the Britons were in their exposed forward position in Berry. Late in 469, or more likely in the first half of 470, Euric pounced on them at Bourg-de-Déols near Châteauroux. This was the fatal battle, and is attested by Gregory of Tours, the sixth-century historian of the Franks. The 'Romans' who failed to arrive would have been troops raised by Syagrius. Euric pursued the British survivors and drove them from Bourges. Riothamus escaped into Burgundy, probably by way of the modern departments of Nièvre and Yonne. There he vanishes from sight.

Some historians have taken the line that these Britons were Bretons, in other words settlers in Armorica, and Riothamus was merely a local chief. This, however, will hardly account for the facts. The Britons came 'by the way of Ocean', the Bretons would not have done. Nor could the small and scattered refugee colonies have put such an army in the field. The number may be exaggerated, but the force was strong enough to hold out hopes of checking the Goths. When Arvandus urged Euric to smash the Britons and split up Gaul he clearly regarded them as the only real obstacle. We are dealing here with soldiers in thousands and a fleet capable of transporting them.

Riothamus, then, may quite well have been 'King of the Britons' in more or less the sense suggested, with Ambrosius as a general in his service. He would doubtless have played his part in the first countermeasures against the Saxons in Britain. His venture abroad fits into a phase in the late 460s when it could have appeared that they were contained. He might then have judged it safe to take an army to Gaul, earning a subsidy from the Roman treasury, and strengthening the Britons against the Saxons on another front — the Loire. Very possibly he would have regarded the emigrants as still being his subjects. It was around that time that the Saxons on the Loire were beaten near Angers. While nothing is said about Riothamus helping the local Britons in the fighting against them, he could have done so. Modern writers have assumed that his troop-carrying fleet arrived in Gaul by way of the Loire mouth. If it did, he could hardly have avoided encountering Saxons there, unless he came too late for that — but the indications are that he came in time. In any case his major action as the emperor's ally would have followed quickly.

Why is Riothamus never mentioned in Britain? The answer is

that he may be, but not in such a way as to be instantly recognizable. Some Britons in that period had two names, one British, the other derived from the Roman milieu. Thus St Patrick's name is 'Patricius', but he was also known by the British 'Magonus' or 'Maun'. 'Riothamus' Latinizes what could be a British name. The king may have had a Roman one also, and be traceable under that.

Or he may appear elsewhere in a different guise because 'Riothamus' was not his name at all, but his title. This in fact is probable. Gildas, it will be remembered, refers to the British sovereign around the middle of the fifth century as the *superbus tyrannus* or pre-eminent ruler. Riothamus is the third of three Britons who are mentioned by designations meaning something like this. Furthermore, they are etymologically linked.

The first of the trio, as already observed, is Vortigern. The syllable *vor* means 'over', the rest means 'chief' or 'king'. Vortigern is literally the 'over-king'. Next comes his son Vortimer — temporarily crowned, according to Geoffrey of Monmouth. 'Vortimer' adapts a Celtic British original which would have been 'Vortamorix'. The first syllable is 'over' again; *tamo* is a superlative suffix; *rix,* akin to the Latin *rex,* is another word for 'king'. Vortimer therefore is the 'over-most' or 'highest' king. As for 'Riothamus' itself, its British original (modified by a slight shift in pronunciation) would have been 'Rigotamos'. The first syllable is the same as the final one of 'Vortamorix', and the last two are the same as the *tamo* part of it. 'Rigotamos' means literally 'king-most' or 'supreme king'. A modern word composed in the same way, from a noun and a superlative suffix, is 'generalissimo'.

So we have three Britons in positions of power, Vortigern, Vortimer and Riothamus. All are referred to in terms which more or less correspond to Gildas's *superbus tyrannus.* All are designated, in various ways, as the High King. The three expressions of that concept are linked, and the second is a transitional form between the first and the third: Vor-tigern, Vor-tamo-rix, Rigo-tamos. Whatever Vortigern and his son may amount to historically, we can see a pattern of royal terminology here. The undoubtedly real Riothamus fits into it in a manner which makes it very likely indeed that we are meeting him under a title and not a name. He may have used the title abroad for official purposes, as Octavian used the style 'Augustus' and is commonly known by it. 'High King' need imply nothing definite as to how far his various princelings had already established small domains of their own. At any rate, if this reading is correct, the question of Riothamus's personal name is open.

He does present a problem. It does seem strange that such a prominent figure should have left no trace in the Britons' history or legends. Hence, there is every justification for looking for this High King under another style, and trying to identify him with someone we know. A recent historian of Brittany has suggested that he and Ambrosius are the same person, and that Ambrosius, as High King, went to Gaul and got back and carried on the struggle against the Saxons. This is a tempting guess. But, it must be repeated, Ambrosius's kingship over the Britons seems to be a product of later legend. It clashes with his traditional status as a *gwledig*, since the men who really held that office had regional powers only. As for waging war in Gaul and returning, even legend says nothing about his doing that. In default of clearer evidence he is best viewed as Riothamus's commander-in-chief in Britain, possibly regent during his absence. Further clues, also incompatible with Ambrosius, will point to another opinion about the High King.

6

After the passing of Riothamus, the Britons' fortunes drifted into another phase of decline, though not catastrophe. The loss of a king powerful enough to be recognized and courted by Rome, together with most of his army, can hardly have failed to make a difference. The Saxons exploited it. According to the *Anglo-Saxon Chronicle* the Kentish host was on the offensive again in 473. Meanwhile, among the continental Saxons, the destruction of the Loire colony turned attention back to Britain. They found new weaknesses and new points of entry. In 477 or thereabouts a chieftain named Aelle landed near Selsey Bill and began the conquest of what is now Sussex, the land of the South Saxons. Bede tells us that he was the first of his race in Britain to wield an *imperium:* he claimed paramountcy among their chiefs, at any rate in the south-east. That status may hint at a more unified effort, a more concerted invasion. About 495 another leader,

Cerdic, sailed in via Southampton Water. Cerdic founded a local dynasty which was to create the kingdom of Wessex. Other penetrations were occurring in other places.

This time there was no British collapse. Gildas speaks of a long fluctuating warfare. 'Sometimes our citizens and sometimes the enemy had the best of it.' Here and there in the *Anglo-Saxon Chronicle,* a petering-out of victory communiqués suggests that a local thrust was halted. It is likely, though, that in many places the Saxons were gaining ground by simply occupying it, without violence. Britain was at last falling apart politically. The short phase when a king of the Britons could be a credible figure was at an end. Almost certainly there were now only *kings* of the Britons, opposing kings of the Saxons with varying fortunes . . . or making treaties with them. Britons still vastly outnumbered Saxons, but in a military sense that meant nothing. The superiority could never be brought to bear.

Lines of demarcation were fluid or non-existent. We know only vaguely what ground the petty monarchies covered. Eventually some of them begin to have names and stabilized shapes — Dumnonia or Dyfneint in the south-west; Brycheiniog, Dyfed, Powys, Gwynedd in Wales; Elmet in south-west Yorkshire; Rheged in Cumbria; Clyde or Strathclyde (Ceredig's kingdom, the prototype); Manau Guotodin bordering the Firth of Forth. But between 470 and 500 most of these regions were beyond Saxon range in any case. The political map of the war zone, and the amount of actual fighting that went on within it, are matters of conjecture.

East Anglia was lost to the Britons and so probably was Essex, but it is not certain who held London. A good deal of speculation has hovered over the Wansdyke. This is a great ditch with a bank of earth alongside, which runs south of Bristol and Bath, vanishes, reappears near Silbury and Avebury, and ends in the neighbourhood of Savernake Forest. Various considerations point to a late-fifth-century date, at least for the eastern section; the western may not be contemporary with it. The ditch is on the north side, so if the Wansdyke is a fortification, it faces north. Yet it is hard to see how such a long line could have been manned effectively for defence. Patrolling is more believable, and patrols could at least have sighted the approach of raiding parties and helped in the concentration of forces to stop them at the line. But the Wansdyke's chief function may have been to mark a frontier. In any case it hints at an organized British kingdom in Somerset and Wiltshire, or, perhaps, an extension of Dumnonia.

One result of the renewed warfare and encroachment was a further drift to Armorica. This was a small, elite migration rather than a mass movement of refugees. Enterprising newcomers began to assume control over areas named after the settlers' homelands. Cornouaille, the Breton Cornwall, acquired a dynasty founded (it is said) by a magnate named John, who came to be known as Riatham. This is a form of 'Riothamus', favouring the view that it was a title, or at any rate a name coupled with other names. But the most important late-fifth-century migrants were the saints coming individually: missionaries, teachers, founders of religious communities, many from Wales, who played a crucial role in forming a new society. The overseas Britain could not become a separate state. It shrank to what is now Brittany, and submitted to the rising power of the Franks. But it kept its local lords, its distinctive culture, and a British language that evolved very much as Welsh did. Fresh waves of settlement in due course confirmed its character. The native Armoricans were absorbed.

Between 470 and 500 many Britons of influence and ability may have turned away from the war zone like the emigrants, whether or not they went abroad. But not all did. A makeshift military cohesion seems to have survived. Ambrosius had successors. Men maintained war-bands, reinforced the kings, concurred in a rough strategy. At length the Britons gained an undeniable victory. Gildas calls it 'the siege of Mount Badon', and describes it as 'almost the last and not the least slaughter of the villains'. He indicates, or is usually read as indicating, that the Britons won the battle somewhere about the year 500 and that after it they enjoyed a spell of relative peace. Thanks to the outcome of this phase of the struggle, their descendants' storytellers gradually improved the breathing-space into a golden, heroic age with stories to match, thereby placing us, today, in a profound historical difficulty.

CHAPTER SEVEN

The Once and Future King

1

IN THE LONG PRELUDE TO MOUNT BADON, AND ITS IMMEDIATE SEQUEL,
THE RECORD OF BRITISH RULERSHIP GOES THROUGH A SHIFT OF BAL-
ANCE WHICH WOULD BE HARD TO PARALLEL ANYWHERE ELSE.
During the Roman phase, we are dealing mainly with historical facts, and legends are incidental. In the Vortigern-Ambrosius
phase we are reduced to scraps only of history, and scraps of
legend which bulk proportionately larger. Now comes a complete inversion. Facts in the sense of hard historical details
dwindle to near-invisibility, while legend becomes familiar, potent, overwhelming. A few modern authors have tried to make
something coherent of the former while cutting out the latter.
How far they have succeeded remains open to debate. Simply to
grasp what this is about, the logical and honest course is to
acknowledge the inversion and work, so to speak, backwards,
giving Geoffrey of Monmouth the first hearing.

On the death of Ambrosius, he says, Britain's crown passed to
Uther, the youngest son of Constantine — Uther Pendragon as
he was called. His first task was to expel the Irish who had
landed in support of Ambrosius's murderer Paschent. After
crushing them and one or two other enemies, he held court in
London at Easter. There his eye fell on Ygerna, the wife of
Gorlois, Duke of Cornwall. He was smitten with ungovernable
desire for her. Her husband noticed the advances Uther was
making and withdrew abruptly from the court. The king treated
this as an insult, and made it a pretext to ravage the ducal lands
in Cornwall.

Gorlois led an army out to resist him, leaving Ygerna in
Tintagel Castle, on a rocky headland approachable only by a
narrow isthmus. Uther besieged Gorlois at Dimilioc, probably
the hill at St. Dennis which now has a church on top. But his real
object was still Ygerna. He sent for Merlin, who, by a magic

potion, made him look like her husband. In that effective dis-
guise Uther passed the guards at Tintagel, entered the castle
where Ygerna was, and made love to her. She conceived a son.
Since Gorlois had just been killed in a sortie, Uther was able to
marry her and recognize her child as his heir. The boy was given
the name Arthur.

Uther reigned for another fifteen years, still with some trouble
from the Saxons, who brought over reinforcements. At last their
chiefs managed to have him poisoned, but they were unable to
prevent the coronation of Arthur at Silchester as Uther's successor. Though still so young, he took command and led a plundering foray against them which broadened into a new war. He
gained a victory over the Saxon field-army, strengthened with
Pictish and Scottish allies, beside the River Douglas. After a
failure at York he won another battle near Lincoln and another
in Caledon Wood in Scotland, the latter against the Saxons
alone, who had retreated north. They surrendered their trea-
sures of gold and silver and promised to return to the continent,
but changed course at sea and reappeared in Devon. Arthur
hastened south and met them on a hill beside Bath. There he
won a decisive triumph, wielding his sword Caliburn which was
forged in the Isle of Avalon. The remaining Saxons in Britain
were now entirely subdued. He marched north again and defeated the Picts and Scots, capturing their last refuges on the
islands of Loch Lomond.

Arthur now married Ganhumara (better known by a later
form of her name, Guinevere), a very beautiful woman of Roman descent. He led expeditions overseas, conquering Ireland
and Iceland. Then he reigned in peace for twelve years. He
founded an order of knighthood, enrolling men of note from
foreign countries as well as Britain. His fame spread through
Europe. Conscious of the awe he inspired, he set out to build an
empire. First he conquered Norway and Denmark. Next he
invaded Gaul, which was governed by the tribune Frollo in the
name of the emperor. He slew Frollo in single combat outside
Paris and wrested most of Gaul from Roman control. At this
point Geoffrey says all of Gaul, but the geography is vague. It
appears from later chapters that Burgundy remained in dispute,
and the country towards the Alps stayed beyond Arthur's reach.

Nine years passed, four of them taken up with the Gallic

conquest, five with the reorganization. Normandy was entrusted to Bedevere, Arthur's cupbearer, and Anjou to Kay, his seneschal. Then at Whitsuntide the king held court splendidly at Caerleon-upon-Usk. Knights and prelates of the realm, kings and lords from foreign lands, gathered for the occasion. 'Britain,' Geoffrey declares, 'had reached such a standard of sophistication that it excelled all other kingdoms in its general affluence, the richness of its decorations, and the courteous behavior of its inhabitants. Every knight in the country who was in any way famed for his bravery wore livery and arms showing his own distinctive colour, and women of fashion often displayed the same colours. They scorned to give their love to any man who had not proved himself three times in battle. In this way the womenfolk became chaste and more virtuous and for their love the knights were ever more daring.'

During the ceremonies at Caerleon, envoys arrived from Rome, sent by Lucius Hiberius, Procurator of the Republic. (This odd title seems to reflect Geoffrey's awareness that there was a period when western Europe was still officially Roman, but its 'emperors' had been reduced to a point where they scarcely counted as such.) The envoys brought a letter reproaching King Arthur for withholding the tribute which the Britons had formerly paid, and for seizing Roman territory in Gaul. Lucius demanded Arthur's submission, failing which he would invade Britain.

Arthur held a council with several of his dukes and the subkings who governed Brittany and Scotland. All agreed that Lucius's demands were unjustified and his threats empty. Arthur recalled the past glories of Constantine the Great and Maximus, both of whom he counted among his relatives. These had ruled in Rome. Far from submitting, he had a good claim to rule in Rome himself. His council concurred. The five-year peace was enough and the best course was to take the offensive. So the king raised an army and returned to Gaul, leaving his nephew Modred in charge at home, jointly with Ganhumara. He turned aside to kill an evil giant who lived on Mont-Saint-Michel, and then marched to meet the force assembled by Lucius from various parts of the Roman world. Having gained the upper hand in several preliminary clashes, he met the Romans between Langres and Autun on the fringes of Burgundy, won a crushing victory in which Lucius was killed, and sent the corpse to Rome, with a message for the Senate saying they could expect no other tribute from Britain.

Arthur subdued the Allobroges (Geoffrey's name for the Burgundians, as his French adapter Wace makes clear) and then prepared to cross the Alps and attack the emperor himself, apparently in Constantinople. However, he was recalled by evil news. His deputy Modred had turned traitor, seizing the crown and persuading the queen to live in adultery with him. Modred had also made a pact with the Saxons, handing over Kent and the country north of the Humber in exchange for their help. King Arthur returned to Britain and drove the traitor's army west, breaking it finally by the River Camel in Cornwall. Modred was killed, Arthur was gravely wounded. He was taken away to the Isle of Avalon for his wounds to be attended to. The year was 542.

2

This is the framework into which the medieval tales of Arthur were fitted. Romancers updated the milieu even more, altered the sequence, cut down the warfare, introduced further themes and characters (for example, the Sword in the Stone, the Round Table, the royal city of Camelot, the Holy Grail, Lancelot, Galahad, Tristan and Iseult). But Arthur as king of Britain, the greatest of them all, begins his known career in Geoffrey of Monmouth.

Where did he get even hints for this feat of imagination? The question, of course, is a literary one, and if it could be confined to literature, the attempts to answer it would rate only summary treatment in history. But through its symbolism and influence the Arthurian Legend became part of history itself. It broke free from a purely Welsh-Breton patriotism and evoked an ancient, glorious unity transcending the divisions of Britain in Geoffrey's day. Henry II and his successors were delighted to see themselves as the heirs of King Arthur, the principal if not the sole rulers in his imperial island. It was such a splendid retort to the kings of France, who plumed themselves on being the heirs of Charlemagne. Arthurian romance, owing much to the patronage of Henry's queen Eleanor, took shape and spread through Christendom. Every region of Britain could find a place in it. Arthur and his knights acquired habitations on the map, all the way from Cornwall to Scotland. Castles and battlefields were assigned in retrospect to Arthurian characters.

The mythos was more than entertainment and morale-building fantasy. It carried political weight, as a factor adding dignity to the monarchy and drawing Britain together. English kings claimed the sovereignty of Scotland on the ground that Arthur had held it. The Tudors exploited their part-Welsh ancestry to make out, with some success, that they were the destined reunifiers and restorers of Arthurian Britain. Even in Queen Victoria's reign, the Arthurian poems of her immensely popular laureate Tennyson gave the Crown a fresh glamour, which helped it to recover from discredit and republican agitation after the death of Prince Albert.

So, once again, where did this creation come from? What elements of fact, tradition, folk-myth and fiction went into it and contributed to its spell? Who was Arthur if he was anybody, and how was it that he could be transmuted into a king with more importance than most real kings?

Geoffrey, according to himself, simply translated the whole story from that 'ancient book in the British language' where he also found Brutus and the rest. On present evidence it is impossible to believe him. The statement is so unlikely that nothing short of the rediscovery of the book could make it acceptable. The utmost serious possibility (and as will appear, there is a case for this) is that he took ideas for King Arthur and his exploits from a book we no longer have. Certainly, however, we no longer have it, and if we survey the pre-Geoffrey matter we do have, the effect is somewhat baffling.

Arthurian traditions were undoubtedly handed down, all along the Celtic fringe where the Britons' descendants managed to preserve their identity: the north, Wales, Cornwall, Brittany. It need not be questioned that the origins lay far back, more or less in the period when the king, supposedly, flourished. The name 'Arthur' is a British form of the Roman 'Artorius'. Geoffrey and others re-convert it into Latin with various spellings, but 'Artorius' is the original. The bestowal of Roman names dwindled in Britain as memories of the Empire receded. With this one, moreover, there was a most unusual extra development. It came back in the century or so after 550 when, amid the fade-out of Roman names, several Arthurs are on record. Someone, the prototype, was seemingly called Artorius when the practice of Roman naming was still normal, and then, after an interval, a spread and increase of his fame led to a temporary revival, with boy-children being named after him when the practice in general had lapsed. Even if the prototype did not exist, and was a bardic concoction, he was concocted early.

Hence we are in contact, however tenuous, with the Britain of the fifth and sixth centuries. Geoffrey's story has its remote origin in something that happened then, whether it was historical fact or an inspired feat of invention. But most of the traces of Arthur's rising fame tell us little about the way he was thought of. He figures in a few old poems in Welsh, not all composed in Wales, as a warrior of proverbial might with a band of famous followers. The chronicle known as the *Annales Cambriae* has two curt entries noting battles in which he was believed to have taken part. One is dated 518:

> The battle of Badon in which Arthur carried the cross of Our Lord Jesus Christ on his shoulders for three days and three nights and the Britons were victors.

This is the 'siege of Mount Badon' mentioned by Gildas, though, in keeping with his habit, he fails to name the British commander. The cross could have been an emblem, or perhaps a relic, one of the fragments of the True Cross retrieved by St Helena. There is reason to think that 'shoulders' is a mistake for 'shield' caused by confusion between two words in Old Welsh. The second *Annales* entry is dated 539:

> The strife of Camlann in which Arthur and Medraut fell. And there was plague in Britain and Ireland.

Medraut is Modred, Geoffrey's villain, though the entry does not say that he was Arthur's treacherous deputy or even that they fought on opposite sides. It is hard to tell when these two items were first written. The *Annales* are a tenth-century compilation, but the compiler copied in material which is much earlier. Nennius is the only pre-Geoffrey Welshman who gives us anything like an account of Arthur's career. In his *History of the Britons* he has a section on St Patrick which takes his story to Patrick's death in about 461. He continues:

> In that time the Saxons strengthened in multitude and grew in Britain. On the death of Hengist, however, Octha his son passed from the northern part of Britain to the region of the Cantii and from him arise the kings of the Cantii [i.e. the people of Kent].
>
> Then Arthur fought against them in those days with the kings of the Britons, but he himself was leader of battles. The first battle was at the mouth of the river which is called Glein. The second and third and fourth and fifth upon another river which is called Dubglas and is in the district Linnuis. The sixth battle upon the river which is called Bassas. The seventh battle was in the Caledonian wood, that is, Cat Coit Celidon. The eighth battle was in Fort Guinnion in which Arthur carried the image of St Mary, ever virgin, on his shoulders and the pagans were turned to flight on that day and a great slaughter was upon them through the virtue of Our Lord Jesus Christ and through the virtue of St Mary the Virgin, his mother. The ninth battle was waged in the City of the Legion. The tenth battle he waged on the shore of the river which is called Tribruit. The eleventh battle took place on the mountain which is called Agned. The twelfth battle was on Mount Badon, in which nine hundred and sixty men fell in one day from one charge by Arthur, and no one overthrew them except himself alone. And in all the battles he stood forth as victor.

Arthur here is portrayed as the Briton's war-leader, *dux bellorum* in Nennius's Latin, fighting alongside regional British kings. Nothing shows whether he was a king himself. The list of battles is thought to be based on a poem in his praise. A recurrence of the possible mix-up over 'shoulders' and 'shield' suggests that it was in Welsh, but this does not help much in dating it. It could have been composed at any time from the sixth century, when the Welsh language was taking shape, to the early ninth when Nennius wrote. Arthur's exaggerated exploit at Badon suggests a prior growth of legend.

The locations are doubtful. 'Glein' could be the Lincolnshire

Glen; it is a tributary of another river, but 'mouth' could mean the confluence. 'Linnuis' is probably Lindsey, also in Lincolnshire. In all that area the Angles were strong from an early date. The 'Caledonian wood', Celidon, formerly covered a large part of southern Scotland. The 'City of the Legion' is Chester or Caerleon. Badon itself, the major victory which gave the Britons a breathing-space, was almost certainly in the south. A good candidate is the hill-fort Liddington Castle near Swindon, which has a village of Badbury beside it, and shows traces of a fifth-century reoccupation.

Several 'Lives' of Welsh saints depict Arthur again as a military leader, and also once or twice as a king, though in an ill-defined sense. They are too full of pious fables and childish miracles to carry weight as history. However, they show that in spite of the stories of Arthur carrying Christian emblems into battle, and winning through divine aid, some Welsh churchmen came to view him in rather a hostile light — possibly because of a notion that he seized monastic property for his troops' maintenance. These 'Lives' were composed at the monastery of Llancarfan in Glamorgan, where the monks may have had different ideas from those of Bangor where Nennius wrote.

Before Geoffrey also, but perhaps not very long before, there was a cycle of Arthurian tales in Welsh. Only one of them has survived in full. This is in the *Mabinogion* and is entitled *Culhwch and Olwen*. 'Culhwch' is pronounced, roughly, Kilhooch, with the *ch* as in 'loch'. It is a savage, colourful affair, replete with marvels and monsters, touches of beauty and touches of grotesque humour. Arthur is a 'sovereign prince' and has a court. But again his power is ill-defined and clearly not absolute, while many of his courtiers are strange beings out of mythology. The theme is a series of fairy-tale impossible tasks which Arthur and his companions perform. Besides *Culhwch and Olwen* we possess written summaries of other tales now lost. They show that the Welsh had a strong and melancholy tradition of the fatal battle of Camlann, and the quarrel of Arthur and Medraut or Modred which led up to it. However, they make it sound like a feud of barbaric equals, not a subordinate's rebellion. Likewise in other settings, Arthur seems to be conceived as very far short of supreme authority. He is imprisoned and has to be rescued; he leads a pig-stealing raid (unsuccessful, at that) on a minor chief.

Arthur is commemorated by a scatter of local legends, and ancient monuments and natural features bearing his name — megaliths called Arthur's Stone, hills called Arthur's Seat, and so forth — all the way from the Isles of Scilly far into Scotland. Nennius, or someone who has tacked an appendix on to his work, mentions two Arthurian sites in the ninth century. At least two others are known to have got their names before Geoffrey. With most of them, there is no telling how old the connection is. One of the best known is the South Cadbury hill-fort in Somerset which mysteriously held out after the Romans conquered the south-west. This has been claimed for centuries as the original Camelot. Another famous site is Glastonbury a few miles away from it, where the fabric of legend is more complex. Both were important places about the time when Arthur is presumed to have lived. We do not know what, if anything, was said about him personally at either, before Geoffrey of Monmouth.

Most of the local legends belong to those parts of Britain where Celtic society was least affected by Anglo-Saxon settlement. Only one story which has any air of being early brings Arthur to London. He dug up the head of Bran on Tower Hill, saying that Britain should not rely on such talismans for protection.

To sum up, what we find in Britain before Geoffrey is a notion of Arthur as a British warrior and leader credited with various exploits, a few of them possibly real, most of them fictitious. None suggests an established national kingship. In some contexts Arthur has power, but its extent and basis are never clear, and in other contexts he is no more than a local chief or guerrilla captain. A few of the lesser characters are mentioned besides Modred — Kay and Bedevere, for instance. One further belief is known to have been current. Arthur was widely held to be still alive. His 'falling' in his last battle was not final. He had been wounded, but he had only gone away. No one could claim any knowledge of his death. A Welsh poem called *The Song of the Graves* declared that his grave was a mystery and should not be speculated about. People along the west fringe of Britain, and in Brittany too, expected him to return as a Celtic Messiah. Before Geoffrey, only the Cornish and Breton hopes can be proved; Wales is less certain.

How much of Geoffrey's story of King Arthur does this older material account for? Not enough. By putting together Gildas, Nennius and the *Annales Cambriae* he could have got the idea of a fresh British offensive against the Saxons, which Arthur led, and which built up to a triumph ending Britain's troubles for several decades. From Nennius he did get the locations of a few battles in the course of the offensive — the River Douglas (Dubglas), though he is not clear where it was; Lincolnshire; Caledon Wood; Bath, his interpretation of 'Badon'. From the *Annales* and from Welsh stories he got the battle on the Camel, his 'Camlann', and the name of Arthur's opponent, though not the theme of Modred's treason as deputy. Welsh sources could also have given him the names of a few other characters, and the idea of an Arthurian court, though the court he imagines is utterly unlike the assembly in *Culhwch and Olwen.*

Finally, he knew of the doubt over Arthur's passing, since he ends with a departure and not a death. However, he has no commitment to a return. In another part of his book he speaks of Arthur's end as mysterious, but there too he goes no further. The Isle of Avalon to which Arthur is taken — *Insula Avallonis* in the Latin — is Geoffrey's version of an Isle of Avallach which figures in Welsh legend as an 'otherworld' place, a realm of fair-folk and enchantment. Its name is usually taken to mean 'apple-place'. Geoffrey has adopted a non-Welsh spelling influenced by the real place-name Avallon in Burgundy, which is Gaulish and has the same meaning.

These details take us a certain way, but not very far. It might be retorted that Geoffrey is a proved adept at spinning a long yarn out of meagre materials. Yet there is a deeper difficulty. It would be easier if the materials were more meagre than they are, and King Arthur could be put in the same class as Bladud, Leir and Belinus. The trouble is that we do have this miscellaneous Arthurian saga, with a setting which is not totally unhistorical. Geoffrey is drawing on something, yet his story, viewed as a whole, is not *like* the saga. Of course this is so scrappy and inconsistent that we might picture him simply discarding most of it, and building up King Arthur out of a few pieces he retained. But the links are very frail, and half Geoffrey's story is taken up with the rise to an apogee in a still-more-or-less-Roman Gaul, for which the Welsh matter gives no hint.

Should we look further, for a missing factor that knits the elements together? Can we find a more cogent continuity between King Arthur's career and the pre-Geoffrey matter, or between either and history?

3

We can certainly venture as far as this: the Arthurian saga is rooted in an Arthurian Fact. The Britons did pass through a phase which had no parallel among other Roman provincials. They alone became independent before the barbarian invasion. They alone opposed it with any energy. They alone checked it, possibly turning it back in places. The stabilization after Badon did not last, but even the jaundiced Gildas witnesses to it, and it was enough to create a legend of a British ascendancy which only internal feud could destroy.

Arthur symbolized the resurgence and was accounted its principal hero — perhaps not at once, but long before Geoffrey. That is the meaning of the term 'Arthurian Fact' as it has been applied to this train of events. It assumes nothing, one way or the other, as to whether Arthur existed. Yet when all the data are passed in review, they give the impression of a real person lurking somewhere. Such things do not happen without leadership, and although Ambrosius is mentioned as well, a great part of the resurgence was plainly not credited to him. If there was no Arthur at all, ever, we have to ask why the actual leaders are not mentioned whereas a fictitious leader is. As a matter of record, no one who has denied Arthur's existence has yet succeeded in giving an adequate and convincing story accounting for the Arthurian Legend without him.

An acceptable original would be a real person somewhere in British history who could be seen as underlying both the Welsh warrior-saga and the literary treatment by Geoffrey. Historians looking for him have nearly all brushed Geoffrey aside and focused on Nennius and the *Annales,* in the belief that these are historical evidence and nothing else is, or very little. Several have stressed the phrase *dux bellorum,* war-leader. Some have argued that it goes back to a specific title, such as *Comes Britanniarum* (Count of the Britains), the designation of a commander who had a function in the island's defence at the very end of its imperial membership. Such a command might have been revived by the pro-Roman leaders of the 460s. This idea is no longer favoured, but it has inspired interesting theories: for instance, that Arthur was a general who turned the tide by the use of cavalry, which the Empire possessed and the Saxons did not. The mounted warrior was far from being as dominant then as he became in the Middle Ages, because the stirrup had not reached Europe. However, horsemen would have had advantages through mobility, surprise and moral effect. British nobles rode to battle a century or so later, when the oldest extant Welsh poetry describes them doing so, and this may reflect a spectral continuity of Roman methods of war and even military institutions.

Results of a more solid kind have come from archaeology. Nothing has been found with Arthur's name on it, but in that age and society, lacking even a coinage, objects with personal names on them are rare indeed. Their presence is not to be expected, their absence has no significance. The achievement of archaeology has been to prove the importance of several places with which Arthur is linked.

Tintagel, the scene of the legendary conception, is known to have been inhabited at about the right time, though opinions differ as to whether the British site on the headland was a stronghold or a monastery. A more striking case is the South Cadbury hill-fort. To judge from a description by John Leland, a Tudor traveller, it was called 'Camelot' at least as early as the reign of Henry VIII. The Camelot of romance is a dream-city which could never have existed. But Camelot in the sense of Arthur's headquarters could have been real. Excavation at Cadbury has disclosed that this Iron Age fort was reoccupied and refortified on a grandiose scale at about the right time, plainly by someone with large resources of manpower. He encircled its eighteen-acre enclosure with a new stone rampart twenty feet thick, and built a new gatehouse and a hall. While other hill-forts were reoccupied, the massive Cadbury defences are unparalleled. It is hard to believe that Tudor folklore, or antiquarian fancy, picked on the aptest hill for a British war-leader by mere guesswork without some genuine tradition. Even a modern archaeologist could not have done it without digging.

However, attempts to put together a real Arthur from Welsh fragments plus archaeology are open to two objections. The first is that, strictly speaking, phrases such as 'about the right time' evade the problem. What was the right time? If we look at Nennius first, it might seem that Arthur's campaigning 'in those days' followed the death of Hengist, which the *Anglo-Saxon Chronicle* assigns to the year 488. But since this way of reading the passage would imply that all twelve battles were fought against the kings of Kent, which is absurd, we should doubtless omit the sentence about Hengist as a parenthesis. In that case the time-reference for 'those days' comes from the previous passage dealing with St Patrick. If any weight can be given to this connection (which is admittedly doubtful, because all Nennius's notions of chronology are widely confused), it pulls Arthur's warfare back to the 460s.

Such a dating has something to be said for it. Battles in Lincolnshire and the Caledonian forest, and at Chester or Caerleon, would fit best as incidents in the revolt of the *foederati* and the consequent anarchy. At that time the Angles had penetrated up the Wash and the Humber; according to Bede, the Picts were involved as their allies; and according to Gildas, enemy forays were extending right across Britain. It is noteworthy that there is no evidence for a Pictish threat, such as might have drawn a British force into the Caledonian forest, at any time after the middle fifth century; and there were certainly no Angles up there.

But other words of Nennius point again to a later period. Whenever these battles actually happened, he regards them as all belonging to the phase leading up to Badon. Badon is loosely dated by Gildas, who is usually construed as putting it about 44 years before the year in which he is writing. That fixes it somewhere about 500. It may have been a little later, but it cannot have been much earlier, because the Saxons were still making progress during the 490s and therefore had not yet suffered their check. Furthermore Nennius's phrase 'kings of the Britons' places the story in a fragmented Britain. His association of this state of affairs with what might be called the run-up to Badon is supported by the other signs of nascent regional kingdoms towards the close of the fifth century, and not much before.

The *Annales Cambriae* carry the perplexity further. By putting Badon as late as 518, they give a date which is workable in itself, but hard to square with Gildas. By putting Camlann in 539, they imply that Arthur was still an active warrior then. So the dating clues are in conflict and stretch his martial career through an incredible span of time, seventy-odd years. This need not actually cause any trouble with the archaeology, which dates the sites within similarly wide limits, but it does confuse the history.

The second objection cuts deeper. A sceptic can argue that advocates of the Historical Arthur have begged the question. They claim to be pruning away the legends and basing their account of him on the early evidence. By this process the best-known of them arrive at a picture of a supreme war-leader, fighting barbarians in various parts of Britain. But the truth is that they are looking at the evidence through the medium of the legends, even through the medium of Geoffrey of Monmouth, however hotly they would deny that. They read it with the notion of a supreme leader already in mind. If we read it without that preconception, we shall have to admit that it cannot sustain the notion in any way which yields reliable history.

To say that it is too distant in time from the events is inconclusive. A text may be based on a much older text, and the case of Cymbeline's father shows that items of this kind may be correct in spite of a very long interval. But the evidence is also too flimsy. We have no proof that all the battles in Nennius's list were fought by Arthur. The point is not that they are too widely spaced for one man. In the next two or three centuries, Britain's history supplies well-attested cases of long marches. The point is that while the Arthur of the battle-list may not be fictitious, he is plainly fictionalized. A hero credited with feats which really are impossible, such as killing 960 men single-handed, could also have been credited with winning battles he had nothing to do with. He takes us into a realm of bardic hyperbole where no fact is firm.

Some critics, following up this line, insist that Badon itself has no convincing connection with Arthur. It was a real event, but neither of the allusions to his role in it will hold water. Some of them go on to propose a different Historical Arthur, not a national commander who won the great victory, but a minor chief in the north, afterwards inflated by legend: bardic hyperbole, in fact. They offer two main reasons for putting him in the north. The first is that his name occurs in some early northern poems and notes of historical tradition. The second is that Camlann is the battle judged to stand the best chance of being authentic, and its name could be a Welsh form of 'Camboglanna', the name of a fort on Hadrian's Wall above the valley of the Irthing. But this solution can also be undermined. The northern material mentions people who were not northerners. As for 'Camlann', it means simply 'crooked bank', and 'crooked' rivers are found in other places, such as the Camel in Cornwall and the Cam in Somerset.

In any case the theory of a minor Arthur is unconvincing wherever he is located, because it fails to explain why he should ever have been enlarged, and to so gross an extent that leaders of genuine stature (such as the real victor of Badon, the real lord of Cadbury) have sunk without trace. In the upshot we have a dilemma. The assumed evidence for a 'big' Arthur is rendered unsafe by fantasy which has not been got rid of. If we try to substitute a 'small' Arthur, it is hard to see why he was fantasized.

A more thorough-going form of the second objection avoids such controversies without loss of force. The pruning-away of legendary matter not only fails to happen in the actual arguments of scholars, it cannot happen at all. None of the items, northern or otherwise, can give us a well-supported Arthur whatever we do with them, because even the earliest are not plain historical statements. We never get such a statement. Everything has at least a touch of legend already except the Camlann entry in the *Annales,* while that sole exception hangs in a void, not giving Arthur a setting which can be checked against history, and is suspect because the date 539 seems improbably late.

The solution of it all could be easy, given even a little documentation. If trustworthy records gave us an Arthur-figure who fulfilled fairly modest requirements — who was a prominent British leader, preferably with some royal title, in the second half of the fifth century; who could have refortified Cadbury; who could be accepted as having won at least a few of Nennius's victories, and done at least a few of the things Geoffrey romanticizes — then the rest would present no difficulty. He would be, quite sufficiently, the 'person lurking somewhere' whose presence is felt. He could have been built up by hero-worship and minstrelsy, sung of as winning battles fought after he was gone, enlarged into a conqueror of countries he never saw.

Nothing in the Welsh matter would then be inexplicable. It would all be legendary development, such as has happened with many heroes. Likewise, Geoffrey's treatment would not be radically different from his treatment of other persons. But we cannot work back to this original Arthur-figure through the Welsh matter itself, because everything it says is already embedded in legendary development. We cannot extract a plain historical statement as a starting-point.

4

Is it deadlock? Not quite. Appraisal of Geoffrey has already suggested that another country harboured materials of its own, which he made use of. Brittany in fact provides what is lacking in Britain, a plain statement. Not necessarily a true statement, but one which can be discussed and assessed as genuine historical matter can.*

Reference was made before to the *Legend of Saint Goeznovius,* with its uncertain eleventh-century date, and its prefatory account by the author 'William' of the first British settlement in Armorica, drawn, he tells us, from something called the Ystoria Britanica. At that point it must be confessed that the history he is sketching is highly dubious and in part legendary. But he moves on towards the time which really concerns him, and as he does so he becomes more factual. He explains about the Saxons' advent in Britain, giving a bald summary of the standard version blaming the usurper Vortigern. The Saxons, he says, got out of control and inflicted much misery on the Britons. But they were not able to go on doing so at will.

> Presently their pride was checked for a while through the great Arthur, King of the Britons. They were largely cleared from the island and reduced to subjection. But

---

* See preface, pp. 7-9.

when this same Arthur, after many victories which he won gloriously in Britain and Gaul, was summoned at last from human activity, the way was open for the Saxons to go again into the island, and there was great oppression of the Britons, destruction of churches, and persecution of saints. This persecution went on through the times of many kings, Saxons and Britons, striving back and forth . . . . In those days, many holy men gave themselves up to martyrdom; others, in conformity to the Gospel, left the greater Britain now turned into the Saxon's homeland, and sailed across to the lesser Britain [i.e. Brittany], some to escape the tyranny of the pagans, more in order that with greater secrecy and devotion, having left all things, they could offer the Lord a pleasing and agreeable service in solitary places.

All of which leads up to St Goeznovius.

The sentences about Arthur are surprising, but straightforward. The author has got clear of manifest legend. Arthur's 'summoning from human activity' may acknowledge the doubt over his end, it does not endorse the belief in his immortality. Moreover the passage as a whole supplies what even the Camlann notice does not, a verifiable setting. Its air of vagueness is deceptive. Studied with care, it turns out to be curiously precise.

'William' puts Arthur's triumphs after the Saxon revolt, but not long after. The word translated 'presently' is *postmodum,* which suggests sooner-rather-than-later. He associates his career with the withdrawal of the freebooting *foederati* from their advanced positions, and the ensuing false dawn when the Britons might have thought them to be contained and dared to take the initiative: 'their pride was checked for a while . . . they were largely cleared from the island and reduced to subjection'. This points to the first British recovery in the 460s.

The dating is borne out by Arthur's exploits overseas. He defeats Saxons (no mention is made of any other opponent) in Gaul as well as Britain. There was only one time when a British leader could have gone on from beating Saxons in Britain to beating them in Gaul. Armed confrontation north of the Loire began after the migration to Armorica towards 460, and ended

143

with the Saxons' collapse near Angers toward 470. Before, there were not enough Britons there. Afterwards, there were not enough Saxons. The indications of serious fighting point to the later 460s and thus fit in after Arthur's British activities. A further detail in support is the title 'King of the Britons' given to Arthur. That, as we saw, accords with a situation which existed in the 460s. It ceased to exist soon after when Britain broke up.

Arthur departs, and the sequel is a renewed invasion: 'the way was open for the Saxons to go again into the island'. That is what did begin to happen in the following decade, whether or not the reason which the author implies is the true one. Vanquished in Gaul, the Saxons reverted during the 470s to settlement in Britain, entering at new points along the south coast. They also pressed forward in other areas. Britain slid into dissolution and the fluctuating warfare recorded by Gildas. That is also as 'William' says when he speaks of 'many kings, Saxons and Britons, striving back and forth'. The same period saw the movement of the saints over to Brittany, and again he is right. To escape from tribulation, they 'left the greater Britain . . . and sailed across to the lesser Britain'.

Whatever the value of the Arthur reference itself, 'William' is doing what no one else does. He is putting Arthur in a context which dates him, with enough detail to impress. He indulges in some clerical rhetoric, but he has no obvious fables to reduce credibility. This story of his with Arthur in it has eight main historical features, and they all seem to be correct in the light of modern knowledge. The Saxons arrive in Britain as mercenaries; they revolt and harry the Britons; they withdraw, or are forced to withdraw, into a confined area; Britons fight Saxons in Gaul as well; the Saxons make fresh incursions into Britain; Britain breaks up politically; a long fluctuating warfare drags on; and the saints emigrate. *Goeznovius* gets it all right, and in the right order.

There are other early accounts of the Britons' fifth-century fortunes which are far longer. None comes anywhere near to being so compactly complete, so straightforward, or so free from elements casting doubt. Whether this was written in 1019 or later hardly matters. Its author could not have got such an acceptable summary from any known text. He might have read, say, Nennius. But he would have needed some other, much better document as a guide, to select and extract the story he tells; and parts of it — especially the sequels and supposed effects of Arthur's demise — he could scarcely have found at all.

So then, what about his allusion to Arthur? Is that a scrap of fiction irresponsibly woven into a fabric of fact? Or is it taken, as all its context suggests, from an older work of serious historical value? If the second answer is likelier, do the clues lead back to firm and early testimony pointing to an Arthur-figure we can be sure of?

Suppose we revert to Geoffrey, not looking for history which is not there, but looking for clues which may be. There is plainly some connection. Like the Breton author, but like none of the Welsh, he makes Arthur campaign in Gaul. Arthur fights against Romans, for no adversary but the Empire itself could be great enough in Geoffrey's eyes. Yet however far he has moved away from reality, the Gallic campaigning is important to him. It takes up half his narrative of the reign. Some have thought that he borrowed from *Goeznovius*. Some have thought that the author of *Goeznovius* borrowed from him. Actually, neither borrowed from the other. Their relationship is more interesting.

Geoffrey's Arthur is the extreme case of the duality in this part of his book. No juggling will make consistent sense of the periods of time. Geoffrey dates the Passing in 542, and if we count back from that, we find that most of Arthur's life must lie in the sixth century. Yet his family background connects him with the earlier of Geoffrey's timescales, and the Breton-oriented story that corresponds to it, the account of the house of Constantine. Constantine is assassinated quite early in the fifth century, and Arthur is his grandson, in the next generation but one. The shortened lives of Arthur's uncle Ambrosius and his father Uther rule out a date of birth for him that would be compatible with his still being an active warrior in 542. At least two medieval writers who drew on Geoffrey were aware of the problem, and solved it by brute force, presenting an Arthur fighting his last battles as a near-centenarian.

As remarked, whenever Geoffrey gives details in this post-Roman phase which link up with documentation outside Britain, we find ourselves in his earlier sequence of events. The reigns of Gracianus and Constantine; Constans's desertion of his monastery; the mission of Germanus and Lupus — however fantasized Geoffrey's versions may be, all these items are in continental records, all are well back in the fifth century, and all produce chronological chaos when he entwines them with the British stories of Vortigern, Hengist and Ambrosius. This remains true with his synthetic career of Arthur. There is one part of it, and only one, where he gives clues to the date which can be checked against known realities. They occur in the Gallic campaigning which he shares with *Goeznovius,* and like Arthur's family relationships they link up with the earlier time-sequence, putting him long before 542.

The Gaul which Geoffrey's king invades is still precariously Roman, and the Western Empire is not defunct. However, while its ruler Lucius is called an emperor a few times, Geoffrey is uncertain about his status. The Senate has power to give him orders. The title of procurator, which he uses in his message to Arthur, belonged historically to deputies of the emperor in minor provinces. Geoffrey in fact mentions another emperor distinct from Lucius. He does not seem to be in Rome. Presumably he is the eastern emperor in Constantinople. And he is the one who really counts. The campaign against him which Modred's revolt prevents would have been the climax of Arthur's military career, with no greater glory conceivable beyond it.

Something like such a state of affairs did exist for a while, but not before 455, when Valentinian III was still fairly effective in the west, or after 476, when there was no Western Empire left at all. Geoffrey's imaginary picture corresponds to the period between, when Roman Gaul was crumbling but not quite finished, and the Western Empire was just surviving under a series of short-lived rulers, the last of the line before its final extinction; whereas the Eastern Empire remained stable.

This dating of Arthur's Gallic warfare, between 455 and 476, is confirmed and tightened by a detail which is much more specific and very curious. Not merely once but three times, Geoffrey says that when Arthur was in Gaul, the 'real' emperor was named Leo. First: 'The province of Gaul was at that time under the jurisdiction of the Tribune Frollo, who ruled it in the name of the Emperor Leo.' Second: 'Lucius Hiberius . . . could not make up his mind whether to engage in a full-scale battle with Arthur or to withdraw inside Autun and there await reinforcements from the Emperor Leo.' Third: 'Arthur immediately cancelled the attack which he had planned to make on Leo, the Emperor of the Romans.'

Leo I reigned at Constantinople from 457 to 474, and he is the only one who can be meant. Leo II was a child who succeeded him and died almost immediately, and there was not another Leo for two hundred years. Thus Geoffrey insists repeatedly and, for the purposes of his story, needlessly, on a date for the Gallic warfare which is hopelessly at odds with a downfall in 542. It makes no sense unless he is handling real and stubborn information — and he defines much the same period as *Goeznovius*. Not only that, he and 'William' do it so differently ('William' through circumstances which Geoffrey does not mention, Geoffrey through an emperor's name which 'William' does not mention) that copying either way is out of the question. They both seem to know an earlier document which placed Arthur, 'King of the Britons' as *Goeznovius* calls him, in Gaul during the 460s and perhaps the early 70s, and contained a good deal of fairly sound material. It may have been the Ystoria Britanica cited by 'William', or the ancient book cited by Geoffrey. They may have been the same work.

The fundamental riddle of Arthur now solves itself. The *Goeznovius* passage is the only piece of straight, largely verifiable history bringing him in, and we already know, or should know, who its author is talking about. We have already encountered a 'King of the Britons' in the right decade. Both 'William' and, in his fashion, Geoffrey, take us back to a man for whom we have factual, early, even contemporary witness. He is Riothamus, that Briton whose style in the continental texts, meaning 'Supreme King' or 'High King', looks like a title, and whose personal name — the one given by his parents — may have been something else: for example Arthur, Artorius.

Riothamus was called 'King of the Britons', and there is surely no room for two Britons so called in the same brief span of time. Riothamus led a British army through Gaul in the late 460s. Riothamus very probably fought against Saxons along the Loire. In late 469 or early 470 Riothamus was 'summoned from human activity', departing from his last fatal battlefield to the neighbouring country of the Burgundians, with no recorded death. Jordanes gives most of this. *Goeznovius* credits the king with victories and Jordanes mentions none, but such discrepancies are normal, and Jordanes, whose concern is with the Goths, has no reason to take any interest in the conflicts of Britons and Saxons.

The connection cuts both ways. It not only solves the basic problem of Arthur, it solves the problem of Riothamus himself and his apparent absence from British records. He is not absent. But Gauls and Romans knew him under one style, while Britons, both on the continent and (it seems) in Britain itself, handed on traditions of him under another.

Once we grasp where to look, light breaks in on several of Geoffrey's other notions. If he is writing with Riothamus in mind, passed down to him as Arthur through whatever channel, we can see why he writes some of the things he does. He is not transcribing history. That is not his way. Apart from anything else, he changes the enemy for the king's greater glory, and ends the Gallic career without defeat. Yet we can now glimpse him running within sight of history, picking up hints, expanding, distorting, very much as we find him doing when he works from historical sources that we know.

Thus, although he turns the Romans from allies (however dubious and untrustworthy) into opponents, he shows that he has some inkling of the real enemy. In the council preceding the major march into Gaul, the sub-king of Scotland speaks of going to the continent to fight Romans *and Germans*. Geoffrey forgets about these 'Germans', evidently Saxons or Visigoths or both, but they are present in his mind at the outset.

Again, while he does not take Arthur to the Burgundian neighbourhood by Riothamus's route, he does take him there. Arthur's march ends in the land of the Allobroges or Burgundians, just as Riothamus's did, if in other circumstances. When Geoffrey tells his story of Arthur's downfall, he adds the theme, which is hitherto unknown, of betrayal by a deputy-ruler. Riothamus actually was betrayed by a deputy-ruler, the Prefect Arvandus, who dealt treacherously with the Visigoths as Modred does with the Saxons. More specific still is the departure of Arthur for Avalon, *Insula Avallonis*. As observed, while Geoffrey is thinking of a Celtic otherworld, the form he gives to its name is not Welsh. He takes it from Avallon in Burgundy. Riothamus's likely line of retreat after his own last battle, from Bourg-de-

Déols to Bourges and thence into Burgundy, would have taken him close to Avallon. An account of his career might well have suggested the name.

Even that inconsistent 542 can be explained. It could have arisen from a type of confusion already mentioned, over the dating of events in the early Christian era — the mistaking of a date counted from the Passion of Christ for a date *Anno Domini,* giving a twenty-eight-year error. That very mistake occurs in Nennius and in the chronological notes following his *History of the Britons.* Counted from the Passion, the year of the departure of Riothamus would probably have come out as 470 minus 28, that is, 442. If the author or copier of the source-book passed this on as A.D., Geoffrey would have realized that even in his elastic scheme, 442 was out of the question for the passing of Arthur. He might have assumed a more obvious error of a hundred years, and emended it to 542, not knowing — or not caring — when Leo actually reigned.

This is a guess, but no other explanation of Geoffrey's date has been offered. If it is correct, an important conclusion follows. The source-book — or, at any rate, the relevant part — must have been written before *Anno Domini* dating became standard. On the continent, that means no later than the sixth century, and even in the British Isles, no later than the early years of the eighth. Geoffrey's 'ancient book' really does begin to look ancient.

5

To accept this as the essential secret of King Arthur does not imply treating *Goeznovius,* unsupported, as trustworthy. Much less does it imply treating Geoffrey so. *Goeznovius* offers clues which have the merit of being plain, Geoffrey offers clues which must be dug for. But their traces of a shared source converge on a solution. The original Arthur-figure is Riothamus the 'High King', who is attested by firm evidence, including a letter to him, the one written by Sidonius. The association of the name with this man is either historically factual or very early. As the point of origin of the Arthurian Legend he explains a whole series of its features — the British kingship, the warfare in Gaul during

Leo's reign, the Burgundian finale to this, the disaster through a deputy's treason, the departure with no recorded death, the name of Avalon, and even, perhaps, Geoffrey's bizarre date for the Passing. At the very least he is the only documented person who does Arthurian things, the only documented person who can be regarded as underlying the Legend.

How far could Riothamus-as-Arthur account for the pre-Geoffrey matter in general — the medley of heroic exploits, battles against the Saxons in Britain, immortality?

The handicap is that we cannot, at present, prove anything about Riothamus on his home ground, before Roman overtures drew him 'by the way of Ocean' into the troubles of Gaul. Still it is a fact that he was 'King of the Britons' and that after him there are only 'kings of the Britons', with no further evidence of an acknowledged central authority. Dissolution followed his passing. Whether this was truly cause and effect is beside the point. Here are the makings of a legend of a national leader tragically lost.

Again, a Riothamus active in Britain, before his venture overseas, would be well qualified to account for at least some of Nennius's battles. Several, as we have seen, would fit the revolt of the *foederati* more plausibly than they fit conditions towards the close of the fifth century, even though Nennius seems to think that they happened then. We have Bede's testimony to an Anglo-Pictish alliance in the revolt, but not later, which could have brought a British force to the Caledonian forest. We have Gildas's testimony to raids across to the western sea in the revolt, but not later, which could have led to fighting at Chester or Caerleon. During the 450s and early 60s Nennius's far-flung clashes are more probable than they are afterwards. Roman Britain had not been left so far behind. The roads would have been in better repair. Cities such as Lincoln would have been more significant, and likelier to have survived as bases. Riothamus could have led his subjects in a brief, scattered resistance, after which the Saxons made their withdrawal to their settlements. It does not appear that Ambrosius did this. He was doubtless an older man as the texts imply, but his emergence as commander was *after* the revolt and withdrawal.

Riothamus could also have been the refortifier of Cadbury-Camelot, or, at any rate, the initiator of that vast work. The dating clues, chiefly imported pottery from the Mediterranean, would just allow this. His expeditionary force proves that he had the large resources of manpower required. The demands of the critical historian should not be ignored: if we were to insist on a soundly documented candidate for the lord of Cadbury, Riothamus would be the only one.

Lastly, the end of his career — so far as known — could have created a doubt about his passing, a mystery over his grave, a dream of his return. Much the same motif attached itself to other heroes besides Arthur, such as Frederick Barbarossa in Germany. In at least one case, it arose from an exit of very much the sort which history indicates for Riothamus. King Sebastian of Portugal led a rash foray against the Moors in 1578 and was routed. His death in the battle was soon being denied. Within a few years four pretenders had appeared, all claiming to be Sebastian. His people's hope challenged the limits of human life. He was still awaited as a national saviour in 1807. In the former Portuguese colony of Brazil a form of Sebastianism lasted even longer, and may not be extinct even yet. Riothamus's cryptic end, far from home, could have inspired just such a folk-belief, which in Arthur's case would have been simply the same belief with the king differently designated. It is worth noting that the earliest and strongest hope was among the Bretons on the continent, and perhaps also the culturally linked Cornish, with the Welsh taking it up from them.

If it is Riothamus who underlies the Arthurian Legend, why should its hero's name be a Welsh version of 'Artorious' and not a Welsh version of 'Riothamus' or rather its British original 'Rigotamos'? The question is all the more pertinent because the apparent title did become a name, as 'Vortigern' did. It turns up in an early Welsh poem transformed into 'Rhiadaf'. That being so, where did the more famous name come from?

There are three possibilities. The first is that while Riothamus was the point of origin in the sense of being earliest, he is not the whole explanation. King Arthur is really two men rolled into one, Riothamus himself and a warrior called Arthur who lived somewhat later. Some of the tradition refers to the second man, and the eventual monarch is a literary creation made up by combining them. Fusions like this do occur in legend. Merlin combines two characters. So, very likely, does Mark of Cornwall in the Tristan romance. Certainly it need not be doubted that as the hero's fame grew, stories of other heroes, perhaps of other Arthurs, were woven in. It could perfectly well be that in its more grandoise form it did begin with an interweaving of characters on a bigger scale. But without hard evidence, it is better to try giving the whole Legend a single starting-point than to postulate another.

The second possibility is that Riothamus was actually named 'Artorius'. As already observed, Britons (St Patrick, for instance) did sometimes have two names; or if 'Riothamus' is purely a title, 'Artorius' could have been the king's personal name. This would be the simplest answer. It is purely a guess, however. We have no direct reason for thinking so.

The third possibility is that whether 'Riothamus' is a name or a title, the king acquired 'Artorius' as another name: perhaps adopted by himself, perhaps bestowed in his lifetime as a sobriquet, perhaps given to him later by story-tellers and bards. This could have happened by reminiscence. It was pointed out many years ago that one real Arthur can be positively proved in Britain before the fifth century. He was the general Lucius Artorius Castus, who led a British army to Armorica in 184. If he left an impression on British folk-memory, as well he might, Riothamus could have been nicknamed 'Artorius' as the commander of a second British force going to Armorica. There is no proof that the general actually was remembered, but we saw reason earlier to think that he may have been, and that the 'Lucius' in his name affected Geoffrey's treatment of the royal convert Lucius of legend.

An alternative way, not ruling out the former, would have been by a sort of word-play. This depends on spelling. While the known copies of Sidonius's letter give the spelling with an *h*, it is likely that the *h* was put in by a Frankish scribe, and the real fifth-century Latinization of 'Rigotamos' was 'Riotamus'. One can scarcely help noticing that 'Artorius' is very nearly an anagram of this. It is easy to see how the one might have suggested the other through a scrambled reading of the letters on (say) a crudely-executed medallion.

RIOTAMUS, plus R for *rex (Britonum)* as in Jordanes, can be arranged so as to give such a result.

RIOTAMUS reads clockwise, with the added R slightly nearer the centre. The reading counter-clockwise, starting from A, gives ARTORIUS M. The M might be ignored, or taken as the initial of *miles*, 'soldier', 'warrior'; Arthur is twice rather strangely called 'Arthur *miles*' in the brief passage about him in Nennius's appendix of local legends. This anagram would be a mere curiosity if it were not that we have so many signs of an Arthur-Riothamus linkage. Given those, it becomes interesting that such an exercise should be possible. The method could not be used to link Riothamus with Siegfried or Roland or any other hero. It works only with Arthur.

If something like this did happen, when would it have been? The anagram implies a time when British names such as 'Rigota-mos' were still being put into Latin forms, and when there were still Britons who could and did do it in writing. Gildas, born about the end of the fifth century, does it towards the middle of the sixth. This is about the latest. The anagram also implies a time when there were Britons who would think of a Roman name in its Roman form — who would notice 'Artorius' as the counter-clockwise reading. Again this would lie within the fifth century and part of the sixth. Riothamus could have acquired the nickname by this route in his lifetime.

6

Whatever the truth may have been in detail, it is now feasible to offer a succinct answer to the question 'Was Arthur real?' Arthur as we know him is a legend, but he has a real original, the British 'Supreme King' or 'High King' who was in Gaul in 469. Or to put it differently, the 'High King' who was in Gaul has been recorded in history under one style and turned into legend under another.

Spain supplies a parallel. Its nearest equivalent to Arthur is known to history as Ruy Diaz de Bivar, but to epic and romance as El Cid. The parallel is imperfect because traditions of him were written down soon after his lifetime, and so the identity was not forgotten. But with Arthur, oral transmission in a dissolving society could easily have lost its grip on the facts. Even with El Cid, the earliest epic has long passages where the name Ruy Diaz never occurs. If it had survived only in scraps, like the Arthur material, subsequent generations might have told of El Cid without knowing who he was.

What then becomes of the Historical Arthur who has been presented in recent years, the war-leader inferred from Nennius's battle-list? Those who have tried to reconstitute him have not been following a false trail, but it may now appear that they have narrowly missed the man himself. What we are getting in texts like the battle-list is the earliest known stratum of Arthurian legend, and it does use traditions of historical fact, but it is not strictly historical. The investigators have been right in inferring the 'real person lurking somewhere', but even the oldest Welsh matter does not quite lead to him.

Afterwards of course he is changed almost out of recognition by a vast and confused literary growth, drawing in the exploits of other heroes, together with a medley of folklore and mythology, some of it far older than any possible Arthur-figure. Arthur develops into a multiple symbol, a human being mythified, transmuted, sometimes lifted above humanity altogether, with different meanings for different generations. That is beyond present scope. The only further problem that demands notice here is the one posed by the bits of early tradition that look authentic, yet cannot be squared with Riothamus. Arthur is associated with the battles of Badon and Camlann. The former certainly happened, the latter almost certainly, and they cannot have been fought by a man who departed from the scene in 470.

Again, obviously, we can conjecture about a second British leader, an Arthur who did fight these battles and came to be blended with the High King in legend. Another possibility is that Riothamus's career was simply prolonged by story-tellers to bring him into later events. That was done with the lives of several Welsh saints and the early chiefs of the West Saxons. But in societies with powerful oral and tribal traditions, the point at which a great man goes may be oddly blurred. I have written elsewhere, on characters such as the Old Testament patriarchs, and figures of the same type among the Arabs: 'They occupy a strange borderland between fact and fiction. A strong leader gathers his kin together, and others join him; the assemblage acts as a unit under his name; and even after his death he is still present, taking part in the affairs of the tribe so that its acts are his acts.' A Welsh poem in a medieval collection, the *Black Book of Carmarthen,* gives what may be the key to a process rather like this, and to the course of the obscure warfare of the late fifth century and early sixth.

The poem salutes the valour of a British king called Geraint. 'Geraint' is the Welsh form of 'Gerontius'. His home country was the Dumnonian realm of the south-west, and he fought a battle at a place called Llongborth. Embedded in many lines about Geraint are three about someone else.

> At Llongborth I saw Arthur's
> Brave men who cut with steel,
> The emperor, ruler in toil of battle.

The poem as it stands may date from about 900. It seems to be a rehandling of an older version. The medieval copyist who gave it a heading thought its subject was a Geraint who lived towards the end of the sixth century, but he cannot be connected with a credible Llongborth. The right person is likely to be one about a hundred years earlier, named, perhaps, after Constantine III's conspiratorial officer.

'Llongborth' means 'warship port'. The place intended is probably Portchester in Hampshire, at or near the scene of a clash which the *Anglo-Saxon Chronicle* also mentions, and assigns to the year 501. Archaeology confirms Saxon occupation of the Roman fort. As for the allusion to Arthur, it is not a late legendary insertion; that would have brought him in with more prominence. Here we may have the only instance of a battle of the Arthurian period recorded by the enemy too. The poem deserves to be taken seriously as being, in some form, very early indeed, and concerned with a real event.

While several Welsh texts dilate on the topic of Arthur's warriors, these three lines are cool, concise and significant. They show what kind of ancient poetic phrases may underlie Nennius's presentation of Arthur, as a war-leader fighting beside British regional kings. Arthur's 'brave men' do fight beside a regional king, namely Geraint. Arthur himself is dubbed 'emperor', *ameraudur* in Welsh, the same as the Latin *imperator* — and *imperator* means, properly, 'commander-in-chief'.

Arthur himself, however, is not present. What the poet gives is a glimpse of a military body called 'Arthur's men', functioning without him and (if he is originally Riothamus) after his vanishing from the scene. Such a body could have existed. A clue may lie in that late-imperial practice of naming military units after persons — the Theodosiani, the Honoriaci, in Britain possibly a force called after Ambrosius. Jordanes says that when the Britons were betrayed in Berry, Riothamus made his escape into Burgundy with 'all the men he could gather together'. What became of them? Some might have found their way back to Britain and continued as a body, at first joining Ambrosius if he was still active, then going on to recruit new members and hire themselves out as auxiliaries against the Saxons. Well before that, the name 'Artorius' could have been attached to their commander and adopted by his veterans; the phrase 'Arthur's men' might even be a rendering of 'Artoriani'. Hence, anyway, the presence of 'Arthur's men' beside Geraint at Llongborth, mentioned in words which could evoke their chief in a *dux bellorum* role.

Could such a motif have been developed if he was not there in person? As a matter of fact, the lines are ambiguous. Modern scholars have disagreed about them, some construing the words as 'Arthur [and] brave men . . . ' Apparently this reading is wrong. But if a doubt can occur now, it could have occurred at any time from the formation of Old Welsh, around the middle of the sixth century. Minstrels' allusions to 'Arthur's men' could easily have been mis-heard or mis-recalled as allusions to 'Arthur and his men', conjuring up a war-leader present in person even when he was not. Once conjured up, he could soon have been endowed with a poetic life of his own.

Arthur's association with Badon, which becomes a major factor in his renown, could have been due not to his being there but to warriors fighting under his name being there, supplying leadership, experience and encouragement. Perhaps someone made a poem about the British victory like the Llongborth poem, praising the deeds of 'Arthur's men', and this became 'Arthur and his men'. If the truth is more or less thus, the basis of the Welsh saga is partly the career of a king remembered as Arthur, but partly also the career of a war-band of which the founder-members were veterans of his, a war-band remembered as 'Arthur's men'; and we cannot be precise as to where the man stops and the men start. Perhaps those semi-comic traditions in which Arthur is a minor figure, stealing pigs and feuding with neighbours, go back to lays like the ballads of Robin Hood and his outlaws — lays about the adventures of the war-band, with Arthur himself being put in by story-tellers where he did not really belong.

In this context of the departure of a king and the living-on of his memory, further possibilities come to mind. Thus, if his vanishing inspired a belief in his indefinite survival, it might have inspired rumours of his reappearing at critical moments, even at Badon. Again, if he refortified the Cadbury-Camelot citadel, it could have been called 'Arthur's fort' and used as a base by 'Arthur's men'. The earliest documented case of an immortal Arthur lying asleep in a cave seems to locate the cave in the Cadbury hill. Near by is the River Cam, an acknowledged candidate for Camlann. That ruinous clash was surely an actual event, which enabled legend-weavers to put Arthur's demise in his native land. But was it a clash between quarrelling Artoriani which destroyed the war-band as a force? A mass burial is said to have been found between the river and the hill.

All this, of course, is speculative. The utmost it can do is to suggest that the traditions can be accounted for without bringing in another principal figure besides Riothamus. That may be the right answer, it may not. Future research may incline the balance one way or another. To return to what is more certain, the *Goeznovius* preface can be accepted as the key, because, there alone, Arthur appears without any of his legendary accretions, in a reasonably convincing context. He coincides so closely with Riothamus that the passage is tantamount to a historical statement. It places him in both Britain and Gaul, so that stories of him could have taken shape in both countries. While it is too far removed in time to be proof in itself, comparison with Geoffrey points to a far earlier record which both authors used. This would have included an account of Riothamus-as-Arthur. Once we have recognized the 'High King', we have arrived at matters for which the evidence is firm and contemporary.

The crucial notion for tellers of tales would have been the unity of Arthur of Britain with the lost king on the continent. This may have dawned first on a Breton chronicler. Wherever and whenever the dawning came, it meant that they could be drawn together. Geoffrey of Monmouth was the genius who did it, re-combining traditions, restoring King Arthur. His restored king incorporated centuries of legend-making. Arthur had already become much more than any original could have been, before Geoffrey took him up. But Geoffrey's imagination transfigured him.

Particularly, he changed the order. He put all the British warfare ascribed to Arthur, up to and including Badon, before the Gallic warfare. He enlarged on a few words of Gildas to evoke a splendid peace in the middle, with the king presiding over a magnificent court. Thus he gave the reign a fictitious length and a new time-sequence, a climactic sweep and a close in tragic glory. His final, brilliant touch was to combine the continental betrayal with the insular Camlann. From this came the story of the Passing of Arthur which, in Malory and others, haunts the memory even when much else may be hazy.

There we may leave Geoffrey of Monmouth, at the zenith of his achievement. He goes on into a post-Arthurian decline, but he has no more major legends to offer.

CHAPTER EIGHT

The Successors

1

EVEN GILDAS TESTIFIES TO THE PEACE AND ORDER WHICH FOLLOWED BADON.

> Both the terrible desolation of the island, and also the unexpected recovery of it, remained in the minds of those who were witnesses of these marvellous events. And for this reason kings, public magistrates, private persons, priests and ecclesiastics all did their duty.

This was the breathing-space which became, in legend, a golden age won by Arthur and his companions. It was not really so very golden. The dissolution had gone too far, the economy had suffered too grievously. Gildas observes that Badon did not put an end to strife among the Britons themselves, and he adds, forty-odd years afterwards.

> Even now the cities of our country are not inhabited as they were before, but are in a wretched state, deserted and wrecked.

That first half of the sixth century was a spell of near-equilibrium among the peoples in Britain. The Picts gave no more trouble. The Britons (still the majority), and the Angles and Saxons, left each other alone in most areas. We have an odd telescopic glimpse of them in the writings of a contemporary, Procopius, at the court of Justinian in Constantinople. For him Britain is a remote and uncanny place, and he knows little about it, except travellers' tales of fogs and ghosts. But he does know some things, if a trifle sketchily.

> Three very popular nations possess the island of Brittia, and there is a king over each of them. And the names of these nations are the Anglii, and the Frisians, and the

Britons who have their name from the island. And so numerous are these nations that every year great numbers, with their wives and children, migrate thence to the Franks, and the Franks give them dwellings in that part of their land which seems most bare of men.

Procopius's 'Frisians' comprise the Saxons and Jutes, the latter by now being more or less assimilated. He names them from their pre-British homeland in the Low Countries; Saxons are called 'Frisians' in a Breton book also. 'A king over each' is an undue simplification. Procopius may be guessing, or he may have heard of claims to superior dignity by Aelle of the South Saxons, and in his own time (as we shall see) the king of Gwynedd. After this paragraph he mentions some Angles who accompanied a Frankish embassy to Constantinople. These may have given him his information.

Information it is, and the really notable point is the triple migration from Britain overseas. The Franks held the whole of what is now France, plus part of Germany. They raised no objection to further British settlement in Armorica, and this period brought the next major wave of it. The chief British leader was Riwalus, who led an expedition from the West Country between 510 and 520. Others followed him during the next few decades, and Brittany became conclusively Brittany. Procopius's migration of Britons is therefore, in substance, factual. His more surprising migration of Angles and 'Frisians' is also factual, and confirmed by continental records. In 531 the Frankish king Theuderich, who was campaigning in Thuringia, received a party of Angles who had sailed over from Britain to Cuxhaven looking for a home. In return for their services he allowed them to live in conquered territory between the Unstrut and Saale. A district in that area is still called Engilin. Place-names and archaeological findings show that the Franks authorized similar colonies in the country inland from Boulogne. Thanks to British resistance, many Anglo-Saxons in Britain had — for the moment — given up expansion within the island. Some of the rising generation were trying their luck elsewhere.

The British recovery had lasting consequences for the Church. With peace and revived morale, it developed a new kind of mission, adapted to a society which was reverting to Celtic tribalism and turning away from urban living. This rebirth was Welsh in its origin, and largely the work of one apostle, St Illtud, who prevented the flow of clerics across the Channel from leaving a vacuum in the homeland. His 'Life' even asserts that he was born in Armorica himself and migrated in the other direction. It makes him out to have been a cousin of Arthur, who went over to serve as a soldier in Britain (could this be a far-off echo of an assembling of 'Arthur's men' after 470?). Entering the priesthood, he founded the monastery of Llantwit Major in South Glamorgan.

Towards the close of the fifth century, Illtud's Llantwit was growing into a school of leadership. One of its graduates was St Samson. His biographer, writing before 615 and much closer to the events than most saintly biographers, pays the founder a lavish tribute: 'This Illtud was the most learned of all the Britons both in the Old Testament and the New, and in all kinds of philosophy — poetry and rhetoric, grammar and arith- metic . . . . Were I to begin to relate all his wondrous works I should be led to excess.' Illtud's pupils presently included Gildas himself and outstanding laymen as well as clergy. Disciples and colleagues of St Samson played a continuing and sustaining role. As the sixth century advanced, more and more followed in Illtud's steps, such as St Cadoc, the founder of Llancarfan.

Illtud's monks anticipated the Benedictines in practical labour. They reclaimed waste land, rebuilt a Roman sea-wall, taught an improved method of ploughing, and used their surplus crops to relieve famine. They, and others like them, were tireless travel- lers and missionaries. Chiefly through them, the Christianity of the British upper classes became the religion of the rest. They ranged from the Pictish borderland to Armorica rendering ser- vices of many kinds — as farmers, teachers, doctors, builders; even, in the Channel Islands, as advisers on how to repel pirates. They opened their schools to Irishmen, and the upsurge of Celtic genius which made Ireland, for a time, the most civilized coun- try of western Europe owed a large debt to them. When St Columba sailed from Ireland in 563 to found his community on Iona, Britain's gifts were returning to Britain wonderfully en- hanced.

A special pattern of Celtic Christianity gradually took shape in both islands. It was the monastic community that counted, rather than the episcopal see; the abbot rather than the bishop. The eminence of the monk meant a corresponding eminence for the nun. In the Christianity of the British Isles, women were closer to being equal. There were communities of both sexes, which normally had female heads. All communities were informal in their structure. Each member had a private cell. They met for worship, meals and discussion, and they enjoyed a certain freedom to wander.

One direction in which they seldom wandered was towards the Saxons. Missionary zeal did not extend to them. They were a scourge inflicted on the Britons for their sins. This idea grew in strength. Under leaders who arose in the later sixth century, such as St David, Welsh monasticism became less literate, more ascetic and inward-looking, because of an obsession with national penance. By then its main achievements were safe, but the recoil from any approach to the Saxons marked a limitation which was to have unhappy results.

The notion that the heathen were in Britain as a divine chastisement was inspired partly by Gildas. He, in his Complaining Book, does not have much to say about the more creditable side, either during the pre-Saxon past or during his lifetime. He pays a tribute to his master St Illtud, calling him 'the polished teacher of almost the whole of Britain'. But although he shows approval of the monastic life (having, after all, embraced it himself), he never enlarges on this promising new trend in the British Church. He has a backward-looking air, still speaking of Latin as 'our language' and of his fellow-countrymen as 'citizens'. Nostalgic for the days of Badonic triumph, he rails at a generation which has grown up forgetful of its fathers' deeds. His main concern is with the alleged wickedness of the rulers and non-monastic clergy. After his unenlightening historical survey, he goes on to a diatribe against five regional kings living in his own time, towards the middle of the sixth century. It would be interesting to know where he was when he wrote. He is said to have lived at Llancarfan, where his 'Life' as a saint was written, and at Glastonbury. Whatever his location, it gave him a narrower horizon than we could wish. He knows a little about the West Country, Gloucestershire and Wales. Everything beyond is a blank.

His first target is Constantine of Dumnonia, who, he says,

swore an oath of good conduct and then, disguised as an abbot, murdered two innocent royal youths in a church. Gildas urges this king to repent, and according to the *Annales Cambriae* he did — more than forty years later. In his reformed guise he may be a constituent of the 'Blessed Constantine' of legend. Next Gildas attacks Aurelius Caninus or Conanus, whose kingdom seems to have been in the lower Severn area and south-east Wales. In this case he has nothing very specific to say, reproaching him for murders and fornications without naming names or giving particulars, and holding it up to him as a terrible warning that his parents and brothers died young and unexpectedly in the midst of their sins.

The third of Gildas's victims is the elderly Vortiporius of Demetia or Dyfed, in south-west Wales. He, it seems, is the unworthy son of an admirable father, and incestuously involved with his own daughter . . . though perhaps she was only his stepdaughter. We know more about this king. A Welsh genealogy gives his father's name as Aircol and his grandfather's as Triphun. These are equivalent to 'Agricola' and 'Tribune', and suggest the family's lingering attachment to the old order before the Celtic-named king himself. Carmarthen Museum has his memorial stone, which was identified in 1895 at Castell Dwyran on the border between Carmarthenshire and Pembrokeshire. It is nearly seven feet high. Under a Celtic ring-cross are the words MEMORIA VOTEPORIGIS PROTICTORIS, the monument of Voteporix the protector. An inscription down the edge in the Irish ogam script repeats the royal name only, in an Irish form. Gildas's spelling of it is a Latinization. Voteporix seems to have been descended from an Irish chief who was put in charge of Dyfed by one of the emperors, possibly Maximus. The title 'protector' was given to officer-cadets in the emperor's body-guard. It looks as if a son of the original Irishman held such a post, and his family treated the title as hereditary.

Fourth on Gildas's list is Cuneglasus or Cinglas, ruling in central Wales. He persecutes monks, and has put away his wife to marry her sister, though the sister took a vow of chastity. One phrase has sometimes been taken as an allusion to Arthur, on whom Gildas is otherwise uncommunicative. Cuneglasus was formerly 'the charioteer of the Bear'. The point of interest is that 'Arthur' would have resembled a Celtic word for 'bear', and is explained by a medieval writer as meaning just that, *ursus horribilis*. If the original Arthur was a man who vanished from the scene in 470, Cinglas could not have been his charioteer. The phrase might refer to some later person nicknamed 'the Bear', and, it must be added, not necessarily named Arthur. But it is too obscure to build any conjectures on. A Welsh genealogy appended to Nennius gives us a piece of information about Cinglas which is not in Gildas: that he was descended from Cunedda, the chieftain given charge of Wales in the early fifth century. Hence his hereditary claim.

Last, and by far the most important, is a king whose name Gildas Latinizes as 'Maglocunus'. He is Maelgwn, ruler of the north Welsh kingdom of Gwynedd. Gildas calls him 'the dragon of the isle', meaning Anglesey. Maelgwn is the only one of the five who stands out as a personality. Educated at Illtud's school, he was a prince of rich promise, tall, brave, generous. But he began his adult career by dethroning his uncle and attacking other princes. Then he reformed and spent some time in a monastery. It did no good. He came out, resumed the crown, and increased his power by aggressive acts. Desiring his nephew's wife, he killed both the nephew and his own queen in order to marry her. Gildas denounces him in sorrow as well as anger. He is a tragically great man, basking in flattery from a crew of sycophantic bards, but dragged down by his own ungoverned energies.

Maelgwn is known to us from several sources besides Gildas. Like Cinglas he was descended from Cunedda, and he was the last British king who tried to assert a hegemony over other kings, though without much success — the days when anyone could be king of all Britons, in the old Celtic sense of that name, were long past. The 'Lives' of Welsh saints portray him alternately quarrelling with monks and endowing monasteries. To judge from the inscriptions in this part of Wales, his subjects were culturally above average and preserved a little more of the Roman heritage. The poet Taliesin is said to have made his début at Maelgwn's court as a youthful challenger to the bards whom Gildas dislikes.

A few generations later the court of Gwynedd was at Aberffraw in Anglesey. In view of Gildas's 'dragon of the isle' epithet, it may have been there already in Maelgwn's reign. His presence is almost certain at another place, the former Roman fort Castell Degannwy, above Conway Bay. Legend says he died in the nearby church of Rhos, where he had shut himself in for fear of plague, with guards posted to prevent anyone from entering. After some days he ventured to peep out. Presently his guards ceased to hear him moving and assumed that he was asleep, but the silence went on so long that they investigated and found him dead of the plague. A Welsh phrase meaning coma or death is 'the long sleep of Maelgwn in the church of Rhos'.

The rest of Gildas's book is a protracted sermon with a plethora of biblical texts. It is an exercise in overkill which can now only annoy, since he could so easily have spent the time giving information. The most informative feature is an omission. He denounces his contemporaries for many sins, but never for apostasy or idolatry. They are all Christians, if, in his censorious eyes, very bad ones. There is no evidence for what has sometimes been guessed at, a resurgence of paganism. There is no evidence even for its effective survival. No doubt the conversion of the kings' subjects still had some way to go, and the old Celtic religion was quietly carrying on here and there in rustic forms. But a reader of Gildas must conclude that the Church's main battle was won. He would have smelt out pagans if he could.

He lived on till about 570 without adding any more. Still, in his restricted Britain, a few other royal characters do emerge dimly. We find them in genealogies, stories of saints and kindred matter, as well as an inscription or two. Little can be said about them historically. One, however, is a certain Marcus who has a romantic interest as the original, or part-original, of King Mark of Cornwall, Tristan's unpleasant but wronged uncle in the tale of Tristan and Iseult. His father, Marcian, may have been named after the mid-fifth-century emperor to whose reign Bede assigns the advent of Hengist. Marcian's home was probably in Glamorgan, since he is said to have given St Illtud a plot of land for his monastery.

Marcus, the son, is extremely hard to pin down. Local legends about him, and place-names with 'Mark' in them, extend from Cornwall through Wales and as far as Kirkcudbright. The Tristan legend as we know it arose from a belief that he was the same person as a Dumnonian king named Cunomorus — Cynvawr — who converted the Iron Age fort of Castle Dore, near Fowey, into a royal residence. This belief in a Marcus Cunomorus in Cornwall is at least as old as the ninth century. The link with Tristan is a sixth-century memorial stone, now just outside Fowey after three or four removals. It bears the inscription DRUSTANUS HIC IACIT CUNOMORI FILIUS — Drustanus lies here, the son of Cunomorus. 'Drustanus' is a Latinization of a name, originally Pictish, which came to be spelt 'Tristan' in legend. If Marcus and Cunomorus really were the same person, Mark was Tristan's father and not his uncle, and Iseult would have had to be a young stepmother. Poets may have changed the relationship to make it less discreditable to the lovers. They also attached the story to the Arthurian cycle. Early versions bring in several place-names in the Castle Dore neighbourhood, but the full facts are beyond retrieval.

In Wales, memorial stones like those of Voteporix and 'Tristan' are numerous. About 140 are known. Their dates extend through the fifth, sixth and seventh centuries. They give a few further sidelights on Welsh kings and their subjects. Latin, the language of the Church, is normal, though sometimes — especially in Voteporix's kingdom of Dyfed — a monument has an ogam inscription. Ogam is rare in Maelgwn's Gwynedd. The memorial stone of his descendant King Cadfan, set up between 625 and 660, uses a script showing continental influence and calls the deceased 'the wisest and most renowned of all kings'. The word for 'wise' is *sapiens*, which meant 'learned', in the sense of being classically educated. Another stone in Gwynedd includes the Roman terms 'citizen' and 'magistrate', hinting at a vestige of Roman-style administration. Another commemorates a doctor, Melus son of Martin.

Yet the information is scanty. Anyone today appraising this period in Celtic Britain may wonder at the lack of trustworthy data. Several reasons can be suggested. No records in British ever existed: it was not used for historical texts, it was probably not a written language at all, and the Old Welsh that developed out of it in the mid-sixth century did not instantly become so. While the Church kept Latin alive, many records in that language were undoubtedly lost, or carried out of the country, or destroyed through raiding and counter-raiding and the lack of proper archives and libraries. Moreover, Celtic society lacked any widespread motivation for writing. More reliance was placed on oral transmission, not only for poetry and tales but for serious matters of law and property rights.

Finally — and this is apt to be overlooked — most people can have had only the haziest notions of what was going on at a distance. Perspectives broad enough for the writing of history were confined to a very few. Even the educated Gildas, 'Gildas the Wise' (like King Cadfan) as later authors call him, has his geographic limits. The royal courts would have known a little about each other through diplomacy and dynastic marriages. Wandering monks, minstrels and craftsmen would have picked up information during their travels and passed it on. But life, on the whole, was parochial, the population was scattered, and barriers were raised on all sides by forests and wastelands covering more of the country than it is now easy to realize.

Though we know so little of individuals and their doings, we can draw inferences about their world from early Welsh poetry and codes of law, and from archaeology. One eloquent fact is that there is no trace of any rebirth of coinage. It was not a money economy. Most of the people lived on the land, growing crops, raising animals, supplying their needs by domestic crafts. A social divide separated freemen and serfs, but the freemen were far from being rich. The nobles' homes were rough timber halls and crude buildings of stone, sometimes, as at Castle Dore, within the enclosures of Iron Age hill-forts. Their mode of life combined a certain culture and luxury with a squalor which today seems incongruous. They had tenants and a few slave labourers. They employed craftsmen. They imported wine and kitchen utensils from abroad, bartering surplus hides and agricultural products. But trade in general was on a small scale, and the nobles themselves did not often go far from home except to ride out hunting and fishing, or to the occasional battle.

As for the kings, men like Maelgwn and the rest, they owed their status to their descent from military upstarts, imperial office-holders, and allegedly, in a few cases, emperors. A British dynasty as far from the imperial centres as Galloway claimed to be descended from Maximus. By Gildas's time, succession through several generations of the same family had created (if with reservations in the mind of Gildas himself) a sense of legitimacy. However, the rules were fluid. Succession from father to eldest son was by no means invariable. It could be traced in the female line, a custom normal among the Picts, though the old Celtic acceptance of female government seems to have lapsed.

Each king had his band of noble retainers, who feasted with him in his hall to an accompaniment of music, finely and colourfully dressed. The court bards were important figures, whose memories were appealed to for customs and precedents. They preserved the family history on which a king's pedigree, and therefore his right, depended. Their poems in praise of their royal patrons were meant to instil confidence. If a king lost support, a stronger rival might oust him. If he suspected that he was losing it, he might try to restore his prestige by victory. Hence, in part, the inter-British fighting condemned by Gildas. It was petty, involving hundreds rather than thousands, and it did little harm to the settled homesteads of the land, but it meant disunion and also instability. Kingdoms were held together by individual qualities, *esprit de corps*, the accidents of success and failure. Brilliant, sustained leadership might still have brought a revival of Celtic Britain; but it was not forthcoming.

2

Gildas's Britain retained geographic continuity for a few decades longer. It was finally torn apart by the kings of the West Saxons.

The West Saxon dynasty is a riddle. Its reputed founder is the 'ealdorman' Cerdic who, in the *Anglo-Saxon Chronicle*, effects the first landing in 495 on the shore of Southampton Water. He comes with five ships, from no one knows where, accompanied by his son Cynric, also an 'ealdorman' and therefore adult. The *Chronicle* next records the landing in 501 of another party of Saxons led by Port and his two sons, and a clash with the Britons at or near Portsmouth. This would have been the seizure of Portchester which is seemingly put on record by the other side too, in the poem about Geraint at Llongborth. Hampshire may then have belonged to his Dumnonian realm. In 508 Cerdic fights a wildly exaggerated battle against the British 'king' Natanleod near the head of Southampton Water. In 514 two more chiefs arrive, Stuf and Wihtgar. In 519 Cerdic and Cynric 'take the kingdom' of the West Saxons. They fight the Britons at that time and again in 527 and 530, invading the Isle of Wight. In 534 Cerdic dies and Cynric succeeds to the kingship.

Most of these details are clearly suspect. It is not so much that they contradict what Gildas says about comparative peace following Badon. They scarcely do. The scanty archaeological remains show that the number of Saxons was very small and that they made only trivial progress inland. The immense majority of Britons, including Gildas, may well have heard nothing about them. But there is too much fantasy. At least three of the names look as if they were invented to account for places: 'Port' to explain Portsmouth, the *Magnus Portus* of the Romans; 'Natanleod' to explain Netley Marsh, *Natan leaga*; 'Wihtgar' to explain the Isle of Wight, *Vectis*. The Saxon landings and movements probably happened, with some of the settlers coasting along from Kent and Sussex. But the *Chronicle* story is a hotchpotch of traditions handed down orally for three or four hundred years in different heroic poems. The dates cannot be trusted and only Cerdic and Cynric emerge at all plausibly as persons.

Even with them, there is yet a further objection. They live too long. If Cerdic already had an adult son in 495 he is most unlikely to have been an active warrior in 530. Cynric does not die in the *Chronicle* till 560. Each leader's career has been stretched to associate him with events he was not involved in. It will be recalled that something of the kind seems to have happened with Arthur. Nevertheless, one single fact makes Cerdic virtually unassailable as a figure of history. Far from looking like an invention, his name is one which no Saxon would have given to a royal ancestor, unless the fact was beyond dispute. It is not Saxon but British. It is the same as 'Ceredig', the name of the Clyde despot denounced by St Patrick; the name, also, of a descendant of Cunedda after whom Cardigan (Ceredigiaun) is supposed to be called; the name of an interpreter at Vortigern's court, according to Nennius, and of a later ruler of Elmet.

Genealogists were to credit Cerdic with a pedigree going back, like those of most Saxon kings, to the god Woden. Yet it is hard to deny him a parentage at least partly British. He may have been a product of local fraternization in Armorica, recruiting followers from Saxon families that remained near the Loire after the defeat and expulsion of the main body. A curious related fact is that names given to Cerdic's people, and to two of his reputed forebears, appear also in the Welsh tradition of Vortigern.

The West Saxons were known as 'Gewisse'. This means, properly, 'allies' or 'confederates', but it was taken to mean 'Gewis's people', and Cerdic's Saxon pedigree includes someone called Gewis. In later times the word was adopted by the Welsh. As we saw, Geoffrey of Monmouth applies it to the people of Gwent and calls Vortigern the Duke of the Gewissei. As we also saw, the inscription on the pillar in Valle Crucis suggests that this title, however fanciful, has some connection with a claim which Vortigern was believed to have derived from a marriage to a daughter of Maximus. The Welsh king who asserted his descent from that marriage, and is the subject of the inscription, was named Eliseg; and Cerdic's father in his own pedigree is Elesa. Did the West Saxon names get into a Welsh context because of some other genealogy giving Cerdic an ancestry among Britons, even a link with Vortigern? We might indulge the fancy that the romance about Vortigern and Hengist's daughter is true, and Cerdic was the offspring of that second marriage, begotten late in the British ruler's life, but not incredibly late. Such a parentage would have given him a foot in both camps.

That, of course, is fancy only. Whatever the reality, Cerdic's heirs began a march towards future greatness when a crushing disaster weakened the opposition. Its origins were far off. The year 542 brought a bubonic outbreak in Egypt, which spread to Constantinople in 543, and to southern Gaul in 544. During the next half-decade the Britons were ravaged, first by the epidemic itself and then by an after-effect called the Yellow Plague. This was the disease that carried off King Maelgwn of Gwynedd, whether or not it happened so dramatically in the church of Rhos. Infection came with imported goods, scanty though they were. It had no equivalent impact on the Saxons. Their own few imports came from northern Gaul and the lower Rhineland, which escaped the worst. Also they had practically no contact with the plague-stricken Britons. The years of truce in most of the country had resulted in a co-existence but not a mingling. British hatred still went too deep. Now it brought retribution. The Saxons, preserved from the plague by being ostracized, gained sharply in relative strength and numbers.

The long-circumscribed group in the south of Hampshire could press forward at last. By about 550 they were near Salisbury, and in 552 they routed a British force holding what was left of the city. In 560 Caewlin succeeded to the leadership of the West Saxons. He created a powerful kingdom, initially by uniting the subjects of the Gewisse dynasty with a mass of Saxons in the middle and upper Thames valley. Nothing in writing tells how they came to be there. An early settlement may have been followed by a withdrawal after Badon, and then by a quiet reoccupation. In 568 Ceawlin fought the first known inter-Saxon battle, moving into Surrey to prevent encroachment by Aethelbert of Kent. He had as his ally a chief named Cuthwulf or Cutha, said to have been his brother, who ruled somewhere north of London, and overran the Britons in Bedfordshire and Buckinghamshire. Such campaigns did not involve large-scale exterminations or clearance. In this second and greater wave of conquest, the Britons survived in varying degrees, more and more strongly as their conquerors left the first Anglo-Saxondom behind. But they had to live with new overlords, new neigh-bours, a new language.

In 577 Ceawlin marched west. He entered the lower Severn area, the kingdom of Gildas's Aurelius Caninus, and won deci-sively at Dyrham seven miles north of Bath. Three prominent Britons were killed, Conmail, Condidan and Farinmail. The *Anglo-Saxon Chronicle* calls them 'kings'. More likely they headed vestigial civic authorities. Several towns hereabouts were still in being: Ceawlin captured Bath, Cirencester and Gloucester.

His realm of Wessex now extended to the Severn estuary, and Wales and Dumnonia were separated. The break was mental as well as geographic. Henceforth the Welsh spoke of the still-independent Britons as Cymry — fellow-countrymen — and they included those of Cumbria and Strathclyde as well as Wales itself, but they did not include those of the West Country. Appar-ently the latter had ceased to count. They held out for many years, but no longer as members of a larger whole. The Saxons sometimes called them West Welsh. 'Dumnonia', in its Celtic form Dyfneint, became 'Devon'. Cornishmen traded and trav-elled across the Channel. In some ways they were closer to their Breton kinsfolk than they were to the Cymry. As story-tellers at least they fought back against isolation, making potent contribu-tions to the Arthurian Legend.

Despite their status as Cymry, the northern Britons suffered much the same fate, and bequeathed a legacy of much the same sort. But the process was more exciting.

North of the Humber everything happened later. That is odd, because Germanic soldiers had been settled between the estuary and Hadrian's Wall before the British break with the Empire. They may even have been Angles. But if this community joined the revolt of the *foederati*, it simmered down afterwards and became passive. The ambitious Angles who were to conquer the north first made their presence felt in 547. On the small coastal hill of Bamburgh, the Britons had an earthwork fort called Din Guayrdi. An Anglian chief, Ida, occupied it. He asserted his independence of the Britons around by fortifying the central area, first with a hedge, then with a wall. It is the only known case of an early Anglo-Saxon fort.

Ida's tiny stronghold was to become the principal royal seat of the great English kingdom of Northumbria. This combined Bernicia, which ran north from a border near the Wall, with Deira, the country between that line and the Humber. Whatever the truth about Deira's first settlers, it certainly had an Anglian population by Ida's time, and chiefs of its own. The ancient character of Northumbria as a region somewhat apart, with a special dignity, has echoes in medieval romance. Its first king's coastal fort underwent a strange literary transformation. The name 'Bamburgh' started as 'Bebbanburh' and was bestowed by a later monarch in honour of his queen Bebba. Before that it was still Din Guayrdi, as Nennius is aware, and the British connection was not forgotten. In romance Sir Lancelot's northern castle is Joyous Gard, and although Malory observes cautiously that 'some men say it was Alnwick and some men say it was Bamburgh', Bamburgh — Din Guayrdi — it manifestly is.

The transition from Britain to England in the north was more a takeover of power by new rulers, less a takeover of land by new occupants, than anywhere else. It was resisted, at one time or another, by four British kingdoms: Elmet south-west of York; Rheged, centred on Cumbria, and extending round the Solway Firth; Strathclyde with its royal stronghold at Dumbarton (otherwise known as Alclud, the Rock of Clyde); and Manau Guotodin around Edinburgh, Din Eydin. Besides these there were minor principalities.

Bernicia took the offensive when its link with Deira was still tenuous. The Angles' first opponent was Outigern, whose domain is uncertain. After him came Urbgen or Urien of Rheged, who reigned in the 570s and 80s. He was the last ruler of the Britons who drew others into concerted action. His chief ally was Rhydderch of Strathclyde. Two lesser ones were Morcant and Guallauc. Urbgen took the offensive himself, driving the Bernicians back to the North Sea, and besieging their king Theodric on the tidal island of Lindisfarne for three days and nights. Near here, however, he was assassinated because of the jealousy of Morcant. His son Owein took command, and held on for a few years longer.

These kings of Rheged were patrons of the first known poets in Welsh, now fully in being as a language distinct from its parent British. Nennius names five of them: Talhaern, Bluchbard, Cian, Aneirin and Taliesin. Verses composed by the last two are still extant, the oldest poetry, some have claimed, in any still-living language of Europe. The wording is curt, staccato, simple. The metres are by no means simple, and imply a developed technique for recitation to music.

Another northern poet, unmentioned by Nennius, attained immortality through a weird transfiguration. In spite of Urbgen's unifying influence, the Britons persisted in fighting among themselves. A battle took place about 573 in the Arthuret district, below the confluence of the Liddel and Esk. The name has nothing to do with Arthur; its early form is 'Arfderydd'. One of the combatants was Gwendollau, and the site of the battle was near his stronghold Caer Gwendollau — today, Carwinley. Two of his own relatives fought against him. The quarrel was over possession of Caerlaverock on the north side of the Solway Firth, and the slaughter was terrible and futile. One result, it is said, was that a British bard who took part was driven half-mad, and wandered off into the Caledonian forest uttering prophecies. Different accounts give him two different names. One is Lailoken, the other is Myrddin. A few verses ascribed to him as Myrddin survive. Despite the anachronism he is the original, or part-original, of the prophet and enchanter Merlin.

The northern bards made other additions to Arthurian legend.

Here Taliesin had a share. So did Llywarch, a cousin of Urbgen. Whatever the truth about Taliesin's début in Gwynedd, satirizing the bards of a previous generation, his surviving poems are in praise of Urbgen and Owein, and extol their generosity and triumphs over the Angles. He outlived both, and composed an elegy recalling how the corpses of Owein's enemies lay staring-eyed on the battlefield:

> His keen-edged spears were like the wings of the dawn . . .
> The host of broad England sleeps
> With the light in their eyes.

A memorable lament ascribed to Llywarch tells how (in imagi-nation if not in reality) he carried away Urbgen's severed head from the scene of his murder, perhaps to save it from deface-ment.

Because of such tributes — some warm, some sad, some grim — Urbgen and Owein were to find their way into Welsh Arthu-rian tales and the romances of the Round Table. Spellings varied. Owein appears in French stories as the knight Yvain. The story-tellers, of course, had their dating wrong as they had it wrong with Merlin, but few of their hearers knew or cared. These paladins obviously belonged at the most glorious of courts. Popular legend located Owein's burial in the Giant's Grave at Penrith. This is a strange-looking assemblage of monumental stones, actually dating from the tenth century, and covering fifteen feet of ground. Local lore declares that Owein was a mighty boar-hunter, and even adds that in the reign of Eliza-beth I the Giant's Grave was opened and his enormous bones were dug up.

Among the Welsh poems, one composed by Taliesin's col-league Aneirin glances at Arthur himself as warrior-hero, in a line which may be the earliest surviving Cymric allusion to him. It comes in a series grouped under the title *Gododdin*, in which the poet tells, obliquely, the story of a campaign launched against the Angles from Manau Guotodin about 598. A force assembled from various parts of Britain. After a period of court attendance and preparation, they went — probably by way of Carlisle — to attack the Angles at Catraeth, the Roman fort of Cataractonium — now Catterick. Its importance lay in its com-mand of the road junction known today as Scotch Corner. It was in Deira, which at that point, after sundry vicissitudes, happened to be more or less separate from Bernicia. The Britons may have had some idea of detaching it for good and breaking the Northumbrian kingdom. Heavily outnumbered, they fought bravely, but all were killed (at any rate, all the aristocratic element) except a handful. Aneirin himself rode with the army and was one of the survivors.

The poems making up *Gododdin* are elegies for the fallen. Such a loose compilation invites the insertion of more matter in praise of favourite characters, and, after Aneirin's death, more was inserted. This puts a query over his reference to Arthur, but there is no specific ground for thinking it a later interpolation. What he says is that a warrior named Gwawrddur 'glutted black ravens on the wall of the fort, though he was not Arthur'. In Welsh poetry 'feeding the ravens' meant killing enemies. The point is not quite clear. It may be that although Gwawrddur was not Arthur, he was equally good at killing. Or it may be that he was a mighty fighter though admittedly no Arthur. In either case the words, if authentic, imply that by the end of the sixth century Arthur was proverbial for prowess in war. They imply nothing further. It has been argued that they support the theory of a minor northern Arthur because *Gododdin* is about northerners. But Aneirin mentions others, including, unfortunately for the argument, 'Geraint from the south'.

Cataractonium was beside the Swale by Catterick Bridge. Presumably the Britons tried to take it by storm. The wall on which Gwawrddur glutted the ravens was seven feet thick, supplying plenty of room for his activities. Aneirin gives many other intriguing glimpses of the three hundred or so nobles (it is not clear how many retainers or auxiliaries they took with them). In time of peace they hunted and fished, and feasted round open fires in halls lit by pinewood torches and rush candles. Their drinking vessels were of horn and glass, silver and gold. They listened to minstrels, they took baths, they went to church. Their clothes were brightly coloured and ornamented with brooches and amber beads. In war they put on cuirasses of leather, and probably a rough sort of chain mail. They carried swords and white shields and used throwing-spears. Heartened by copious draughts of mead, they rode to battle and seemingly fought on horseback.

The men went to Catraeth, they were renowned, wine and mead from gold cups was their drink for a year, in accordance with the honoured custom. Three men and three score and three hundred, wearing gold necklets, of all that hastened out after the flowing drink none escaped but three, through feats of sword-play — the two wardogs of Aeron, and stubborn Cynon; and I too, streaming with blood, by grace of my blessed poetry . . . .

The men went to Catraeth in column, raising the war-cry, a force with steeds and blue armour and shields, javelins aloft and keen lances, and bright mail-coats and swords. He led, he burst through the armies, and there fell five times fifty before his blades — Rhufawn the Tall, who gave gold to the altar and gifts and fine presents to the minstrel . . . .

The warriors arose together, together they met, together they attacked, with single purpose; short were their lives, long the mourning left to their kinsmen. Seven times as many English they slew; in fight they made women widows, and many a mother with tears at her eyelids . . . .

It is grief to me that after the toil of battle they suffered the agony of death in torment, and a second heavy grief it is to me to have seen our men falling . . . . After the battle, may their souls get welcome in the land of Heaven, the dwelling-place of plenty.

Gododdin is the requiem of Arthurian Britain. It was not actually quite defunct, but a Northumbrian king was soon to deal the final blows. Aethelfrith had begun to reign in Bernicia in 593. It was he who renamed Ida's coastal fort Bebbanburh after his queen. During his first decade of power he was slowly gaining ground in Rheged. Owein contested his advance, but was killed. The northern Britons appealed for help, desperately, to King Aedan of Argyll. He ruled over a colony of Scots, the nuclear settlement of that Irish people in the country to which they were to give their name. Though Aedan was not British, he had called one of his sons Arthur, another sign of the growth and spread of the saga. Apprehensive about Aethelfrith on his own account, he marched south in 603 under the delusion that Anglian malcontents would support him. Aethelfrith routed him at an unidentified place called Degsastan, Degsa's Stone. Aethelfrith's army suffered heavy losses, but Aedan's was almost wiped out. The Welsh, ungraciously, were to blacken him in retrospect as a traitor.

In 605 Aethelfrith occupied York and re-established the union of Deira with Bernicia. In 614, or a year or so after that, he turned towards Wales. At Chester he met the army of Powys under the Welsh king Selim or Solomon. A host of monks had gathered to pray for Christian success. When the heathen Aethelfrith asked what they were doing, and was told, he replied that praying was tantamount to fighting. Like Jerry Cruncher's wife in *A Tale of Two Cities*, the monks were 'flopping agin him'. He ordered his soldiers to put them to the sword. Brocmail, the Welsh officer detailed to protect them, deserted his charges and twelve hundred were killed. Aethelfrith went on to complete his victory.

It was the northern equivalent of the battle of Dyrham, splitting the Cymry apart. The gap which had been opened in Cheshire and southern Lancashire was not immediately filled by the Angles, but it was a power-vacuum which presented no obstacles when they did fill it. To the east the little kingdom of Elmet was clearly doomed. Most of the shrunken remnant of Rheged was soon to be swallowed up by Strathclyde. Strathclyde itself still had a long life ahead of it, and the Celtic character of the region around Carlisle remained stubborn enough to pass on the name 'Cumberland' — the 'land of the Cymry' — into English. From Wales itself, one amazing counter-attack was yet to come. But Wales and the northern Cymry were separated and out of touch. Arthurian Britain was beyond re-assembly.

CHAPTER NINE

The Makings of a Monarchy

1

IN THE LATER SIXTH CENTURY, FRAGMENTATION HAD REACHED ITS EXTREME POINT. Besides the British kingdoms there were eight Anglo-Saxon ones: Kent, Sussex, Wessex, Essex, East Anglia, Mercia, Deira, Bernicia, the last two still oscillating between separateness and union in a single Northumbria. Their cohesion reduced the total to seven, which were to endure as such for a long time. That is the reason for the term 'Heptarchy' sometimes applied to Anglo-Saxondom. But several minor groupings existed also, such as the Hwicce in Gloucestershire. Some of the political units owed their origin to dealings with the Britons followed by independence and growth. Some had been independent from the beginning, as lands seized by adventurers without consent. At least one had arisen out of post-settlement developments in Britain itself.

Mercia, covering the Midlands, has almost no early history. 'Mercians' means 'borderers' — the same word occurs in the expression 'Welsh Marches' — but it is not certain what area they bordered upon. Their kingdom seems to have started as an outgrowth from an independent Lindsey created by the Angles of Lincolnshire, and to have come into being with its Mercian identity about 584. The Britons of the Midlands had no powerful rulers and offered no resistance. Hence, Mercia's expansion was swift and peaceful. It absorbed or dominated other Anglian territories and became the largest kingdom of all.

The kings of the Anglo-Saxons claimed loftier antecedents than those of the Britons. As heathens they were at liberty to do so. All were of divine descent. All but one of the royal pedigrees went back to the god Woden. The East Saxons preferred to be descended from another god, Seaxnot. Each royal house had in fact begun with the chief who headed the pioneer settlers. Only with the Mercian dynasty is it known that any ancestors (that is, human ones) were rulers on the continent before the migration: here the key figure is Icel, a chieftain of the Angles who can be traced outside Britain in the fifth century. The other founders may have been simply freebooters. But as power and territory grew, divine ancestry was invoked in each case to prove that the founder had had a god-given right from the outset and that it passed to his descendants.

Surprisingly, the divine ancestors were not put far back in a mythical once-upon-a-time. A count of generations does not give consistent results, but it shows that Woden would have lived in the third or fourth century A.D. In his ancestral role he may have been a real person, for example a deified chief, or a chief who was named after the god and supposed to embody his spirit, thus perhaps being a northern counterpart of Brennus the Gaul who sacked Rome. As for Woden's immortal nature in the Anglo-Saxons' pantheon, very little is known about this, or indeed about their religion in general.

The English names of four weekdays — Tuesday, Wednesday, Thursday and Friday — are taken from deities: three gods and a goddess. But the Anglo-Saxons did not originally use the seven-day week, and the only reason for the four names is that when they adopted it, they replaced four Roman deities with four of their own. The days of Mars, Mercury, Jupiter and Venus became the days of Tiw, Woden, Thunor and Frig. It is doubtful whether the correspondence between the two quartets went much beyond gender. However, Tiw had something to do with war, like Mars, and Thunor had something to do with thunder, like Jupiter. Woden was a being of vague and colossal power. The name 'Wansdyke' means 'Woden's ditch' and was bestowed on the earthwork by Saxons who thought it superhuman.

Gods were represented by images, or idols, in Christian parlance. Their shrines were in woodland clearings or on mounds, natural or artificial. Place-names in parts of England which were settled during the heathen period show where some of these were. Woodnesborough, Wednesbury, Wednesfield, recall Woden just as Wednesday does. Thursley, Thunderfield, Thundersley, were sacred places of Thunor the Thursday-god. The priests were medicine-men and wizards. Their main rituals were concerned with everyday welfare, which the gods gave if they were pleased, or at least propitiated.

The year followed a seasonal and ceremonial cycle. It began when the sun had just passed the winter solstice, on what is now 25 December. The night after that day was 'the night of the mothers'. The first month was Giuli (whence 'Yule'). The second was marked by a festival in which cakes were offered to the gods. The third and fourth were called after the goddesses Hretha and Eostre (whence 'Easter'). The pattern of the late spring and summer is not so clear, but the ninth month was 'holy', the time of the harvest festival. The tenth was the month of the full moon heralding winter. The eleventh was 'the month of sacrifice', when animals were slaughtered in preparation for the season of cold and food shortage, and some were devoted to the gods. The twelfth was Giuli again, so that Yuletide extended over two months. Besides the communal events related to the calendar, there was a great deal of individual magic, spell-casting and so forth.

To revert to the kings, the claim to a divine pedigree was inseparable from family kinship. A man who was to rule had to be of the right birth for it, and anyone who was outside the family lacked the pedigree. Whether or not the theological notion was present from the beginning, the hereditary notion certainly was. In the first two centuries of settlement it seems never to have been defied, and it was observed as the norm long after that. But as with the Celts, the rules were flexible. A king's successor was not necessarily his eldest son, or even his son at all. Others of the blood royal could qualify. Sometimes the king chose an heir during his lifetime. In any case, when he died, the nobles were free to make a short-list of eligible members of the family and award the crown to the one they judged best fitted. Since some of the families grew and branched out widely, there might be candidates with a merely cousinly kinship who could still be considered and who, if appointed, broke the direct line. The actual ruler had to be male, but women who had blood-ties with kings, or married them, could inspire great respect and wield enviable influence. Their sex did not condemn them to nullity.

A royal household, in those earlier days, was a group of warrior-nobles who stood in much the same relationship to their sovereign as Welsh retainers did to theirs. Specific court posts were hardly known. Government was at a rudimentary stage.

No distinction was drawn between king's revenue and state's revenue. The court lived on the produce of royal estates or, when it travelled, was supported by taxation in kind, levied on the neighbourhood and paid over directly. A single important place might be informally the capital, but not as a fixed seat of authority or as the home of a civil service or treasury, even though some of the kingdoms were using coinage of foreign origin (they began striking their own in the seventh century). Justice, order, the raising of troops for war, were all very personal matters and in the hands of the king and aristocracy. Some kings did well out of plundering expeditions and overseas trade, but without employing full-time professional officers or agents.

While each ruler had a royal council, the *Witan*, it was little more in practice than a committee of the household. If issues arose affecting large numbers of people, a king could enlarge it into a consultative assembly. The assembly was not a permanent body, no one but the king could insist on its meeting, and no one outside the household had an *ex officio* right to attend when it did; the members were invited. It was not till many years later that assemblies began to be held often and to foreshadow the parliamentary idea. Local government, apart from the powers and responsibilities of local lords, did not exist.

Most Anglo-Saxons lived in villages and tiny rural communities, or on farms. The towns had not recovered and were thinly populated, or in some cases deserted. The typical Anglo-Saxon was not a citizen or a serf but a landowning peasant. He might be quite a well-to-do peasant, owning slaves as well as land. One has the impression of a people who were hard-working and tough but rather dull. Their immense latent gifts were not yet emerging. They used the roads but built none themselves. They cultivated wheat, rye, barley and oats as Britons had done in Roman times, and kept much the same livestock, but there is little evidence for the wide range of fruits and vegetables which Roman Britain produced. Houses were cramped, crude and dirty, made of wattle-work or of logs at best. Clothes were largely utilitarian — tunics, hooded mantles, trousers with cross-gartering for men, long simple dresses for women, stereotyped brooches and clasps. Society had well-defined grades, but no extreme polarization of rich and poor, ruling class and ruled. That was to come later with economic growth.

2

The persistence of so many distinct kingdoms was due, in part, to the events of the Badonic period. In those days Aelle of the South Saxons had briefly asserted his *imperium* over other chiefs. Victory might have put his little realm at the head of a confederacy. Procopius's statement about the 'Frisians' having a single king may even be a distant, belated echo of his claims. But in the upshot they came to nothing. Badon checked the Saxon advance and perhaps, in places, reversed it. If Aelle was still on the scene at all, the defeat may have discredited him. We hear no more of any such over-king for a full lifetime. Yet although the Anglo-Saxondom of the late sixth century was divided like the land of the Britons, it was developing an inner dynamic which was the very opposite.

The Britons had started out with their imperial unity. They all belonged to Britannia, which covered most of the island, contained most of its people, and was the only serious political entity within its shores. Vortigern maintained that unity after a fashion, and it lingered, however spectrally, into the 460s when a king of the Britons could still be recognized in Rome. Then came the falling-apart. The British states confronting Aethelfrith and his colleagues were the offspring of decline, discord and failure. Some could produce warriors, poets, saints, even statesmen of a sort, but the constructive energies needed for even a semblance of reunion were lacking.

For the British kings and their subjects the concept of Britain-as-a-whole survived only as nostalgia. They were already well on the way to what was to be an orthodox falsification of history: that 'the Cymry had lost dominion over Lloegyr', the Welsh name for England. They could still dream of a change for the better. It was the hope which later attached itself to Arthur and kindred immortals. But they conceived it only in terms of a revenge and reconquest, bringing Lloegyr back to its imaginary Cymric subjection. Such notions drifted steadily away from the facts, taking the form, at last, of prophesyings ascribed to Myrddin and other seers about a pan-Celtic alliance including Brittany which would crush the English. After the death of Urbgen of Rheged such an alliance was a fantasy only. The abiding reality was the falling-apart.

While the Anglo-Saxon kingdoms were as numerous as the British, it was not for the same reason. They were not dissevered remnants of a previous unity. They had begun in separateness and continued so. Therefore they carried no burden of loss and disintegration. Strangely perhaps, the Anglo-Saxons too had a notion of Britain-as-a-whole. For them, however, it held no connotation of vanished glory. It was not depressing or discouraging, it was something which they half-consciously moved to realize.

Its clearest expression was a title, 'Bretwalda', Britain-ruler. This was given to a series of kings, and passed through five royal houses before it showed signs of coming to rest in one of them. The compound word has a flavour of German heroic verse, which coined epithets like 'deed-doer' and 'bracelet-giver'. It may have begun in the panegyrics of royal minstrels, but it grew to denote an actual superior dignity. Bede has it in mind when he speaks of the *imperium* of Aelle, who counted, in retrospect, as the first Bretwalda: not as having ruled Britain — obviously he did not — but as having first made the claim to an over-kingship in the island. The claim was more or less abortive with Aelle himself, but it acquired substance in the course of time. During the long pause following Badon the *imperium* lapsed. Then the West Saxon conqueror Ceawlin revived it. He was the second Bretwalda, and had immediate successors.

This conception of one Anglo-Saxon king as the overlord and focus of Britain helped in the making of a centripetal trend and, after many years, a united monarchy. One noteworthy aspect is that the Bretwaldaship seems to have depended on more than brute force. It involved a kind of consent, and agreement on spheres of influence. Early Bretwaldas made no claim to suzerainty beyond the Humber. That was where Aethelfrith ruled. He was the greatest conqueror of all, yet he did not break into the system or displace the Bretwalda contemporary with him. The latter, whose tenure coincided closely with Aethelfrith's reign, was king of a far smaller realm and a defeated king at that: Aethelbert of Kent, whom Ceawlin had pushed back from Surrey.

Aethelbert became Bretwalda on Ceawlin's death in 593, being the first Anglo-Saxon ruler with any air at all of returning civilization. He produced the first written English laws. Most of these were framed for a pre-Christian society. If the original writing-down was pre-Christian, his scribes would have used the runic letters of Nordic paganism. Vernacular writing of any kind was uncommon in Britain. Apart for a stray word preserved by Gildas (*cyula*, 'keel', meaning a ship), there is no specimen of Anglo-Saxon prior to a copy of Aethelbert's laws as published about 600. He made them for his own kingdom. The extent of his power outside, as Bretwalda, is a matter of conjecture. At that time the title may still have been little more than honorary. However, Kentish ornaments scattered through southern England, and Kentish-type burials in the Midlands, have been held to show the presence of garrisons and royal representatives. It is on record that King Raedwald of the East Angles accepted the status of a vassal. Perhaps this was a matter of policy and self-commendation, because when Aethelbert died in 616, Raedwald became the fourth Bretwalda.

His name is best known on account of the ship-burial at Sutton Hoo and the theory that it was his. Whether it should be assigned to Raedwald himself or to a king soon after him, it is the richest archaeological legacy of Anglo-Saxondom, witnessing vividly to the tastes of the East Anglian court. It includes Anglo-Saxon jewellry, decorated bronze bowls of Celtic workmanship, Frankish coins, a silver dish from the Mediterranean; drinking-horns, a lyre, a board game; a helmet and shield; finely ornamented golden buckles and clasps; royal emblems such as a wrought-iron standard and a ceremonial whetstone, symbol of the king as sword-giver. The ship which held this treasure rotted away long ago, leaving only rusty nails, and stained patches in the sand of the burial pit. But it can be reconstructed from what is known of other ships. It was almost ninety feet long, and propelled by thirty-eight rowers with help from sails.

3

One problem raised by the Sutton Hoo burial is the absence of a body. Various clues suggest that there was a body originally which decomposed into near-nothingness, but they are inconclusive. It remains possible that this is not strictly a burial at all, but the ritual treasure-deposit of a king buried somewhere else . . .

in a Christian graveyard, for instance. On the other hand, would a Christian have passed into the next world with such a lavish pagan display? The finds, and the non-find, put a query over the character of the king's religion.

The Christianization of Anglo-Saxondom was launched by Pope Gregory the Great during the Bretwaldaship of Aethelbert. Gregory had been dreaming of a mission to the Anglo-Saxons for years. The famous anecdote of the boys in the slave-market, who, he said, would be 'not Angles but angels' if they had the Faith, belongs to a time when he was a monk in Rome long before his election to the papacy. He wanted to go himself but was prevented. The slaves had come from Deira. However, when he launched the mission in 596, its destination was Kent. Kent was closer, with more continental links. Moreover Aethelbert's wife Bertha, a Frankish princess, was a Christian herself and had brought over a chaplain. The ground was in some degree prepared at the court.

Gregory entrusted the mission to the monk Augustine. This was not an entirely happy choice. Augustine was timid, afraid of taking decisions. After making a start he tried to turn back, and the Pope had to write and urge him on. Later he asked Gregory for rulings on a whole series of points, all of which had to be sorted out in writing. In public Augustine tended to over-compensate by arrogance. That trait in him was the cause of a crucial failure.

With forty companions, Augustine landed at Ebbsfleet in Thanet in 597. Aethelbert came to meet him. The king insisted on parleying in the open air, fearing that if they were indoors, Augustine could employ magic against him. He agreed to the missionaries' coming to his chief town, Canterbury, and provided lodgings. He also gave them the use of a church dedicated to St Martin, which, after long emptiness and decay, had been adopted by Bertha as her oratory. A few weeks of probation went by and Aethelbert was impressed. He received baptism at Whitsun with some of his nobles. Thenceforth he favoured the new religion warmly, approving the conversion of temples into churches. But he did not exert pressure. Paganism retained plenty of vitality and, in fact, Kent largely relapsed for a while after his death.

Augustine became the first Archbishop of Canterbury. In 603

he approached the ecclesiastics of Wales. Through the Bretwalda's good offices he was able to arrange a conference at Aust-on-Severn. The Welsh, however, had diverged in various ways from the practices of Rome . . . or in their own view, had preserved the correct practices while Rome had shifted. In particular they fixed Easter differently, an issue which was to become a rallying-cry in later disputes. They were not disposed to fall in line with a foreigner's dictates, or become junior partners in his new-fangled establishment. Furthermore they were suspicious of his intentions. He was inviting them to help in converting the hated Saxon, and this they had never attempted, or wanted to attempt. The Saxon could go to a well-deserved perdition.

At the first meeting, according to Bede, a blind man was cured in response to Augustine's prayers. The Welsh spokesmen declined to budge, but agreed to more discussion, and demanded a fuller conference. Seven bishops attended and a number of monks, chiefly from Bangor. In the Welsh Church it was still the monks who supplied most of the energy and learning.

Before coming to Aust the party visited a much-revered hermit and asked whether they should renounce their own ways and comply with Augustine. The hermit said: 'If he is a man of God, follow him.' They asked how they could tell. He replied that they should make humility the test. They should arrange the conference so that Augustine would arrive first and sit down to wait. Then, when they arrived themselves, he would either stand up politely to greet them or remain seated. If he stood up, it was a sign of humility and they could accept his authority. If not, it was a sign of pride and they must refuse it. When the confrontation occurred, Augustine stayed in his chair and all was lost. They rejected him and broke off discussions. He is said to have foretold that divine judgment would fall on them at the hands of their enemies. Aethelfrith's massacre of Welsh monks at Chester, a few years afterwards, was regarded at Canterbury as fulfilling the prophecy. It is unlikely that many of the monks who died in the massacre had taken part in the conference, but the guilt was doubtless collective.

The Welsh had opted for introversion. Augustine, however, had restricted his own success. At his death in 604 his mission had made virtually no progress outside Kent itself. One of his last acts was to consecrate Mellitus as Bishop of London, which was then the principal town of Essex, the kingdom of the East Saxons. Mellitus converted their king, Sabert, who was a nephew of Aethelbert, and Aethelbert built a church in London dedicated to St Paul, the original St Paul's Cathedral. Raedwald of East Anglia, then still Aethelbert's vassal, submitted to baptism during a visit to Kent. However, when he went home, his wife convinced him that he had gone too far. He is reputed to have set up a double temple, with an altar of Christ and an altar of the old gods side by side. The story is quite in keeping with the doubts over Sutton Hoo. The East Saxons backslid also. Laurentius, Augustine's successor in his archbishopric, made a second attempt to win over the Celtic Christians, extending his appeal beyond Wales, but accomplished nothing.

Augustine's only solid achievement was his creation of the see of Canterbury. This was to become a centre of Christian unity from the Channel to Scotland. The Church which its archbishops governed was to strengthen the movement towards a common Englishness and a single monarchy. But that was still some distance ahead. The new religion had to prevail first, and its triumph was to be gradual and circuitous, taking a course unforeseen by Gregory.

16

TOMB OF THE VENERABLE BEDE (A.D. **673-735**) IN
DURHAM CATHEDRAL.

17

OPENING PAGE FROM BEDE'S *ECCLESIASTI-
CAL HISTORY OF THE ENGLISH PEOPLE*,
WRITTEN IN A.D. **731** AT JARROW MONAS-
TERY, NORTHUMBRIA. IT CONTAINS A GREET-
ING AND DEDICATION TO THE KING AT THAT
TIME.

THE BORDER DESIGN
IS TAKEN FROM A
VINESCROLL ORNA-
MENT ON THE ACCA
CROSS IN HEXHAM,
NORTHUMBRIA, AND
DATES FROM C. A.D.
740.

COINS FROM BRITISH HISTORY

18A

18B

COIN FROM THE REIGN OF THE ROMAN EMPEROR ANTONINUS PIUS, SUCCESSOR TO HADRIAN.

18C

COIN USED IN BRITAIN AT THE TIME OF HADRIAN'S VISIT C. A.D. 122.

18D

GOLD *SOLIDUS* OF BRITISH 'EMPEROR' MAGNUS MAXIMUS (A.D. 383-388). ON THE REVERSE SIDE, TWO EMPERORS AND A FIGURE OF VICTORY. THE MINT SIGNATURE AT THE BOTTOM (AVGOB) INDICATES THE COIN WAS STRUCK AT 'AUGUSTA'—ONE OF THE EARLY 4TH-CENTURY NAMES FOR LONDON.

18E

GOLD *THRYMSA* FROM THE CRONDALL HOARD, OXFORDSHIRE (C. A.D. 650-675). THE REVERSE CARRIES THE ABBREVIATED NAME OF LONDON, WHERE THE COIN WAS STRUCK.

18F-G

SMALL SILVER *SCEATTAS* (PROBABLY CALLED 'PENNIES') WERE A DEBASED FORM OF THE 7TH CENTURY GOLD *THRYMSAS*, THIS COINAGE WAS USED UNTIL THE MID-700S.

18H-I

SILVER PENNIES WITH OFFA'S NAME AND PROFILE, 18H STRUCK IN CANTERBURY.

18J

COIN OF CYNETHRYTH, OFFA'S WIFE, WITH THE NAME OF THE MONEYER 'EOBA' ON ONE SIDE. OFFA'S COINS, ON THE ROMAN MODEL, WERE INTENDED FOR OVERSEAS TRADING.

18K

ONE OF ALFRED'S SILVER PENNIES, STRUCK BY THE CANTERBURY MONEYER, HEAHSTAN. AS RULER OF WESSEX, ALFRED WAS RESPONSIBLE FOR ESTABLISHING A GOOD COINAGE OF PENNIES THERE.

18L

ANOTHER OF ALFRED'S PENNIES. EARLIEST ISSUES BORE HIS PORTRAIT AND THE MONOGRAM OF THE CITY OF LONDON, TO COMMEMORATE ESTABLISHMENT OF A GARRISON THERE. REVERSE SHOWS THE MONEYER'S NAME.

ARTIFACTS FROM THE EARLY CHRISTIAN PERIOD IN ENGLAND

19

EARLY DRINKING GLASS FOUND IN A CHRISTIAN CEMETERY IN BUCKINGHAMSHIRE.

20

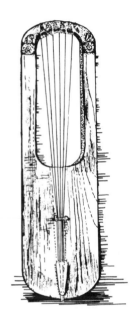

ANGLO-SAXON LYRE OF THE TYPE FOUND AT THE SUTTON HOO SHIP BURIAL (C. A.D. 650).

21

BRONZE BUCKET, ABOUT **9** INCHES HIGH, FOUND IN OXFORDSHIRE IN **1847**.

22

BRONZE BOWL, SHOWING INFLUENCE OF ROMAN ART, DISCOVERED IN KENT IN **1843**.

ST PATRICK'S BELL, NOW PRE-
SERVED IN THE NATIONAL LIBRARY,
DUBLIN.

23

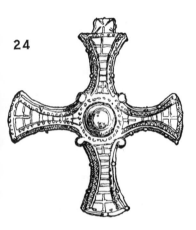

24

ST CUTHBERT'S CROSS. A PECTORAL
CROSS OF GOLD SET WITH GARNETS.
THE TECHNIQUE USED IS SIMILAR TO
THAT IN JEWELRY FROM SUTTON HOO.
THIS RELIC WAS FOUND INSIDE ST
CUTHBERT'S COFFIN, AND REPRESENTS
ANGLO-SAXON JEWELRY AT ITS FINEST.

25

ST CUTHBERT'S COFFIN. THIS ORIGINAL WOOD COFFIN WAS DECORATED WITH
CARVINGS OF THE TWELVE APOSTLES, THE VIRGIN AND CHILD, AND THE SEVEN
ARCHANGELS. IT IS NOW HOUSED IN A PLACE OF HONOR EAST OF THE HIGH ALTAR IN
DURHAM CATHEDRAL.

26

St Laurence Church, Bradford-on-Avon (Wiltshire). In Victorian times it was first identified as being of Anglo-Saxon design from the early 8th century and claimed to be the oldest such church in England. A more recent assessment places its construction in the 10th century on what was probably the site of an earlier chapel founded by St Aldhelm.

Restenneth Priory Church, Angus, is an example of early Anglo-Saxon architecture in Scotland. The lower part of the tower, with arched doorway, was built by Northumbrian masons after A.D. 710 for the Pictish king, Nichtan (or Nechtan II).

This picture of King David, taken from an early English psalter, shows a type of regal costume from the late Anglo-Saxon period (note the cross-gartering), along with the clothes worn by musicians and jugglers of the court.

29

An Old English huntsman from an early manuscript. The style here is less elaborate or sophisticated than the previous illustration, reflecting the difference in subject matter.

30

SKETCH OF A 9TH-CENTURY GOLD AND NIELLO RING FOUND NEAR SHERBURN, YORKSHIRE. INSIDE IT BEARS THE INSCRIPTION 'EATHELSWITH REGINA' AND REFERS TO THE QUEEN OF MERCIA, SISTER OF ALFRED THE GREAT.

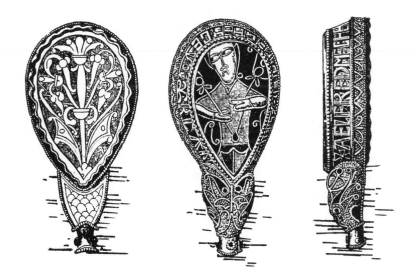

31

THE ALFRED JEWEL FOUND IN 1693 NEAR ATHELNEY, DEPICTING 'SIGHT', ONE OF THE FIVE SENSES. CARVED AROUND ITS PERIMETER IN LATIN IS THE MOTTO 'ALFRED ORDERED ME TO BE MADE'. THE JEWEL IS MADE OF ROCK CRYSTAL OVER CLOISONNE ENAMEL SET IN GOLD.

32

Statue of Alfred the Great at Wantage, erected to celebrate the millenary and location of Alfred's birth. This statue was the work of Count Gleichen, a relation of Queen Victoria. As there were no likenesses of Alfred, aside from stylized portraits on coins, Count Gleichen used a local landowner, Lord Wantage, as his model.

CHAPTER TEN

Northerners Ascendant

1

RAEDWALD'S MOST IMPORTANT ACT WAS HIS HARBOURING A FUGITIVE FROM THE NORTH. Edwin was a prince of Deira. A Bernician effort to bring Deira under control, perhaps Aethelfrith's or perhaps an earlier one, forced him into exile. He is said to have found haven with the king of Gwynedd, a defection to the other side which could have planted ideas at the Welsh court about splitting the Angles. If it did, the results were one day to be fatal to Edwin himself.

In his twenties he wandered on from place to place, coming at last to East Anglia, where Raedwald received him hospitably. Aethelfrith at this time was supreme throughout the north. He had married Edwin's sister Acha, apparently as his second wife, since Bebba was the first. Mistrusting his brother-in-law as a pretender and a menace, he sent envoys offering Raedwald a bribe to put Edwin to death. When they returned with a refusal, Aethelfrith assumed that the East Anglian king was merely holding out for more, and offered a larger bribe coupled with a threat of attack. At this third attempt Raedwald gave way, and decided either to kill Edwin or to hand him over to Aethelfrith's envoys. Warned by a friend, it is said, Edwin passed an anxious night, in which he had a half-waking dream about a visitant who promised him rescue and good fortune if he pledged himself to obey a man who, in some unspecified future, would lay a hand on his head. Without understanding, Edwin gave the pledge. His friend reappeared and told him that Raedwald's wife had persuaded the king to honour his obligation as Edwin's protector. This was the same queen who persuaded Raedwald to compromise on Christianity. She seems to have been a strong-willed 'good pagan'.

Raedwald, now Bretwalda, dismissed the northern envoys and raised an army to restore Edwin. Aethelfrith, taken by surprise, was routed and killed on the east bank of the Idle. So ended his long career of triumph. His sons fled into exile among the Picts and the Scots of Argyll. In Dalriada, as the little Scottish kingdom was called, three of them were taught Christianity by spiritual heirs of Patrick. These were Eanfrith, Oswald and Oswy.

In 617 Edwin established himself in Deira and quickly gained control of the entire Northumbrian realm. Then he began extending it. He annexed the vestigial British state of Elmet in south-west Yorkshire; its last ruler, Ceretic, died in 619. He pushed his northern frontier towards the Firth of Forth, smashing Manau Guotodin too, or possibly displacing Picts who had already done so. Edinburgh is sometimes alleged to have been named after him, but as the British Din Eydin it is older.

After the death of Raedwald, towards 625, Edwin was his natural successor as Bretwalda — the fifth. East Anglia recognized him almost at once. With a Northumbrian moving into this role, the confinement of Bretwaldaship to Anglo-Saxondom south of the Humber came to an end. Edwin, however, limited its scope in another way. Kent counted as an ally and not a vassal. This privilege was linked with his marrying a Kentish princess, Aethelburga, Aethelbert's daughter. Her brother Eadbald, now king of Kent, had renounced Christianity but been reconverted by Archbishop Laurentius. Aethelburga was also a Christian. Eadbald raised difficulties about his sister's marriage to a heathen. Edwin assured him that she could practise her religion freely, and that he would give thought to it himself.

In the summer of 625 she arrived in Northumbria with her chaplain Paulinus, newly made a bishop at Canterbury. Paulinus is one of the few persons in this period for whom we have even the sketchiest of descriptions. He was tall, slightly bent, with black hair and an aquiline nose and a gaunt, ascetic face. He came hoping to win converts, but at first made no impression. Then a public crisis gave him an opening. In 626 the West Saxon king Cwichelm, who resented Edwin's claim to overlordship, sent an agent named Eumer to murder him. On Easter Day Eumer found the king and queen at a country-seat by the Yorkshire Derwent. Edwin was preoccupied with his wife's approaching motherhood. Eumer obtained an audience by pretending to have a message from Cwichelm, and then rushed at the king with a dagger. A courtier sprang to interpose, Edwin was only slightly wounded, and the assassin was seized.

The same night Aethelburga gave birth to a daughter, safely and with little pain. Paulinus declared that although the king had prayed for her to the old gods, it was her own God who had answered. Edwin consented to have the child baptized. He added that he would lead a punitive expedition against Cwichelm, and if it was successful he would listen to Paulinus's teaching with favour. It was very successful indeed. He beat the West Saxons, killing several of their regional sub-kings. The victory confirmed him as the fifth Bretwalda.

On the religious issue, however, he still wavered and said he needed fuller instruction. The Pope, Boniface V, wrote to him urging him to abandon his idols, and also wrote to Aethelburga urging her to influence him. The importance of royal wives in conversion, either towards Christianity (as with Aethelbert) or away from it (as with Raedwald), is a notable feature of the time. The decisive moment is said to have come when Paulinus laid a hand upon Edwin's head and asked him if he remembered that sign. Edwin recalled his vision, and accepted that he must do as Paulinus bade him. It may be suspected that he had told Aethelburga about it and she had passed the word to her chaplain.

Early in 627 Edwin summoned a council to debate the proposed change. It met at Goodmanham, just north-east of Market Weighton. Here the gods of the Angles had a temple. Their high priest Coifi remarked that as they had never been kind to him, their loyal servant, he was willing to try an alternative. Another councillor drew the famous parallel between human life and the flight of a sparrow through a firelit hall in winter: darkness before, darkness after. A doctrine which could shine a ray into the darkness deserved attention. When others had concurred, Coifi invited Paulinus to address the meeting. Then, pronouncing himself satisfied, he mounted a stallion and took up weapons — thus breaking taboos laid on him as high priest — and profaned the temple by casting a spear into it. Having made that symbolic gesture he ordered it to be burnt down.

On Easter Day, 12 April, Edwin and his nobles were baptized at York in a makeshift church of timber, afterwards enclosed in a stone basilica. Paulinus became the first bishop of York. The royal couple took him to their Bernician residence at Old Yeavering by Kirknewton. There he preached to large crowds of commoners, and baptized them in the Glen, a tributary of the Till. Old Yeavering is below the hill-fort Yeavering Bell. Its site is windswept and cheerless, and may have been chosen because of a pre-existing British centre. Excavation has revealed that the builders employed British techniques and Roman measurements. The chief structure was an aisled timber hall nearly a hundred feet long. Around it were smaller buildings and, in Edwin's time, a church, which was possibly an adapted temple. Fire damage caused several reconstructions. Outside was a curved wooden grandstand with several hundred seats, rising tier above tier like a segment of a Roman theatre, with a dais for speakers at the foot. This would have been used for public meetings, and here, surely, Paulinus preached.

A tantalizing footnote to the conversion of the Northumbrians is a Welsh claim that a bishop from Rheged, Rhun, had a major share in it. He may have come forward in belated response to the appeals of Augustine and Laurentius. The populace remained largely of British stock, and many may have been lapsed Christians rather than pagans.

Paulinus conducted a successful mission in Lindsey. In East Anglia Edwin himself persuaded Raedwald's son, Eorpwald, to revert to the faith his father had backed away from. However, East Anglia was not to be retrieved thus. Eorpwald was murdered and several years of reaction ensued. The kingdom's conversion came finally in 631. Its ruler at that time was Sigbert, a brother of Eorpwald. He had become a Christian while an exile in Gaul. His accession was followed by the arrival of a Burgundian bishop, Felix, who reported to the Archbishop of Canterbury and then proceeded to East Anglia. He set up his see at Dunwich. For many years this was a coastal town of importance, but most of it has crumbled into the water. Sigbert, while abroad, had been impressed by Frankish education, and he founded a boys' school staffed by masters whom Felix imported from Canterbury. Some have maintained that this was the germ of the University of Cambridge. The school is more likely to have been at Dunwich. Sigbert was popular, and had proved himself in the conventional way as a warrior, but preferred study and the religious life to kingship. He not only founded a monastery but abdicated and retired to it himself.

During his reign a learned Irish missionary named Fursey came to the East Anglian court. Sigbert made him welcome and gave him land for a monastery of his own at Burgh Castle near Yarmouth. Whatever the truth about Bishop Rhun of Rheged, here at least we begin to encounter a Celtic factor in the Christianization of Anglo-Saxondom. Because of King Edwin, though against his intentions, this was to appear after his death in Northumbria as well.

Edwin's conversion had not checked his aggrandizement of the kingdom. Men like the pragmatic Coifi, and others who were not so pragmatic, regarded it as proof of divine favour. He even extended a protectorate over the Cymry. When he went ceremonially on foot, a standard of Roman type called a *tufa* was carried before him as the emblem of Bretwaldaship. It took the form of an upright spear surmounted by a winged globe. Later generations were to look back on his reign as a brief golden age. In the words of a proverbial saying, a woman could carry her newborn child from sea to sea without fear. A king was expected to maintain order and enforce justice, and Edwin did those things unusually well. But he did more, being credited, for instance, with a pioneer measure of public welfare, the provision of brass bowls attached to posts near springs of clear water, so that wayfarers could drink in comfort. Perhaps it is the highest tribute paid to any early king of the English that the bowls were not stolen.

From 630 to 632 Edwin was busy occupying Anglesey and the Isle of Man. In the course of his operations he besieged Cadwallon, the king of Gwynedd, on Puffin Island off Anglesey's east tip. But by seizing Anglesey itself, with the kingdom's chief royal seat at Aberffraw, he ventured too far. When all seemed to be over, Cadwallon, who was descended from the redoubtable Maelgwn, launched a staggering counter-thrust. This was the one great Welsh *revanche*, the one bid to recover Lloegyr. He recaptured Anglesey and burst out of Wales into Northumbria, with a prince of the Angles, the Mercian Penda, as his subject ally. Edwin had returned, and stationed an army in the way, but without effect. On 12 October 633 the allies routed and killed him at Hatfield Chase near Doncaster. One of his sons also perished. Another surrendered to the Mercian, who imprisoned him and put him to death.

Cadwallon had triumphed partly by setting the English against each other, and it looked as if their divisions would soon go further. Under his blow Deira and Bernicia fell momentarily apart again. A cousin of Edwin, Osric, assumed the crown of Deira, while the eldest son of Aethelfrith, Eanfrith, returned from his Scottish exile to take Bernicia. Both were nominal Christians, both apostatized. Cadwallon of course was himself a Christian, by inheritance and not conversion. However, his ally Penda was a pagan, and the Welshman advanced to ravage Northumbria with a fury which undermined Christianity in the most deadly way — by discredit. Showing no sign of statesmanship, he threw the north into an anarchy that deprived him of support from its Cymric inhabitants. His sole aim was to exterminate the English of both sexes and all ages. Edwin's widow Aethelburga escaped, fleeing to Kent with several royal children and Edwin's treasure. Paulinus accompanied the party, leaving his church in York in the charge of James, a deacon and specialist in plainsong, who remained quietly at his post with a faithful few. Edwin's severed head, retrieved from the battle, was subsequently enshrined there.

Cadwallon's contempt for the two kinglets of the north was total. He surprised a force with which Osric of Deira was foolishly counterattacking, and annihilated the entire body with its leader. Then Eanfrith of Bernicia came to parley with him, displaying even more foolishness by bringing an escort of only twelve. The interview was fatal. Meanwhile Cadwallon's regime of frightfulness continued. It probably included the destruction of the royal complex at Yeavering, and with it the only Christian centre in Bernicia.

However, by his treatment of Eanfrith he overreached himself. In 634 Eanfrith's more capable brother Oswald, known to the Welsh as Oswald White-blade, arrived with a small but loyal army. He found the enemy near Hexham, just south of Hadrian's Wall. Oswald, during his own exile, had been converted by monks of St Columba's Iona community. During the night he set up a wooden cross on the field. At dawn he attacked Cadwallon's host and dispersed it. Cadwallon himself fell in the battle. The place was afterwards called Heavenfield and attracted many pilgrims. Splinters of Oswald's cross, which remained standing, were prized as relics and credited with healing powers, as was the moss which grew on it.

Oswald was thirty. As Aethelfrith's son and Edwin's nephew, he reunited Northumbria without trouble, completed the occupation of the Edinburgh area, and was acknowledged as the sixth Bretwalda. With the Welsh threat nullified, he was the first to be paramount in an England which had no doubts overhanging it, though many years were still to pass before anyone gave it that actual name. He made two punitive assaults on the Welsh. New rulers in Gwynedd and Strathclyde were amenable, so Edwin's protectorate over his Celtic neighbours revived. Meanwhile Oswald was concerning himself with the religious issue. Since he ascribed his success to the help of the Christian God, he wished to make Northumbria irreversibly Christian. Paulinus's mission had never had time to take full effect. Now, moreover, a fresh obstacle had arisen. A British Christian king, like Ceredig of Dumbarton in St Patrick's time, had dealt a traumatic shock to neophytes of another race.

James, Paulinus's deacon, was still in York, but Oswald seems to have had no use for him except as a music teacher. Instead he sent to his friends in Iona. A Scottish bishop soon arrived. He was rigid and austere, unwilling to adapt himself to his audience. When the English refused to listen, he went back grumbling that they were 'an uncivilized people of an obstinate and barbarous temperament'. The Iona community tried again with a much better choice, the tactful and kindly ascetic Aidan. With royal approval, he and his companions made their home on the island of Lindisfarne. Oswald travelled about with him, interpreting his sermons, since the king was fluent in Gaelic but the saint at first was halting in Anglo-Saxon.

Aidan was the only adequate retort to Cadwallon. He made converts by example. He and his fellow-monks, and others who came after them, won people over by simple, humble and charitable lives. The Christianity of the north blended the best of Celtic and Anglo-Saxon ways. It was democratic in spirit, it gave women a high place, it was active and effective without a too-powerful hierarchy. For a while the court of the sixth Bretwalda eclipsed Canterbury as the Christian headquarters of Anglo-Saxondom. Stories of Bishop Aidan, and the king's friendship with him, were lovingly passed on. Once, it is said, they were at dinner together. A silver dish full of food was placed before Oswald, when his almoner came in and reported a gathering of the poor outside. Oswald told him to take the dish out to them, distribute the food, and break up the dish itself so that a piece of silver could be given to each. Aidan clasped his right hand and said, 'May this hand never perish!' After the king's death, his right arm with the hand was enshrined at Bamburgh in a silver casket, and remained uncorrupted.

2

In 635 Oswald was present at the baptism of Cynegils, king of Wessex. The apostle of the West Saxons was Birinus, a mysterious prelate, possibly Irish, sent from Italy by Pope Honorius I. The Pope's action might have been construed as bypassing Canterbury. He seems to have intended Birinus to go outside its jurisdiction, perhaps to Dumnonia. However, when the papal missionary reached Wessex he elected to stay there. His mission prospered. Oswald adopted Cynegils as his godson and married his daughter. The two monarchs sponsored an episcopal see at Dorchester-on-Thames, which was the chief town of the West Saxons.

Then the balance began to shift as Mercia recovered. Cadwallon's ally Penda was now its king, still heathen, still predatory. Disputing Northumbrian suzerainty over East Anglia, which he hoped to bring within his own orbit, he inverted the arrangement of 633 by attaching a subsidiary Welsh corps to his army. The Welshmen came from a petty state, a dependency of Powys in Shropshire, where the Roman town of Wroxeter had survived to an unusual extent, remodelled in timber for a British population. They were led by their prince Cynddylan. With his combined force Penda challenged Northumbria again. On 5 August 642 Oswald came to meet it in northern Shropshire, and was defeated and killed. Oswestry, Oswald's 'tree' or cross, is named after him, doubtless because the battle was fought thereabouts, and he set up a cross as he did before his Hexham battle. If so, it is a sign of progress since Edwin that the emblem's apparent failure on this occasion was not seen as refuting his religion. He was accounted a saint and martyr, and was reported to have died praying for the souls of his men.

His brother Oswy, the last of Aethelfrith's sons, succeeded to the crown of Northumbria. He had to cope with an invasion by the triumphant Penda before he was allowed to reign in semi-peace. Whatever the virtues of his deceased brother, the new king was by no means a saint. He permitted a relative of Edwin named Oswin to govern Deira, and then, after a spell of co-existence, tried to suppress him. Oswin had no desire for a futile struggle, and went to stay unobtrusively with a friend, who betrayed him. Thereupon Oswy had him executed. The crime aroused all the more disgust as Oswin was a man of high character, and a good friend of the beloved Aidan. Reputedly he gave Aidan one of his best horses and did not complain when the saint gave it to a beggar . . . or, at any rate, complained only briefly. Aidan foresaw that Oswin would not survive long in the milieu where his birth had placed him, and was so depressed when this foreboding was fulfilled that he died himself soon afterwards, on 31 August 651. Oswy evinced repentance. He endowed a monastery in atonement at Gilling, the scene of the execution, near Richmond in Yorkshire.

Penda meanwhile had pursued his martial adventures. Soon after withdrawing from Northumbria he made his bid for power over East Anglia. Its king, Aecgric, successor of the popular Sigbert, was no match for him. A deputation waited on Sigbert in his monastic retirement and begged him to come out and hearten the troops. On his declining they dragged him to the battlefield. He refused to bear arms, and confronted Penda's host carrying only a stick. The Mercians charged, Sigbert and Aecgric were both killed. This invasion was not a conquest. Penda raised no objection to the East Angles having another king, so long as he was compliant. The new one was called Anna, a male name among the English, who were not yet adopting saints' names from the calendar.

About 645 Penda turned on Wessex. Its Christian ruler Cynegils had recently died. His son and successor Cenwalh had remained pagan and married Penda's sister. Most imprudently Cenwalh divorced her to marry someone else. Penda treated this affront as a *casus belli* and marched into Wessex, occupying a large part of it. Cenwalh fled to East Anglia, where King Anna's court was firmly Christian. During a three-year exile he was baptized. Penda, deciding that Anna was not compliant enough, returned with another army and killed him too, installing his brother Aethelhere, who reigned as Penda's subject ally. Cenwalh managed to get back to Wessex unscathed and asked Agilbert, a bishop from Gaul, to reorganize the Church.

Oswy showed his penitence for the death of Aidan not only by religious benefaction but by trying to convert the king of Essex, another Sigbert. The East Saxons had been relapsed pagans for a long time. Sigbert, however, was friendly with Oswy and often visited Northumbria. Oswy urged him to smash his idols. In 653 Sigbert yielded, and was baptized at the royal village of Atwall or Walton. After he went home, Oswy sent missionaries to the East Saxons under the leadership of Cedd, a monk of Lindisfarne, brother of the more famous St Chad.

Then Penda began stirring again. He was the last major standard-bearer of the old gods, surrounded by Christian kings on all his frontiers. Only Sussex was untouched, and Sussex carried little weight. The new faith, moreover, was biting deeper. In Kent it was now the only authorized religion. Penda's aggressions may have been a sort of counter-attack, a pagan crusade, but it is hard to be sure. In Mercia he did not persecute or forbid preaching. Nor did he veto the conversion of his son Peada, who governed the Middle Angles, even though Peada had agreed to it as the price of a marriage to Oswy's daughter, and even though the baptism took place at Walton under the Northumbrian's auspices. Penda asserted that his only animus was against those who professed Christianity but did not observe its precepts. His experience of Cadwallon may have soured him. Whether because he saw his opponent Oswald as a fraud of this kind, or out of pure vindictiveness, he had had the corpse's head and arms cut off and impaled on oaken stakes.

He made two attacks on Northumbria in addition to the one following Oswald's death. In either the first or the second of the three, he reached Bamburgh and laid siege to it. Repulsed, he tore down the houses in the neighbourhood and used the wood to fuel an enormous fire, hoping that the flames and smoke would be blown over the citadel. At first they were, but according to legend St Aidan (who was then still living) saw the conflagration from Farne Island and exclaimed, 'Lord, see what evil Penda does!' — whereupon the wind changed. In one of these expeditions Penda swept through to the Firth of Forth, where he made a princely distribution of spoils to his followers.

The third attack was in 655. Penda entered Northumbria with an immense army. It comprised thirty contingents under eminent leaders, including his client king of the East Angles, a renegade northern prince, and some Welshmen. This invasion was more than a raid. Penda announced his intention of crushing Northumbria altogether, and spurned Oswy's attempts to buy him off. Oswy made a vow that if he could drive the enemy out he would endow twelve more monasteries, and place his infant daughter Elfleda in a convent, as a virgin dedicated to God. On 15 November the Northumbrians fought the Mercian horde by a river known as the Winwaed, near Leeds. Oswy was victorious. Owing to heavy rain the river had flooded, and more Mercians were drowned in flight than were killed in the battle. Most of their commanders fell including Penda himself. Whatever he really stood for, it expired. His only lasting memorial may be the word 'penny', which has been explained as meaning 'Penda's coin' from his minting the first.

Oswy duly endowed his monasteries, six in Deira, six in Bernicia. Elfleda grew up to accept her destiny. She was entrusted to St Hilda, Abbess of Hartlepool. When Hilda took charge of a new community at Whitby, the princess went through her novitiate there and remained till her death at sixty. Whitby was a double foundation on the Celtic plan, with inmates of both sexes under female headship. Caedmon, the first named poet in English, was one of its lay-brothers in Hilda's time. Elfleda and her mother became joint abbesses, and several members of the Northumbrian royal house were buried within the precinct.

After the Mercian débâcle, Oswy was more or less generally acknowledged as the seventh Bretwalda, the third Northumbrian to hold that position. He tried to rule Mercia directly, while northern priests carried out its evangelization, setting up a diocese which was to be centred on Lichfield and governed by St Chad. Penda's son Peada worked with the new regime as a sub-king in the southern part of Mercia, but was assassinated. In 658 the Midland nobles rebelled and enthroned Wulfhere, another of Penda's sons. Oswy acquiesced. Wulfhere was a Christian and did not revive the anti-Northumbrian vendetta.

About this time Penda's Welsh ally Cynddylan apparently perished in a clash with a band of Angles. It is not certain who they were. The Welsh enclave in Shropshire became part of Mercia. Wales was reduced within roughly its present borders, and the passing of Penda blotted out the last faint hope of regaining ground through Cadwallon's policy of pitting the English against each other. This point in history is marked by a poet's elegy on Cynddylan and his companion-in-arms Elvan.

> Cynddylan's hall is dark tonight,
> There burns no fire, no bed is made,
> I weep awhile, and then am quiet.
>
> Cynddylan's hall is dark tonight,
> No fire is lit, no candle burns,
> God will keep me sane.
>
> Cynddylan's hall. It pierces me
> To see it roofless, fireless.
> Dead is my lord, and I am yet alive.
>
> Cynddylan's hall is desolate tonight
> Where once I sat in honour.
> Gone are the men who held it, gone the women.
>
> Cynddylan's hall. Dark is its roof
> Since the English destroyed
> Cynddylan, and Elvan of Powys.

With the small principality erased, the field where King Oswald died was securely English ground. Thanks to the growing tradition of his heroism and holiness, miracles were said to be worked by earth from the spot where he had fallen. So much was taken away by pilgrims that the site was soon identifiable by a pit. Oswy favoured the cult. He retrieved his brother's head and arms from the stakes where Penda had transfixed them, and took the arms to Bamburgh and the head to the church on Lindisfarne. Oswald was thus enshrined at both the main centres of Northumbria, the royal and the ecclesiastical, and his uncorrupted right hand at Bamburgh recalled the tale of his gift to the poor. The rest of his remains were eventually conveyed to Bardney Abbey in Lincolnshire and entombed there. With the

Shropshire place of pilgrimage in addition, his cult flourished and became popular. Even splinters from Penda's stakes came to count as relics, and were dropped in water to give them curative powers. Veneration of Oswald spread through the British Isles, Germany and Switzerland, where the English king is the patron saint of Zug.

3

Another result of Penda's death was that Cenwalh of Wessex no longer felt threatened from the Midlands. He was free to advance his frontier at the expense of the 'West Welsh' of Dumnonia. They still held central Somerset. In 658 he drove them back to the River Parrett. The chief prize of this campaign was Glastonbury. There Cenwalh made a momentous and symbolic decision. In the marsh-girt cluster of hills surmounted by Glastonbury Tor was the monastery. This was a British foundation, still surviving and even flourishing. Cenwalh treated it reverently and allowed its abbot to stay in charge. Over the next few years he introduced Saxon monks, and appointed a Saxon successor to the abbot, but the changes were advanced gently. The king not only spared Glastonbury, he refrained from violently altering it. In 671 he made it a grant of land.

This was the first and indeed the only instance of a major centre of British Christianity being absorbed into Anglo-Saxon Christianity without a break. The earlier waves of conquest and settlement had effaced the bishoprics of London and other cities, which only reappeared after a long gap and in a new form, as products of the papal mission. Glastonbury, however, was so far west that the effacement never happened. It simply went on, and passed from the old possessors to the new after the latter had become Christian themselves and left their phase of total unsympathy behind. Here alone was a visible continuity.

Continuity of what? The most remarkable feature of the place was a building, around which a body of legend was to gather. It was a plain monastic church, sixty feet long by twenty-six feet wide, made of wattlework reinforced with timber and perhaps a lead roof. Its dedication, then almost unparalleled in Britain, was to the Virgin Mary. All the indications are that it had stood on

201

the spot for a long time — so long that it was already called the Old Church — and no trustworthy records or traditions stated how it had come to be there. In later years, stories were to be written down about the church having been planted miraculously by God himself, or built by disciples of Christ, Joseph of Arimathea being the favoured candidate. No one knows when these stories began to be told, or whether the monks of Cenwalh's day already held such beliefs.

We have a possible clue, if an oblique one, in Gildas more than a century before them. He is supposed to have lived for a while at Glastonbury, and he may have done so. At least he shows signs of an acquaintance with it. In his onslaught on Constantine of Dumnonia as an oath-breaker and murderer, he speaks of the king as having committed his crime disguised as an abbot, and in a church. To make the sacrilege worse, Constantine had taken his oath with the saints to witness and the *genetrix*, 'mother', presumably the Mother of Christ. Nennius uses the same word when he speaks of Arthur winning a victory by Mary's aid. Gildas, then, seems to allude to a monastic church in Dumnonia and to the practice of the Marian *cultus*. These particulars would point to the Old Church at Glastonbury, so he may well have known it.

Now we can fairly juxtapose that fact with another thing he says — that the Christian faith was first brought to Britain during the first century A.D., soon after Boudicca. With his habitual avoidance of helpful detail he does not say who brought it, or where. But he could be thinking of a story of early Christians at Glastonbury, which already existed in some form, and was told him by the monks. When the West Saxons arrived, such a story would have had time to improve. Certainly an idea of Glastonbury as uniquely sacred and important was established long before the Norman Conquest. Some of the greatest British saints — Patrick and David, for instance — were said to have come as visitors, even residents. Paulinus, too, was said to have made a vast detour on his travels to see the Old Church. According to the monks, Paulinus was responsible for the lead roof-covering.

The problem of Glastonbury's origin cannot be solved with present knowledge. In the early centuries A.D. there was much more water round about. At times it would have been almost an island. Finds at two Celtic lake-villages show that this area was a centre of the La Tène culture. Recent years have brought a gradual accumulation of evidence that the Tor was a numinous hill to pre-Christian inhabitants and a focus of myths about the Otherworld. If so, the sacred character of the place is thousands of years old, and the continuity is more than a purely Christian one. As for the Christian presence itself, this may, in some form, be very ancient. The Old Church may have marked a spot which was hallowed in Christian eyes almost indefinitely early. But the monastery cannot be dated farther back than the advent of monasticism in north-west Europe under the auspices of St Martin of Tours. Nor were churches dedicated to Mary before the fifth century. The fifth century is possible, though the community may not have lived at first on the site where Cenwalh found it, and where the abbey ruins stand today. This whole question is bedevilled by legend, bogus history and spurious documents.

Cenwalh's conduct at any rate was statesmanlike. In the words of a Somerset historian, he made Glastonbury a temple of reconciliation between Saxons and Britons, where, for the first time, they worked together in a respected institution. Here in a token sense, long before its political realization, the United Kingdom was born. Glastonbury attracted Irish as well. Hemgisl, who became abbot in 678, had studied in Ireland. Irishmen who joined the community and conducted its school promoted the lore of its early saints, especially some who could attract pilgrims from their own country. They also improved on it, even claiming that St Patrick was buried in the Old Church, and exhibiting his tomb. Texts of the ninth and tenth centuries speak of the place as 'Glastonbury of the Gaels', to which they 're-sorted' as to a sanctuary of their own.

That phase was finally superseded under the abbacy of St Dunstan in 943. Glastonbury grew into a Benedictine house on the grand scale, a centre of cultural fusion for the peoples of the British Isles, and a literary fountainhead during the Middle Ages, making a rich contribution to the Arthurian Legend. Its far-off Christian beginnings became involved with the story of the Holy Grail. Arthur himself was said to have come there to save Guinevere from an abductor; this was the first form of a romantic episode in which her rescuer is Sir Lancelot. Arthur was also said to have been buried there, a claim challenging the belief that the king's fate was unknown and his grave a riddle. In 1191 the monks dug in their graveyard and produced what were asserted to be Arthur's bones, with an inscribed cross identifying them. This event raises complicated issues. If the original Arthur was a king whose career ended in Burgundy, the grave seems unlikely to have been authentic. But the finds of archaeology, and certain peculiarities about the inscription, suggest that it was not simply a twelfth-century fake and that the cross and other objects had a more mysterious provenance.

4

Soon after Cenwalh's gesture at Glastonbury, King Oswy presided over another act of unity, though this one was not so amicable. The part played by Iona in his people's conversion had meant that the Church in the dominant northern kingdom was still under a strong Celtic influence, and committed to observances which were non-Roman. A similar difficulty had arisen through every part of the British Isles outside the range of Canterbury. The Celtic Church had never broken with Rome, or challenged the primacy of the See of Peter, or embraced doctrines opposed to Catholicism. But its long semi-isolation had led to divergences. In some cases the Celts had changed, in others they had failed to adopt Roman changes.

The conflict reached a crisis over two issues. One was the method of fixing Easter. The persistence of Celtic practice meant that the most holy day of the year was kept on different dates in different places. Even Christians living in the same area might disagree. The other issue was the shape of the priestly tonsure. Clerics under Roman discipline shaved a round patch on top of the head. Celts shaved the front of the head from ear to ear.

Both disputes sound like mere procedural squabbles. However, the clash over Easter had practical importance. Pilgrims might make a long journey to a shrine only to find that the ceremonies were over. Or neighbouring Christians might observe different Lenten fasts, so that one group was feasting while the other was still condemned to hunger. This problem was acute in the highest Northumbrian circles. The deacon James, who had stayed in York when Paulinus left, was still alive and had formed a cell keeping the Roman Easter. Oswy's queen, whose chaplain was Kentish, did likewise together with her attendants at court. Oswy himself did not, nor did most of his subjects.

Beyond these manifest problems, the two points of dissension were rallying-cries in a deeper conflict of attitudes. The Roman party insinuated a dark symbolism in the Celtic tonsure by calling it the 'tonsure of Simon Magus', Simon being the magician denounced by St Peter in *Acts* 8, reputed founder of the multifarious heresy known as Gnosticism. The Celts made no serious attempt to rebut this charge. They defended their Easter reckoning by appealing to a tradition supposedly handed down from the apostle John. That too, however, might be viewed as suspect, because there was something a shade elusive and off-beat about John. In the Fourth Gospel (21:15-23), while Christ entrusts his flock to Peter, he seems to reserve John for some other task.

The Celts palpably stood for a Christianity of their own. It was not heretical, but it was less formal and patriarchal, less tightly administered, simpler, plainer. It was less subject to censorship: the Celts read apocryphal books which Rome tried to suppress. Also, as remarked before, it was less dismissive of pre-Christian myths and beliefs. The Irish, for instance, were reluctant to shed the idea of reincarnation. An early poem even equates St Brigit with the Mother of Christ. Celtic Christians thought in less black-and-white terms than Roman ones. Poets and story-tellers, if not priests, continued for centuries to adopt the old gods as heroes and heroines, and to evoke a world where enchantment could be benign and even angels could be ambiguous.

For many seventh-century Christians the conflict took on a bitterness out of proportion to the nominal issues. With those of British stock, centuries of warfare and dispossession had made it worse. Some of the Welsh turned Celtic Christianity into a xenophobic patriotism. When Christians of Roman loyalty came among them, they forced the strangers to do penance for forty days, refused to take meals with them, and scoured the dishes after the papists had eaten. Bede claims that when Cadwallon overran Northumbria in 633, his savagery was all the more unrestrained because for him Paulinus's converts did not count as Christians.

That was an extreme view, and it softened somewhat with the passage of time. In the Celtic lands generally — Ireland, Scotland, ultimately Wales itself — the main problems were adjusted by regional steps over many years, without set-piece confrontations. The northern Picts, whose Christianity had come from Iona, complied with the rest. By the early eighth century papal authority was plainly winning, though still far from prevailing everywhere, or enforcing uniformity.

In Northumbria, however, the disagreements had led to such difficulties that a confrontation did occur. Oswy insisted on favouring Celtic usages, in spite of his wife, or perhaps because of her. But a son of his was under the spell of Wilfrid, the abbot of Ripon, a learned cleric of Roman education and fiercely Roman convictions. Family pressure induced Oswy to summon a conference. It met in 663 at St Hilda's abbey of Whitby, where Oswy's daughter Elfleda, dedicated to God after the victory over Penda, was now about nine years old. The king took the chair. The Celtic case was presented by Colman, a monk from Iona who had joined the Lindisfarne community and was now primate of Northumbria. Agilbert, Cenwalh's bishop, led the Romanist group accompanied by the veteran James. Agilbert was a poor linguist, a shortcoming which was to lead, in Wessex, to his dismissal. Preferring not to rely on Oswy's interpreter, the pro-Celtic Bishop Cedd of the East Saxons, he deputed his task to Wilfrid.

Colman was courteous, Wilfrid domineering. Colman appealed to the long-held customs of the Christians he knew, including St Columba. Wilfrid appealed to the general practice of the Church in Europe, Asia and Africa, and abused the Celts as 'people stupid enough to differ from the whole world'. Colman spoke of the tradition inherited from St John. Wilfrid retorted that John had changed his mind, and unleashed a barrage of calendric technicalities and precedents. How far Oswy followed any of this is open to question. But he understood one thing, that Wilfrid spoke for the Pope, Peter's successor. His opportunity came when Wilfrid quoted the words of Christ: 'Thou art Peter, and upon this rock I will build my Church, and the gates of hell shall not prevail against it, and to thee I will give the keys of the kingdom of heaven.' Oswy turned to Colman and asked:

'Is it true that Our Lord said this to Peter?'

'Yes,' answered Colman.

'Did he say anything like it to Columba?'

'No.'

'Then,' said the king with a slight smile, doubtless relieved at having hit on a way to end the debate, 'I must rule in favour of Peter and obey his orders, or I may get to the gates of heaven and find he has locked me out.'

That concluded the Synod of Whitby. Northumbria conformed to Rome. Colman and his monks refused to accept the ruling, and went back to Iona. There the community held out for another fifty years, unmoved by Oswy's argument. The argument was not forgotten, however, and St Aldhelm of Wessex used it in an attempt to persuade a king of Dumnonia.

All the Christian English were now obedient to Canterbury, as the seat of Roman authority in their island. The ecclesiastical centre of Northumbria was shifted from Aidan's Lindisfarne to Paulinus's York, where, predictably, the bishopric was bestowed on Wilfrid. Together with an artistic and scholarly friend, Benedict Biscop, he began to enrich the life of his diocese in the spirit of continental Catholicism. Wilfrid and Benedict imported books, pictures, relics. They started the construction of larger and finer churches made of stone. The arch-cantor of St Peter's came to England to teach the Roman method of chanting. Masons and glass-workers came from Gaul, and craft schools were founded for Englishmen.

In 669 an erudite Greek, Theodore of Tarsus, became Archbishop of Canterbury. Appointed by the Pope at the age of sixty-six, he had studied in Athens, and profited from a last flowering of art and learning in Syria which preceded the Arab conquest. During his long tenure (he lived to be almost ninety) Theodore unified the Church's administration in England, and gave it a single code of canon law. He met little opposition. However, one of his measures — the division of Northumbria into four dioceses — ironically estranged the arch-Romanist Wilfrid. Wilfrid appealed to Rome and was banished. Even this worked out advantageously for him. About 680 he found his way to Sussex, where the king had been converted under Mercian auspices, and converted the king's subjects. The process begun by Gregory was thereby completed. Or nearly so. The Isle of Wight defied Christianity until 686, and, as will appear, was never actually converted at all.

CHAPTER ELEVEN

Midlanders Ascendant

1

OSWY DIED ON 15 FEBRUARY 670 AND NORTHUMBRIA BEGAN TO FLAG.
While his supremacy had never been challenged in plain terms,
the vigour of Mercia under Wulfhere had weakened it. The main
forward thrust of Oswy's reign had in fact been in the other
direction, at the expense of the Picts and their neighbours.
There he had been successful. But English failure after his death
marked a turning of the tide, and was crucial for the future of
Britain.

The maxim of policy which he bequeathed was, in substance,
that Northumbria need not stop at the Firth of Forth. On the far
side of it was the Pictish heartland. The Picts' recorded history is
scanty and not always convincing. We cannot feel much confidence in the statement that a fifth-century king, Drust son of
Erp, 'reigned a hundred years and fought a hundred battles'.
These are merely poetic clichés meaning that he had a long
reign and was a famous warrior. Still, Drust puts in a more
plausible appearance in Irish annals; he may have been the
instigator of the attacks which induced Vortigern to recruit his
Saxons. In his time the effects of the mission of St Ninian seem to
have dwindled, but under Nectan Morbet, who reigned from 462
to 486, Christianity recovered.

Pictish kingship was a confused institution, because the ancient custom of inheritance through the mother had survived in
this northern land, combined awkwardly with actual government by men only. About 554 it seems that the Picts brought in a
foreigner to be their king. He was Bridei son of 'Maelcon', and
Maelcon is said to have been none other than Maelgwn of
Gwynedd. During a thirty-year reign this part-Welshman extended his power widely, becoming overlord of the Orkneys and
part at least of the Western Highlands and Isles. Meanwhile the
more northerly Picts, those whom the influence of Ninian had

never reached, became Christian also. The principal figure here is St Columba, who made several missionary journeys from Iona. He travelled as far north as Inverness to meet the king, and is said to have rebuked a water-monster which upset a boat on Loch Ness, an incident dear to monster-hunters in the twentieth century. Bridei's reign saw a lively development of Pictish art, with much skilful carving on memorial stones.

South of the Clyde-Forth isthmus there had never been a significant Pictish presence. Early in the seventh century, however, one of Bridei's successors may have overrun the British remnant around Edinburgh. If so, it was a fleeting conquest, soon lost to the advancing Northumbrians. But the main Pictish kingdom north of the Firth continued to flourish. This was the kingdom which Oswy tried to subdue and which confronted his heir as unfinished business.

The situation was made more complex by the two other kingdoms on Northumbria's flank. Between the Clyde and the Solway Firth the Britons of Strathclyde had expanded, taking over some residual scraps of Rheged. Strathclyde too has little recorded history. Its Christianity was doubtless as old as Ninian's church in Galloway, and Dumbarton has been claimed as the birthplace of St Patrick himself, though not with much likelihood. Another saint of the region was Kentigern, otherwise Mungo, who was recalled from exile by King Rhydderch in the latter part of the sixth century, and became the patron of Glasgow. Kentigern is reputed to have had dealings with the wild prophet Lailoken or Myrddin, the proto-Merlin. During the decades after him, Strathclyde was fairly quiet and stable.

Alongside it was the erratic Scottish kingdom of Dalriada. The Scots had been in Kintyre for fully a century and a half. The motive for their original move from Ireland is obscure. It has been suggested that the Clydeside Britons allowed Scots to settle as *foederati* at a time when Pictish energies were threatening the Dumbarton area rather than the south. Towards the close of the sixth century, when the Scots had multiplied and expanded considerably, their king Aedan emerged from his rocky citadel of Dunadd on the Crinan isthmus, and marched in various directions. But his defeat by Aethelfrith in 603 ended his adventures, and after that, according to Bede, 'no king of the Scots ever dared to meet the English in the field'. Aedan's grandson

Domnall did fight the Picts, and looked like a conqueror for a while, but finally failed. Much more important than the campaigns of these Scottish kings were the activities of St Columba and his Iona monks from 563 onwards.

During Oswald's reign the northern peoples had allowed him a courtesy suzerainty and been left alone. Oswy's aim was to make English power tangible. After his Mercian stabilization he crossed the Firth of Forth, killed the Pictish king, and installed a puppet. Most of the Picts were made tributary. So were the Scots. He also killed the king of Strathclyde and installed another puppet, his own brother-in-law (English and Cymric royal families were beginning to intermarry).

Such a political legacy depended on a Bretwaldaship which, towards the close of his reign, was crumbling as Wulfhere grew more powerful. The Mercian king resumed pressure on Wessex and mastered some of his smaller neighbours. He outlived Oswy by five years. On his death Oswy's son and successor Egfrith tried to re-assert Northumbrian overlordship, but was forced in 679 to accept the permanence of his southern border and acquiesce in Mercian control of Lindsey. Meanwhile the Picts had been showing signs of independence under another Bridei, son of one of the kings of Strathclyde. Egfrith turned his back on England and set out to restore the northern arrangements.

In 684, somewhat cryptically, he sent an army to Ireland. It was the first English aggression in that quarter, and for many years the only one. Irish resistance, and protests from his own churchmen, brought the foray to a swift end. In the following year he marched north, rejecting the advice of his councillors and the wise St Cuthbert, whom he had just made bishop of Lindisfarne. The Picts lured him on to Nechtansmere — Dunnichen Moss, just east of Forfar — and pounced. On 20 May 685 the king of Northumbria was routed and slain, and his father's edifice in the north collapsed.

Nechtansmere was the first victory of Caledonia over invasion from England, a precursor of Bannockburn. It made a profound impression. A bizarre by-product, centuries afterwards, was a local transplantation of the Arthurian Legend. The real battle was turned into a clash between Arthur and Modred. Dumbarrow Hill a few miles to the east became Arthur's Seat, like the better-known hill beside Edinburgh, and a legend of Arthur,

Modred and Guinevere overspread the broad valley of Strathmore. Barry Hill near Alyth became Modred's fortress, to which he carried off Guinevere. In this version of her abduction she went all too willingly. On recapturing her, Arthur put her to death for adultery. She was torn apart by stallions. In the eighteenth century a Pictish carved stone in Meigle churchyard was alleged to portray her execution, though actually it portrayed Daniel in the Lions' Den. A farm called Arthur's Fold, a stone called Arthur's Stone, and an Arthurbank, were all located hereabouts. This displacement of one heroic tradition by another, totally different, could apparently happen because the Picts and their folk-memories had passed into oblivion. Nothing lingered but a rooted awareness of a 'battle long ago', which some Arthurian story-teller embroidered after his own fashion.

Shaken by the disaster in Pictland, Northumbria memorably changed course. The new king was Egfrith's scholarly half-brother, Aldfrith. He had studied at Iona under Adomnan, St Columba's biographer, who was abbot of the community. In his twenty-year reign the best talents of the kingdom were steered into the paths of peace. For the church it was a real golden age, productive not only of saints and scholars but of pioneer English missionaries, such as Willibrord, a monk of Wilfrid's Ripon community who spent forty years evangelizing the Frisians in Holland, and founded the see of Utrecht. Women still played a distinguished part despite the movement away from Celtic practice. Music flourished. So, for the first time in Anglo-Saxondom, did verbal and visual arts. Caedmon, as a lay-brother at Whitby, had just made the transition from minstrelsy to literature with his verse paraphrases of scripture. Others made copies of his works and followed in his steps. The old Anglo-Saxon epic *Beowulf* may have been moulded into its final shape at about this time. It was also the period of the Lindisfarne Gospels, written and illustrated by a bishop, bound by another bishop, and enclosed in a jewelled case by a hermit-craftsman. The volume's noble lettering, its scrollwork and animal ornaments and interlacing linear patterns, all show Celtic influence going lustrously on.

A religious project of Oswy's, which he never carried out himself, was adopted by other kings and took them along new paths. It was Oswy's desire to go to Rome as a pilgrim and end his life there, among the holy places. The allure of this idea was strengthened by the example of Sebbi, king of the East Saxons, who, like Sigbert of East Anglia, abdicated and entered the cloister. A king of Mercia and a later king of Northumbria followed his example. Two kings of Wessex, two kings of Mercia, and another member of the East Saxon royal house, actually did what Oswy had dreamed of doing and made a humble ending in Rome.

After Aldfrith's death in 705, the Northumbrian monarchy declined into an age of repellent nonentities. But the Northumbrian civilization which Aldfrith had promoted still had its greatest glories to come. Bede, 'the Venerable', was born in 673 and sent to school at the age of seven, in a monastery founded at Wearmouth by Wilfrid's friend Benedict Biscop. Benedict lived long enough to know the boy personally as a pupil. When he founded a second monastery at Jarrow, Bede was transferred to it. There he became a monk and stayed all his life. His talents and force of personality were displayed early. When only thirteen he reorganized and retrained the choir after most of the experienced choristers had died in a plague. These new houses observed the continental rule of St Benedict, and Benedictine respect for scholarship enabled Bede to spend most of his time in teaching, study and literary work. When Adomnan came to visit his former pupil King Aldfrith, Bede persuaded him to accept Roman usages instead of Celtic. Adomnan tried to win over his diehard brethren at Iona, but their submission was delayed for a few years longer.

Bede was a minor Renaissance in himself. He studied Greek and Hebrew as well as Latin, classical literature as well as ecclesiastical, and history, medicine and astronomy. He compiled commentaries on scripture, composed and translated biographies, and wrote books on versification, spelling and chronology. His masterpiece is the *Historia Ecclesiastica Gentis Anglorum*, best translated a little freely as *A History of the English Church and People*, which supplies most of the documentation of Anglo-Saxondom up to 731. He has defects due to his time and background — a bias against the Britons, a fondness for the would-be edifying and the dubious supernatural. But to compare his book with those of Gildas and Nennius, or with any historical writings in Britain before his time or during several centuries after, is to appreciate his amazing stature.

Bede's character and outlook appear vividly in an eyewitness account of his last illness in 735. To the very end he was toiling at two translations, one from the Gospel of John and one from the Spanish encyclopaedist Isidore of Seville, saying he did not want his students to read anything erroneous. On the last day of his life he was still dictating, and he died a moment after supervising the writing-out of a final sentence. Bede is the only Englishman whom Dante explicitly gives a place in Paradise.

In the year of his death was born another Northumbrian who also achieved European fame. Alcuin was a native of York, and became head of its school. In 781 he met the Frankish king, Charles, better known as Charlemagne, and joined his court at Aix-la-Chapelle. Subsequently he settled at Tours, where he gave a new impetus to education throughout the Frankish domains, and organized a supply of books from England. As a political thinker he had a large share in forming the project of a united Western Christendom, which Charles attempted to realize in 800, and which survived as an ideal through the Middle Ages in the Holy Roman Empire.

2

When Bede wrote his *History,* Northumbria was still independent, but no more than that. Its obscure monarchs had made no attempt to resume power-seeking, and the priests and teachers overshadowed them. In 731 Bede says that 'all the kings south of the Humber are subject to Aethelbald, king of the Mercians'. The only kingdom other than Mercia which might have aspired to Northumbria's lost hegemony was Wessex. Wessex, however, had passed through a similar shift of emphasis, though with sovereigns who had not held the Bretwaldaship for a hundred years the transition was less abrupt.

Having seized central Somerset in 658, Cenwalh paused for a while and then seized a large part of Devon. He also tried to dominate the South Saxons. But he was not left undisturbed. Wulfhere of Mercia attacked him in 661, freeing Sussex and detaching the Isle of Wight from Wessex. When the South Saxon king Aethelwalh was baptized (this was the king under whose aegis Wilfrid converted the populace), the ceremony took place in Mercia. Wulfhere was his godfather and handed over the Isle of Wight as a christening gift. It may have been in Cenwalh's reign, and because of this harassment, that Winchester became the chief royal town of Wessex and an embryonic capital. It was farther away from the Mercians than Dorchester-on-Thames.

Cenwalh died in 672. A phase of internal contention followed, in which his son or grandson Centwine failed to establish himself. Aethelred of Mercia, Wulfhere's successor, attacked again. The rule of the West Saxons passed from Cenwalh's immediate family. A minor prince named Caedwalla became king in 685. He was about twenty-six. His reign was brief but extraordinary. Before his accession he had led a raid on Sussex and slain Aethelwalh. As king he pursued the same aggressive policy, crushing a South Saxon recovery and imposing his own rule. In 686 he moved to recapture the Isle of Wight from the prince who had been in charge of it during the South Saxon annexation, and who now stood alone.

This episode is the one hideous blot on the record of Christian progress among the Anglo-Saxons. The islanders were the last heathen English population. Caedwalla was unbaptized himself, but he vowed that if he conquered the island he would devote a quarter of the land and spoils to the Christian God. Having overrun the island he slaughtered all the inhabitants and replaced them with West Saxon settlers. He kept his vow by handing over a quarter of the land to Wilfrid, who arrived on a well-timed visit and accepted the donation on behalf of the Church. Two brothers of the prince had escaped to the Hampshire mainland. They were betrayed and taken prisoner. Caedwalla, who was convalescing after being wounded in the campaign, sentenced them to death. A priest asked for a stay of execution while he instructed them in the Christian faith. The king consented, the priest instructed them, and they were then put to death.

Soon afterwards Caedwalla experienced a revulsion, perhaps a genuine repentance. He decided to be baptized. He wanted it to happen in Rome, at the shrines of Peter and Paul, and when it was done he wanted to die as quickly as possible. In that state of mind he performed what Oswy had planned. He abdicated after a three-year reign and made his pilgrimage. The baptism took place on Holy Saturday before Easter, in 689. Less than a week later, while still wearing his white baptismal robe, he was taken ill. On 30 April he died. Pope Sergius had him buried with a long verse epitaph telling how he had 'come safely from Britain's distant shores' to gain a heavenly crown.

His successor, Ine, held on to the Sussex dependency, and pursued Cenwalh's forward policy on his western borders. However, the tempo was leisurely. He completed the conquest of Somerset and Devon in 710 and entered Cornwall in 722. Ine was a conqueror with a difference. His Cornish invasion was half-hearted, and the remnant of the Dumnonian kingdom survived for more than a century. Its reduction had never been very important to him. Several of his laws echo Cenwalh's conciliatory action at Glastonbury. His subjects of British stock are given recognized status. Some are clearly men of substance: a 'Welshman' owning five hides of land ranks with the middle grade of Saxon aristocracy, and five hides — in Wessex, hardly less than one-third of a square mile, and perhaps considerably more — would be a fair-sized holding, refuting any notion of dispossession.

Ine enrolled 'Welshmen' in his service, even in his bodyguard, a sign of good relations and trust. He showed his attitude further in his fixing of *wergild*. Among the Anglo-Saxons this was the sum that could be claimed in compensation by the relatives of a man who was killed. It was used to define social standing generally. Thus, the fine for 'breaking and entering' varied according to the *wergild* of the householder. Ine's laws fixed the *wergild* of a free tax-paying Welshman at 120 shillings, as against 200 for a free tax-paying Saxon. It was not equality, but it was recognition. Even Welsh slaves had compensation-value of 50 or 60 shillings and a degree of legal protection.

There is a story that Ine married twice and that one of his wives was a Welsh princess. The point about this is not its truth or otherwise, but the fact that it could be told. Wessex was outstanding among the English kingdoms in its power of absorbing without obliterating. Behind the enigma of the founder Cerdic, with his British name, there may be a racial blending at the source. Caedwalla's name has the same un-English character.

At some stage Ine too underwent a conversion, though it was

not as cataclysmic as Caedwalla's. A nominal Christian, he is said to have been made a sincere one by his wife (that is, his authentic wife) Aethelburga, another queen in the notable succession of king-persuaders. Legend credits her with a practical parable. She and her husband were staying once at a comfortable, well-appointed hunting lodge. After they had left it and gone a few miles, Aethelburga made some excuse to take Ine back. The servants, on her instructions, had thrown the place into chaos, upsetting the furniture, emptying refuse on the floor, and putting a sow in the bed. Ine was horrified. Aethelburga said: 'Take a lesson from this. All earthly delights will pass away.' The author who tells the story says nothing about the views of the servants who had to clean up after she had pointed her moral.

Legend aside, Ine encouraged the best of the Church's activities in Wessex, very much as Aldfrith did in Northumbria. Cenwalh had fostered an atmosphere of goodwill, and been on friendly terms with Benedict Biscop and Archbishop Theodore; Caedwalla had ended his reign and life in a blaze of devotion; and now Ine gave form to the Christian spirit, not only by making enlightened laws, but by promoting education and the monastic order.

While he was growing up, the fountainhead of scholarship in the kingdom had been a school in Selwood Forest, conducted by Mailduibh, an Irish missionary, who also founded Malmesbury. The etymology of 'Malmesbury' is complicated, combining Mailduibh's name with that of Aldhelm, his best pupil, who was abbot from about 683. Aldhelm was related to Ine and became his adviser in Church matters. He was a good choice — an able administrator, a fluent speaker, the architect of a fine if eccentric Anglo-Irish scholarship. He was also a musician and poet, in the vernacular as well as Latin; some of his English verses were known and loved by King Alfred. He also made up riddles. In his priestly apprenticeship he is said to have attracted an audience for his sermons by singing ballads on a bridge people had to cross, and then addressing them as they stopped to listen. In Ine's reign he built a church at Bradford-on-Avon, identified by some with a church which is still standing, and tried to convert the Dumnonian king Geraint from Celtic to Roman ways. In this he was unsuccessful, but he managed to win over many of the

'Welsh' within Ine's kingdom.

His writings give a glimpse of the elegance which, to his disquiet, was spreading among those vowed to the religious life: 'In both sexes the costume consists of a fine linen under-garment, a red or blue tunic, a headdress and sleeves with silk borders; their shoes are covered with red dyed leather . . . . Instead of head coverings they wear white and coloured veils which hang down luxuriantly to the feet and are held in place by headbands sewn on to them.'

Ine made Aldhelm Bishop of Sherborne in 705. Another Wessex churchman whom he picked out, and whose achievement eclipsed both his own and Aldhelm's, was St Boniface. His baptismal name was Winfrith. He was born about 680, probably at Crediton. This was in country recently annexed, his father being doubtless a pioneer Saxon colonist. From a school at Exeter he went to the abbey of Nursling near Romsey, and made a reputation as a brilliant and popular teacher. When he was in his early thirties, Ine employed him as his representative in some dealings with the Archbishop of Canterbury. He now had an assured career. But he had heard of the Frisian mission of Willibrord, and became convinced that he was called to evangelize the heathen in Germany.

With a commission from the Pope — by coincidence, another Gregory — he began to do this in 719, changing his name to Boniface. He first joined Willibrord in Holland, then moved to Hesse, then to Thuringia. The Irish were already there, but Boniface's success was much greater. In 747 he became Archbishop of Mainz. Seven years later he resigned and returned to Holland, where he was killed after a few months by pagan bandits at Dokkum near Leeuwarden.

Boniface is rightly known as the Apostle of Germany. His work among the Germans, and among the Frankish rulers of Gaul, was administrative as well as missionary. He kept in touch with Anglo-Saxon bishops and kings, sending them presents of continental wine, and carrying out little commissions such as the purchase of falcons. A letter of his to an archbishop of Canterbury casts a sidelight on the fashion for pilgrimage to Rome set by King Caedwalla. He urges that women, both laity and nuns, should be discouraged from going (as they often did) alone and without adequate funds. 'Many of them die, and few keep their virtue. In most towns of Lombardy and Gaul, most of the whores are English.'

He also had an interesting dispute with Bishop Ferghil of Salzburg, otherwise Virgil, an Irishman who governed his diocese from a monastery like a true Celt. Boniface objected, and also complained to Pope Zacharias of Virgil's teaching that the earth was round and had people on it at the antipodes. The Pope thought this doctrine might be heretical, but on reflection he decided that it was not. Virgil became a canonized saint in the Roman calendar. While Irishmen might be ahead in science, Boniface's labours in other fields prepared the way for a new political order in western Europe, as Alcuin's did on the level of ideas. The principal scene-setters for Charlemagne were these two Englishmen.

Ine lived to see his protégé's rise. His own dearest religious work was the enrichment and enlargement of Glastonbury, which he began early in his reign. Aldhelm suggested it to him, and may also have encouraged the influx of Irish scholars which so stimulated its life. The monastery was still in appearance what it had been for a long while, a community on the Celtic pattern. It comprised the famous but very simple Old Church, on the site now occupied by the Lady Chapel; the burial plot on the south side of it; a cluster of wattle cells and tiny oratories; and a boundary bank and ditch. In the burial plot were — perhaps — a few monumental stones marking British graves, one of which was — perhaps — a stone eventually taken as marking Arthur's. The monks farmed the less water-logged acres of the surrounding land.

The king made no attempt to remodel the Old Church, which was sacrosanct. For the use of a growing community, however, and for pupils and pilgrims, he built a bigger church to the east. This was of mortared stone. Its plan was a compact continental one, introduced into Britain via Kent. It was dedicated to Dominus Salvator (the Lord our Saviour) and the Apostles Peter and Paul. Outdoors, Ine put up a stone cross with pictorial carvings. Late in his life he embellished both churches with gold and silver. He endowed Glastonbury with several square miles of land, and may also have given it certain exemptions from episcopal authority. In 725 he judged that his earthly task was done. Like Caedwalla he gave up his crown and went to Rome, together with his wife, and spent his last year in retirement visiting the holy places. Shortly afterwards, as Bede testifies, Wessex submitted to the supremacy of Mercia.

3

It should not be supposed that the Mercian kings themselves were immune to the new religious influences. Aethelred became a monk in 704, resigning the crown to his nephew Cenred. In 709 Cenred himself resigned it and followed the path to Rome, accompanied by an East Saxon prince. Both also became monks in the papal city.

But the atmosphere was different. Mercian kings might abdicate out of personal piety, no Mercian king reigned like an Aldfrith or an Ine. The Christianity of the Midlands failed to produce an Aldhelm, a Bede, a Boniface or an Alcuin. One reason was that it lacked the Celtic dimension. St Chad, the first bishop of Lichfield, had been a pupil of Aidan and was imbued with the spirit of Lindisfarne, but chiefly in the sense of humility and simplicity. After his death in 672 the Midlands were not fertile of scholars or missionaries, and claimed only one saint, Guthlac, whose career underlines the difference. Guthlac was a nobleman and former soldier of Aethelred. He went to Crowland or Croyland, then a desolate island in the Fen country, and lived as a hermit and ascetic making friends with the wildfowl. He was beset by demons described as 'ferocious in appearance, with great heads, long necks, thin faces, yellow complexions, filthy beards, shaggy ears'. It is thought that they were Britons, descendants of people who had hidden in the Fens from the Angles.

Little distracted by a religion thus typified, Mercia's kings were ready to pursue power with an energy and efficiency which their neighbours were not equalling. Their main interest lies in their nearly creating a permanent monarchy of England. Aethelred himself, in his early, pre-monastic days, moved into territory belonging to Kent and Essex, and captured London. In 716 Aethelbald entered on a long and successful reign. It has been conjectured that he is the same person as a similarly named pupil of Aldhelm, and if he was, he retained an interest in the composition of Latin verse, but not much else in the way of learning. During a phase when he was out of favour, he had visited Guthlac in his dank retreat and been assured that he would become king, though he must mend his ways. When he did become king he met the saint's requirement after his fashion by founding an abbey on the site. This was the Aethelbald who, when Bede wrote his *History*, was overlord of 'all the kings south of the Humber'. In 740 he partly repaired the obvious omission by invading Northumbria, leaving it ravaged and cowed.

On his death in 757 the next king was Offa, who reigned almost as long — till 796. These two were the eighth and ninth Bretwaldas. A list in the *Anglo-Saxon Chronicle* leaves them out, but the compiler may have been prejudiced. They unquestionably held such a position. If the Mercians did not adopt the actual title, it may have been because their kingdom was formed long after it originated, by settlers whose awareness of 'Britain' was minimal. Yet as a matter of fact, the title 'King of Britain' occurs in a charter of Aethelbald dated 736.

Offa came to be known abroad more accurately as *Rex Anglorum*, 'King of the English'. *Angli* was now increasingly used to mean English-in-general, including Saxons; that function had migrated from one word to the other. The title *Rex Anglorum* had been applied by popes to two previous Bretwaldas, Aethelbert of Kent and Edwin of Northumbria, perhaps mainly as a courtesy. Offa, after a faltering start, set out to give it more substance. His aim was to draw the minor kingdoms into a Mercian empire which would completely overshadow the other two major ones. The minor kingdoms were to become, not subordinate states, but provinces. This programme included secure control of London and Canterbury. London, as such, did not carry political weight; the East Saxon kingdom which had long possessed it was the only one which had never held the Bretwaldaship. But it was growing important economically. Canterbury of course was now the undisputed capital of the Church.

Sussex, Essex and Kent succumbed, the rulers of Sussex being allowed only the style of *duces*, 'dukes'. In 774 we find Offa referred to as 'king of the whole land of the English'. That was premature. It was not until 794 that East Anglia was finally quelled, with the decapitation of its king. Meanwhile, however,

Offa had defeated Wessex, and forced the West Saxons and the Northumbrians to accept the rule of nominees of his own, married to his daughters. The only rebellion was in Kent, and it failed. He had sown bitter resentments which were to work against Mercia later, but his personal triumph was complete. As far, that is, as the English were concerned. Neither Aethelbald nor Offa himself reasserted the Bretwaldaship over other peoples, and Welsh harassment on the frontier was a recurrent problem.

It was Offa's misfortune that the poverty of Mercian learning denied him a biographer or historian. He does not live in imagination as, if sketchily, the Northumbrians do. He is recorded as having founded abbeys, including Bath, and as having added to Glastonbury as an ingratiatory move with Wessex. But ironically his chief monument is Offa's Dyke, marking limitation rather than growth. It defined the Welsh border. Today its northern section has vanished. It emerges into plain view near Tryddyn, on the hills between the Alyn and Clwyd. It passes Wrexham and meets the Dee, then crosses the lower part of the Berwyn mountains to the Severn, six miles below Welshpool. A stretch of the river is here the frontier. Leaving it at Buttington, the Dyke runs north of Montgomery to the Clun forest, and keeps mainly to high ground for twenty miles. In Herefordshire it ceases to be continuous, and for some distance it gives way to the Wye as the frontier-line, but further fragments can be made out near Chepstow.

Apart from its primary purpose the Dyke, if adequately patrolled, could have presented a barrier to raiders and doubtless did. Parts of its course, however, imply local English withdrawals and therefore negotiation rather than edict, recognition of the Welsh rather than total hostility. Curiously, the Anglo-Saxon poem *Widsith* mentions an Offa who fixed a boundary on the continent in the fifth century, before his people moved to Britain. He may have been an ancestor of Offa of Mercia. Perhaps a minstrel sang this poem before the Mercian king and put the notion of the Dyke in his head.

What was happening on the other side of it? Mercia's neighbour along a good deal of the line was Powys. One of its restless kings may have been the Eliseg of the Valle Crucis pillar, with its inscription tracing his ancestry to Maximus. To the north-west was Gwynedd. In the seventh century this kingdom had held a primacy of honour under the descendants of Maelgwn, the most famous being Cadwallon, the conqueror of Edwin. His son Cadwaladr, who died of plague in 664 or 684, was venerated as a saint. He also came to be regarded (it is not clear why) as the last royal embodiment of the old pre-Saxon Britain. Poets prophesied his return to lead the Cymry to victory. Geoffrey of Monmouth confuses him with Caedwalla and, as a result, makes him die in Rome in 689 — Geoffrey's third precise date. The house of Maelgwn did decline after Cadwaladr's death, and by Offa's time it had only a shaky authority outside Anglesey. As for southern Wales, it was divided among several minor states extending from Dyfed to Gwent.

More interesting than the kings' dynastic affairs are the laws they made, and what these reveal about their courts. A code of law for all Wales, compiled in the tenth century under the auspices of King Hywel Dda, assembles much matter from earlier times and various places. A conspicuous feature is the literary element due to the royal bards. They were key figures, and far more than entertainers. Bards were heirs to a large portion of the druidic tradition. Property and power depended on knowledge they preserved — knowledge of pedigrees, customs, precedents. Hence, the kings' secretaries and lawyers worked closely with poets and story-tellers. They acquired a clear-cut, well-stocked vocabulary, mainly native, not Latin. The code of Hywel Dda testifies to a literacy in Welsh government which was quite other than the literacy of the Church.

Few modern Acts of Parliament can match the style of a law defining the penalty for killing or stealing the cat which guards a royal barn. The thief must pay a fine which is assessed by measurement of the cat.

> Its head is to be held downwards on a clean, level floor, and its tail is to be held upwards; and after that, wheat must be poured over it until the tip of its tail is hidden, and that is its value.

In view of the trouble which this method would cause if the animal were still alive, we might almost suspect a sly joke. Out of sheer overflow of spirits, a clerk has added his criteria for a good cat:

It should be perfect of ear, perfect of eye, perfect of teeth, perfect of claw, without marks of fire, and it should kill mice, and not devour its kittens, and should not go caterwauling every new moon.

The Welsh Church, turned in upon itself by the refusal (however understandable) to work with Augustine, had declined a long way from its monastic founders. Still it was far from negligible. In 768 its practices were at last brought into Roman conformity. The reformer's name was Elfodd. He became 'chief bishop in the land of Gwynedd'. Nennius of Bangor, compiler of that chaotic *History of the Britons* which is such a perplexing companion in earlier times, was a disciple of his.

To revert to Offa: his wars, however unprincipled, hurt only a minority, and his peace made many of his subjects richer. He minted golden coins copied from an Arabic dinar. English merchants were spreading through western Europe. In 796 Charlemagne complained that they were trying to evade paying tolls by mingling with parties of pilgrims who were exempt. He also complained that cloaks made in England were too short for continental tastes. Though the Englishman Alcuin was supplying an ideology for Charlemagne's empire, Offa had no intention of joining it. He claimed diplomatic parity, and pursued the first English foreign policy, keeping in touch with Charlemagne himself and the Pope. Throughout most of the eighth century, the England of St Boniface had been the base for papal operations in a large part of Europe, and Rome acknowledged its debt.

Yet Offa's achievement remained a personal one. It always rested on force rather than consent. He failed to found a dynasty. The son who succeeded him in 796 reigned for four months and died. A distant relation, Cenwulf, became king and continued to assert Mercian supremacy, even styling himself *imperator* like Charlemagne. But the foundations were breaking up. And even before, while Offa lived, a grimmer portent had appeared on the horizon.

Norse raiders were prowling about the coast in their ships, and in 793 they destroyed the monastery on Lindisfarne. The following year they did the same to Bede's Jarrow. They were not to return for several decades, but Alcuin appraised the peril correctly. Offa's prolonged wars had united the English after a fashion, but the unity was bogus. They had created unhealed antagonisms — fighting, indeed, was still going on in East Anglia — and they had blotted out old families and loyalties. Alcuin saw history as repeating itself.

> An immense threat hangs over this island and its people. It is a novelty without precedent that the pirate raids of heathens can regularly waste its shores. Yet the English are divided, and king fights against king. Saddest of all, scarcely any heir of the ancient royal houses survives, and the origin of kings is as dubious as their courage . . . . Study Gildas, the wisest of the Britons, and examine the reasons why the ancestors of the Britons lost their kingdom and their fatherland; then look upon yourselves, and you will find among you almost identical causes.

Like Gildas, Alcuin detected a moral failure. The summer of Aldhelm and Bede and Boniface was gone. He wrote to the survivors at Lindisfarne inquiring tactfully whether they had been faithful to the sobriety and simplicity of the past. He also wrote to Aethelred I, the king who governed Northumbria by Offa's leave. His letter reproaches the court with its luxury and fine living. But while there are touches here of a dubious puritanism which could regard the Norse raids as divine punishments, Alcuin sees a deeper flaw, an irresponsible callousness of the ruling class which is a symptom of decay.

> Some labour under an enormity of clothes, others perish with cold. Some are inundated with delicacies and feasts like Dives clothed in purple, and Lazarus dies of hunger at the gate. Where is brotherly love? Where the pity which we are admonished to have for the wretched? The satiety of the rich is the hunger of the poor . . . . Be rulers of the people, not robbers; shepherds, not plunderers.

225

CHAPTER TWELVE

Cerdic's Legacy

1

MERCIAN IMPERIALISM COLLAPSED FIRST IN WESSEX. Offa had settled
its affairs, as he thought, in 786 when the throne fell vacant. A
prince named Egbert, related to both the West Saxon and the
Kentish royal houses, put forward his claim. Offa vetoed it in his
capacity as lord of Kent, excluding Egbert in favour of his own
candidate. Egbert went into exile at the court of Charlemagne.
In 802 another chance presented itself, and he returned to
become king of Wessex unopposed.

Elsewhere Cenwulf maintained Mercian power, skirmishing
with the Northumbrians and hitting the Welsh. But when he died
in 821 the crown passed to his unsatisfactory brother Ceolwulf,
who was deposed after a two-year reign and replaced by the
rebel leader Beornwulf, a person of suspect pedigree. Mercia's
internal strife unleashed the pent-up grievances of its victims. In
825 the East Angles, whose king the relentless Offa had killed,
rose in revolt and restored their dynasty. About the same time
Egbert declared against Mercia and won a victory at Ellendun,
probably near Swindon. Ellendun has been called 'one of the
most decisive battles of Anglo-Saxon history'. Immediately after
it, Sussex, Kent and Essex broke free from Mercia and entrusted
themselves to Egbert's care, becoming provinces of Wessex
instead. He took over Surrey, always a doubtful area, and he
supported the East Angles, becoming their overlord. In 829 he
conquered Mercia itself. Thereupon the Northumbrians acknowledged his paramountcy. So did the Welsh.

Thus, without having to try very hard, Egbert of Wessex
became the tenth Bretwalda. His advisers stressed the ancient
title because it made him heir to an over-kingship which had
existed before Aethelbald and Offa. It impressed on his subjects,
none of whom could remember farther back than those two,
that the rulers of Mercia were not the first of their kind. Egbert,

of course, had not created another empire. Northumbria's homage was mainly a placatory gesture, Mercia shook off his direct control, and the Welsh protectorate did not mean much. But his Bretwaldaship, if diluted, was never directly challenged, and his own greatly enlarged Wessex was an authentic and powerful state. As it turned out, Wessex had the capacity to do more than Mercia had done.

It did not yet include Cornwall. In 815 Egbert had renewed Ine's push westward. Dumnonia seemed to be expiring at last. But the Cornish fought back. In 823 they were still holding Launceston, and a battle beside the River Camel, just above Camelford, was inconclusive. The battlefield has a place in legend through what was almost certainly a mistake. Later generations identified it with Camlann, and the dim recollection of a conflict helped to establish it as the scene of the fatal clash between Arthur and Modred. This was not the only case of Arthurian tradition being located in Cornwall, a country of British-descended people who were still holding out and keeping their stories alive when most of their compatriots had been absorbed into Anglo-Saxondom.

Geoffrey of Monmouth knew the tale. Or perhaps he started it. The bridge over the river was (and still is) called Slaughter Bridge. Here, reputedly, the dead and dying fell in the water till it ran red with blood. John Leland, the Tudor traveller who published the first account of Cadbury-Camelot, visited the place and wrote down what he said was the story as he heard it. Arthur and Modred fought on the bridge hand to hand, and Arthur slew Modred, but not before the traitor had wounded him with a poisoned sword. Arthur staggered away upstream along the river bank and was gone. Leland adds that 'pieces of armour, rings, and brass furniture for horses are sometimes digged up here by countrymen'. If so, they probably dated from 823. At the spot where Arthur might be supposed to have fallen, there lies a stone slab with a memorial inscription in which local fancy once deciphered his name, but erroneously.

Since the real battle failed to break Cornwall's doughty Arthurian remnant, Egbert, as Bretwalda, still had them on his remoter flank. At the time they did not look dangerous. A few years later they did, because they found alarming allies. Forty years after the first descent on Bernicia the Norse returned.

Their marauding in Britain was part of a wider onslaught extending through western Europe and Russia. They are called both 'Vikings' and 'Danes'. The terms are not synonymous, but they overlap. In ninth-century Britain, 'Dane' was the usual word. The cause of this vast explosion was the growth of population in Scandinavia. Early settlers who crossed over to the Shetlands and Orkneys were land-seeking peasants and gave little trouble. After them, however, came waves of aristocratic freebooters and their henchmen — tough, enterprising heathens with a love of wealth and show and few scruples, who went to many places besides the Shetlands and Orkneys. Poetry gives us illuminating glimpses of the court of Harold Fairhair in Norway when these expeditions had been going on for some decades: of the king's 'glorious champions' with their splendid swords, their fine chessmen, their gold and female slaves from the East. Fashions in clothing were copied from the English and Franks, and made more colourful. Silks came from Asia, military hardware from the Rhineland. Harold's picked warriors did not marry; the provision of prostitutes was part of the royal system. This was a male society, where women like the great ladies of Anglo-Saxondom were unthinkable.

During the first half of the ninth century a stream of Norwegian pirate-nobles rounded Cape Wrath and overran the Hebrides and much of Ireland. The Danes, encouraged by divisions in Charlemagne's empire, assailed the Low Countries and Gaul and Spain. They went up the rivers — the Rhine, the Seine, the Garonne. Their penetration of England by way of the Thames and Humber began as one aspect of the wider adventure. At first, like the Saxons themselves in Roman times, these Danes sailed in as plunderers only. A raid in 834 brought them to Sheppey. In 836 another party swooped out of their longships into west Dorset, where Egbert's troops were no match for them. In 838, farther west still, the Cornish accepted Danish aid and the raiders remained ashore as auxiliaries. This time, however, Egbert was better prepared. At Hingston Down near the Tamar he defeated the Danish-Cornish army and, as a bonus, completed the conquest of Dumnonia. Cornish 'kings' survived obscurely in remote places till at least 875, but faded into oblivion.

Egbert's son Aethelwulf succeeded him in 839. Aethelwulf was never Bretwalda, but he enlarged Wessex by incorporating what is now Berkshire. After a brief breathing-space, he had to cope with the beginnings of a national crisis. The Danes continued to appear in various parts of England. In 842 they raided London, and in 850 they made their first prolonged stay ashore. It happened in Thanet, the legendary starting-point of Hengist and Horsa four centuries earlier. Having wintered there, they advanced to storm Canterbury and to put London through a second ordeal, expelling the king of Mercia. South of the Thames, however, they were on West Saxon ground. In 851 Aethelwulf found the Danish host, which was composed of 350 ships' companies, and routed it. The Danes withdrew. Henceforth Wessex was to lead the English resistance.

Even now the real test was some way off. When another Danish force wintered in Sheppey in 854, Aethelwulf took little notice. He had other concerns. He had recently sent his youngest son Alfred to Rome, for a papal blessing. Alfred was then four years old. In 855 Aethelwulf made the pilgrimage himself. Unlike some of his predecessors he had no notion of giving up his crown for good. But his eldest son Aethelbald, supported by a faction among the nobles, organized a coup with a view to preventing him from resuming it. On the way home he strengthened his rebel son's hand by marrying a second wife, Judith, the young daughter of the Frankish monarch Charles the Bald. Public opinion backed Aethelbald in objecting to a thirteen-year-old stepmother. Aethelwulf managed to patch up an arrangement for a shared sovereignty. He died in 858. Aethelbald survived him by only two years (though in those two years he married Judith himself). The next son, Aethelbert, succeeded to the throne unopposed by the third, Aethelred, and the fourth, Alfred; and when Aethelbert died in 865, Aethelred too succeeded without Alfred's making any difficulties. The loyalty and forbearance of that last royal boy prepared the way for his own reign, and foreshadowed its quality.

In the year of Aethelred's accession the storm broke in earnest. Up to now there had been at least twelve Danish raids in force, but nothing like a full-scale invasion. In 865, however, a composite horde recruited largely from Danes settled in Frisia, and known to history as the Great Army, landed in East Anglia and showed no sign of any intention to go away. Few of its members ever did, and their descendants still form part of the English nation. The king of the East Angles, Edmund, bought peace while the Great Army wintered in his kingdom. For a large part of the following year it did not seem to be doing much more than blackmail Edmund . . . and then it stirred, and a time of tribulation began.

The picture we have of this whole period of raiding, settlement and eventual warfare is confused. Chroniclers in England and on the continent surround the Norsemen with an atmosphere of unalloyed horror. They evoke dreadful images of ships with striped sails and dragon prows gliding suddenly into peaceful inlets; of huge foreigners slaughtering harmless peasants, drinking their blood, dragging them through fires for amusement; of horses seized in their pastures and ridden recklessly across country; of priests and monks murdered, churches looted, crosses chopped down for firewood; of pillage, rape and enslavement everywhere. There is no need to question any of this, yet the story has another side. The Danes in England were limited in their objectives. They had little hunger for political power. They were in no hurry to set up governments of their own in occupied territory. This meant anarchy in the short term, but as time went on, many proved their willingness to live with the English and not dominate them, so long as they could manage their own affairs locally. Where co-existence was achieved, trade and crafts flourished, and towns revived as they had not done since the Roman Empire. Yet the transition was slow and agonizing. It fell to a king of Wessex to inflict on the Danes what the Britons had once inflicted on the Anglo-Saxons themselves — a reverse which prevented their triumph in the anarchic and destructive phase, and preserved potentialities which might otherwise have been stamped out.

The Great Army in East Anglia was led by two sons of Ragnar Lothbrok, the most celebrated ninth-century Viking. Their names were Ivar and Halfdan. Ivar was called 'the boneless', seemingly because he was a contortionist, reputed to have gristle instead of bone in his limbs. The invaders spent much of the time collecting horses. When they had enough to be mobile, they headed north plundering. On 1 November 866 they occupied York. Northumbria was embroiled in a civil war between two royal claimants, and the Danes were content to let the rivals wear down each others' forces. On 21 March 867 the claimants at last combined against them, attacked York, and were killed. The Danes allowed a non-entity named Egbert to rule over an enfeebled Northumbria, and moved off to plunder Mercia.

There the Army made its headquarters at Nottingham. The Mercian king, Burgred, had married a sister of Aethelred of Wessex. He asked for help, and Aethelred arrived with his younger brother Alfred, but the Danes simply avoided a major battle and Burgred bought peace with them. Now they retraced their steps, first to York where they remained for a year, and then, in the autumn of 869, to East Anglia. There they seized Thetford. This time King Edmund tried to resist, but was routed and taken prisoner near Hoxne in Suffolk, being then twenty-eight years old. On 20 November the Danes put him to death. According to very early tradition he died a martyr. Ivar made demands which, as a Christian with a duty towards his people, he would not accept. The Dane called upon him to abjure his religion. Edmund refused, whereupon he was tied to a tree, flogged, shot at with arrows so as to wound but not kill, and, after this protracted torture, beheaded. St Edmund the Martyr became a popular saint in medieval England. The abbey of Bury St Edmunds was named after him and possessed his remains.

Soon after this, Ivar drops out of history. He died, or retired, or went to another country; no one knows. Under Halfdan the Army prepared for more sweeping conquests. But it made a false start which was to leave subsequent Danish chieftains with unfinished business. In 870 it probed Wessex, where, at the hands of Aethelwulf, the Danes had suffered their only serious defeat hitherto. His surviving sons proved that Wessex was still different from the rest of England.

From its East Anglian base at Thetford, the Army moved to Reading. Aethelred and Alfred attacked its camp and were repulsed. The Danes followed up their success by ascending Ashdown, the central ridge of Berkshire, which gave an easy route westwards. Finding this blocked by the royal troops, they drew up for battle on the highest ground in two divisions, one led by Danish 'kings', the other by earls. Aethelred responded by dividing his own army, opposing the 'kings' himself, and leaving the earls to his younger brother. He opened the action by hearing mass in his tent and praying. The prayers went on and on while the Danes edged closer and closer. At last Alfred could wait no longer, and ordered a charge. His men had to charge uphill, but they reached the enemy and engaged them. When Aethelred had completed his devotions, and arrived with his own force, the Danes were unable to handle the fresh assailants. They fled back to their camp at Reading with heavy losses.

Ashdown was significant without being decisive. The Danes recovered and won a battle at Basing. That was not decisive either. In April 871 Aethelred died. Though he left children, the situation demanded an adult, and so at twenty-two Alfred was king of Wessex. His reign had a depressing start. While he was attending his brother's funeral at Wimborne, the Danes, reinforced from abroad, won again at Reading. They maintained their advantage yet failed to crush him, and after a few months he was able to negotiate peace, paying a price as other kings had done. In the autumn of 871 the Army withdrew and spent the winter in London, squeezing out an enormous tribute, and minting coins with Halfdan's name on them. The Wessex incident seemed to be closed — a mere hiccup, in modern jargon — and the enriched Army headed north again.

Northumbria had expelled its nominee Egbert. However, any loss in that quarter was more than compensated by total triumph in Mercia, where the Danes planted themselves in 872 and stayed for some time. King Burgred fled from them, taking the old path to Rome. They installed a 'foolish thegn' as Ceolwulf II, on the understanding that he would be compliant and, in particular, would let them into his kingdom whenever they wished.

In 874 the Army divided. Halfdan took part of it to the mouth of the Tyne. Having briefly harried the Picts and the Strathclyde Cymry, he moved into the York area and parcelled out land among his followers. Most of Deira became an improvised Danish state. Obscure Englishmen ruled the rest of a crippled Northumbria. The Army's southern division had a new leader, Guthrum. His base at first was Cambridge. In 877 he showed what the Mercian treaty meant by ripping away half of Ceolwulf's puppet kingdom. That land also was handed out to Danish settlers. But throughout this display of power Alfred was still hovering, not yet reduced to the status of a vassal. Guthrum

was not allowed to forget that the English still had one independent ruler.

2

Towards the middle of the ninth century Scotland and Wales
were both moving towards a single monarchy, just as England
had been, if erratically, before the Norse onslaught. With them
too the Norse advent was an ordeal, but it did not throw the
process into reverse.

Scotland, containing as it did four distinct nations, was the
more complicated case. The battle at Nechtansmere had saved
the Picts and made them supreme over most of Caledonia north
of the Clyde-Forth line. It had not expelled the Northumbrian
Angles from the country between the Forth and the present
Border. Throughout the eighth century the British-descended
people of Strathclyde, with their fortress at Dumbarton, had
remained resilient. As for the Scots of Dalriada, they were
subordinate to the Picts, but growing in numbers and importance. They wielded influence through the Church, which still
had its northern headquarters on their island of Iona. The Picts
tried to control them politically through client rulers, and a
Pictish king showed his religious independence by adopting the
Roman Easter before Iona did.

The king in question was Nechtan II, who began to reign in
706, with Inverness as his chief town. He sent messengers to the
abbot of Wearmouth asking for guidance, and received a reply
going over the Whitby arguments and explaining the Roman
practice, both calendrically and symbolically. At a council presided over by Nechtan the letter was read, translated and approved, and Nechtan ordered the change. This happened in 710.
It opened a phase of royal supremacy in the Pictish Church, with
the king pursuing a policy of orientation towards Rome, and
curtailing the influence of Iona. As for Iona itself, the community
at last conformed about 716.

Nechtan abdicated in 724, and went to live as a hermit in a
remote cave by the sea-shore outside the Cromarty Firth, on the
far side of Nigg. It is still called the King's Cave, and the path
running down to it from the Hill of Nigg is Nechtan's Path. After

two or three years he emerged to intervene in a disputed succession. A tangled civil war finally put Angus I on the Pictish throne. Angus came closer than anybody to uniting the north as Pictland instead of Scotland. In 741 he conquered Dalriada and brought it under his direct rule. In 756 he captured Dumbarton and abridged the power of Strathclyde. During his reign the country acquired its future patron saint. The cult of St Andrew the Apostle may have been known before, but it became popular when some reputed relics were enshrined at the place now called St Andrews. According to legend, Andrew appeared to King Angus in a vision and gave him victory in battle.

Angus I died in 761. Three undistinguished reigns were followed by another spell of confusion, in which the only notable royal figure is a man whose interest lies in romance rather than history. His name was Drust, and he is briefly glimpsed about 780. 'Drust' is the original form of 'Tristan'. It was borne by princes before this one — Drust son of Erp in the fifth century, for instance — and adopted among the Britons. Cunomorus of Cornwall gave it to the son whose monument stands near Fowey, and the love-story of Tristan and Iseult struck root in that neighbourhood. But whether or not this Cornish prince is the 'original' Tristan, the legend incorporates a tale about the eighth-century Pict.

He is known as Drust son of Talorc. In Welsh it becomes Drystan son of Tallwch. The story tells how he came to an island in the Hebrides with several companions, and learned that the daughter of a local chief was to be handed over to three sea-robbers as a tribute. He slew the robbers, suffering only a wound himself, which the maiden bound up with a strip of cloth torn from her dress. Later, when other guests claimed the credit for the deed, she ordered a bath to be made ready and proved who the true champion was by uncovering the bandage. In medieval romance, this tale becomes the episode in which Tristan slays Morholt and is identified while taking a bath. It gives no hint of the love-story itself, but it was current very early, within a few decades of the actual lifetime of Drust.

The next Pictish king of any historical note was Constantine I. In his reign the Norse raiding started. Exploratory crews threaded their way through the Hebrides and attacked Iona three times — in 795, 802 and 806 — killing many monks and causing others to flee to Ireland, with the golden shrine containing St Columba's remains. Constantine intensified Pictish rule over Dalriada and strengthened the defences. The monks returned. So, in 825, did the Norse. They searched in vain for the shrine, which had been buried, and slew the abbot at the altar. Despite this, Iona survived. The Pictish kings continued to struggle against the growing flood of Norsemen. In 839 one of them died in a sea-battle. The Dalriadic Scots under King Alpin shook off Pictish control.

Alpin inherited a state of affairs in which the balance of population had shifted. A century of Dalriadic absorption into the Pictish kingdom had resulted in many Scots going to the richer regions lying eastwards, taking service with Pictish kings and receiving lands on which they settled. They were now numerous in the Forth valley and in Fife. Alpin's mother may have been a Pictish princess; that would have been socially feasible. His reign was short and of no great interest. But his son Kenneth, known to history as Kenneth MacAlpine, succeeded him in 841 and created Scotland as a kingdom in 843.

His action was sudden, conclusive and mysterious. Somehow or other the whole Pictish structure tumbled down. There is no clear evidence for a war of revolution or conquest. If Kenneth had a Pictish grandmother, the Picts' matrilinear customs might have given him a claim to the crown. The strongest tradition is a grim one, and concerns the 'Treachery of Scone'. Kenneth, it is alleged, summoned a conference about the succession. The Pictish nobles assembled as his guests. They sat down to a banquet on benches with bolts which could be pulled out. When Kenneth's agents withdrew the bolts, the benches became trap-doors dropping the nobles into pits where his men slaughtered them.

No king could have seized a realm as large as Pictland by a massacre alone. Presumably Kenneth had a bloc of supporters. These would have included the Scottish immigrants. He formed a party in the Church by reviving the Iona connection, favouring priests of that disposition, and bringing the relics of St Columba to the church at Dunkeld. His reign was efficient, and Norse attacks were few and not very successful. A reference to him as owning 'many stables' suggests that he countered the mounted raiders with mounted units of his own. He made inroads into

Northumbria and Strathclyde, and then formed an alliance with the latter by marrying one of his daughters to its heir-apparent. Two other daughters married Irish princes and became the mothers of Irish kings.

Kenneth MacAlpine died about 858 and was buried at Iona. Much turbulence was to follow, and worse trouble with the Norse, but the combined kingdom remained in being. It was Scotland, but it was not immediately called so. Writers in Latin adapted the ancient name of Britain, Albion. The kingdom became — oddly to a modern reader — Albany or Albania.

For Wales, the prime unifier was a resurgent Gwynedd. In 825 the direct line of Maelgwin came to an end. Power passed to a dynasty founded by Merfyn Frych, 'the Freckled', despite a doubt over his hereditary claims. He may have come from the Isle of Man. Merfyn pulled the kingdom together and married a princess of Powys. Norse raids on Wales may have begun during his reign, and were certainly under way soon after. They were often severe, but the marauders seldom went far inland, and never stayed for long or on a large scale. When Merfyn's son Rhodri succeeded him in 844, the problem was growing but not, as it became in England, catastrophic. His astuteness and energy ensured that it would never become so. In the course of his career as architect of Welsh self-defence, he united most of the country.

Twice during his reign the Danes ravaged Anglesey, where he had his principal residence. The second time he was forced to escape to Ireland. Yet he recovered from every blow. Politically, he appealed to the need for defence against English as well as Danes, and thus gained the support of Cymry who lived away from the coast and were not threatened by the longships. In 855 the aged king of Powys, brother of Merfyn's queen, died on a pilgrimage to Rome. Rhodri, as his nephew, assumed the protectorate of Powys. His prestige was decisive. Powys had seldom felt at ease with its English neighbours, Dyke or no Dyke, and its people accepted the new overlord. In 872 another of the regional kings died by drowning. Rhodri, whose wife Angharad was the dead man's sister, assumed control over a large area of central and southern Wales.

In 877, soon after his return from Ireland, he was murdered by some Englishmen. He passed into Welsh tradition as Rhodri

Mawr, Rhodri the Great. For centuries afterwards, royal status depended on being of Rhodri's blood. Many aspirants were, because he left six sons. These, or some of them, unfortunately shared out their patrimony. But the idea of cohesion was too firmly implanted to destroy. During the following century the union of all Wales was achieved — temporarily, but genuinely — under Hywel Dda of Dyfed, the king who made the aforementioned code of laws. 'Hywel Dda' means 'Hywel the Good'. This is the only Welsh monarch who was ever so called.

3

When Alfred came to the throne of Wessex, in 871, the tiny Hampshire settlement of his ancestor Cerdic had grown into a kingdom stretching from Cornwall to Kent. But unlike the monarchies of Kenneth and Rhodri, it seemed to be past its best days, and doomed to early destruction. Alfred's grandfather Egbert had held the Bretwaldaship, but lost it, for practical purposes, before his death; Alfred's father and brothers could never even aspire to it; and now, with the rest of England submissive to the Danes, the submission of Wessex itself could surely not be far away.

The next round, like the campaign of 870-1, was indecisive. In 875 Guthrum's division of the Great Army reappeared in the kingdom and marched across to Dorset. This was a limited operation, though a prolonged one. The Danes remained within Alfred's territory for two years, extracting money in return for a promise to leave, and then seizing Exeter instead. Alfred at last forced them to retire to Gloucester. Guthrum's next action was his partition of Mercia. When that had been dealt with he turned south again for a final blow. His force was much less numerous than the original Army, not only because of the split, but because many Danes were now making homes on Mercian land and abandoning the life of plunder. But the host which pounced on Chippenham in January 878 (a surprise move in mid-winter) was still very formidable.

At this new shock, many of the West Saxons lost heart and surrendered. Others fled overseas. The Danes poured southwestwards. Alfred, with a few loyal followers, was reduced to wandering among the woods and swamps of Somerset, living off the land and harried even by subjects of his own, who desired peace at any price and resented his keeping up a hopeless resistance. The legend of the burnt cakes belongs to this desperate nadir of English fortunes. About Easter a roving band of Danes reached Glastonbury and sacked the monastery, but did not stay. A few miles beyond, Alfred was in the Isle of Athelney. With the draining of the Somerset marshes Athelney has long ceased to be an island, but the ridge of high ground is still distinct, with a not very impressive monument.

By every rule of probability all was over, yet the embers refused to be quite stamped out. For seven weeks the king harassed the conquerors from his Athelney base. Then he moved across past Frome, and assembled levies from Somerset, Hampshire and Wiltshire. They met at Egbert's Stone near Penselwood, 'and when they saw the king they received him like one risen from the dead, after so great tribulations, and they were filled with great joy'. The English army met Guthrum's main force at Edington, twelve miles south of Chippenham, and routed it. This was the turning of the tide. Guthrum got the survivors back to Chippenham and withstood a two-week siege, but morale was low and he finally accepted terms. He was to give hostages, undergo baptism as a Christian and evacuate Wessex. Some weeks later he brought thirty of his chief men to Alfred for the ceremony. It was held at Aller, across the marsh to the east of Athelney. Alfred stood godfather to him. This time the Danes really did leave Wessex. The offensive spirit had not deserted them — they began an intensive occupation of East Anglia — but the crisis of imminent annihilation was past.

In 884 a new Danish host swooped on Kent and some of Guthrum's veterans helped it. Again Alfred was driven into war, and he evicted the Danish garrison from London and took the city. He did not annex it, but respected its Mercian status — now more than a century old — and handed it over to a noble named Aethelred who was governing what remained of Mercia. Aethelred married Alfred's eldest daughter Aethelflaed and accepted him as overlord. The return of London to English control had a crucial moral impact. It proved that the Danes could be rolled back, and it made Alfred the natural and acknowledged leader of all who still hoped. A treaty with Guthrum defined a boundary, conceding Danish settlement in a large part of England, but also forbidding it outside. The line ran up the Thames to the point where the Lea flows into it; then up the Lea to its source; then across to Bedford and along the Ouse; and then along Watling Street. The arrangements to the north are less clear, and other bodies of Danes undoubtedly held Leicester and York. However, the main point was the security of the land on Alfred's side as English.

He was an extraordinary person, one of the few truly extraordinary kings, and amply deserved to be called 'the Great'. His childhood had been distracted; he did not learn to read till he was past his twelfth birthday. All through his arduous life he was plagued by a disordered stomach. Yet he plodded on and on with a doggedness and a curious sober versatility which made his reign an achievement hard to parallel.

His normal surroundings and mode of living were in no way spectacular. Beside the flamboyant Norsemen, he might have looked as drab as most of his subjects. His manor at Cheddar covered a mere two acres. Its main timber hall was 78 feet long and 20 wide, with porched entrances in its long sides, and probably an upper floor. There were two smaller buildings, 25 feet by 14, and 30 by 24. The latter may have been a workshop. In this and similar dwellings, when he was not campaigning, Alfred followed the pursuits of a country gentleman with a broadening of horizons which was new. He hunted and hawked, and was expert enough to give advice to his falconers and kennelmen. He collected Anglo-Saxon poems and songs, such as he had heard, loved and learned by heart before he could read. He entertained travellers and listened to their tales of remote countries. One of his visitors was a Norwegian, Ohthere, who had sailed round to the White Sea. He planned his time by inventing a kind of clock — a lantern made of horn planed so thin as to be transparent, with a socket inside for a graduated candle. This burned down at a constant rate because it was shielded from draughts whichever way they blew.

In the spell of peace after the capture of London he launched a programme of education, aimed especially at the clergy. Alfred was devout but extremely critical. With a view to raising standards, he brought foreign scholars to his court. They included Grimbald, a Frank; John, a German; and Asser, a Welshman.

Asser became a close friend and wrote the king's biography. English scholars had become few, but several joined the project, including at least four Mercians. The king took the lead in person. He learned Latin and presided over the translation of a number of books into 'the language which we can all understand' — an obvious thing to do, yet almost unprecedented, and not to be paralleled on the continent until centuries later.

One of the books was Bede's monumental account of the English Church and people. Another, which the king himself translated, was a fifth-century compilation of world history by Orosius. He did more than translate it, he added notes of his own, recording, among much else, the geographical matter which he had picked up from travellers like Ohthere. Another translation he made in person was a version of the *Consolation of Philosophy* by the sixth-century statesman Boethius. Its special interest for him lay in Boethius's attempt to show how a man in a responsible position could best cope with disaster and rise above it. Boethius was no armchair preacher. He wrote the book while in prison under sentence of death.

So that his work and his team's should not be wasted, Alfred founded a school at his court for the sons of nobles from all over the kingdom. His own sons attended it. This was not a scheme for democracy or equality. It was, in modern language, élitist. What Alfred wanted to do was to improve the quality of the élite, both clerical and lay. He cherished a hope that the social extent of education might widen, but it was a guarded hope. In a letter to Werferth, one of his assistants, he voiced his cautious ideal — that 'all the youth of freemen which now is in England, who are rich enough to be able to devote themselves to it, be set to learn as long as they are not fit for any other occupation'.

To enlighten the English on their own past, he sponsored the first version of the *Anglo-Saxon Chronicle*. He also published a code of laws which brought together what he judged to be best in the laws of Aethelbert of Kent, Ine of Wessex and Offa of Mercia. (Geoffrey of Monmouth, it will be recalled, claimed that Alfred got them from the early British king Molmutius and the early British queen Marcia, the latter being conveniently named to account for the Mercian part of the code.) Alfred added more laws of his own, aimed at protecting the underprivileged, limiting the custom of blood-feud, and promoting a more cooperative, less violent society. His code was meant to apply wherever the English accepted his supremacy. Many did, outside Wessex as well as within it. Several minor princes in Wales also placed themselves under his protection. Rhodri's eldest son Anarawd, who ruled in Gwynedd, paid a state visit to his court and became his ally. Hywel Dda in the following century seems to have taken Alfred as a model, codifying the laws as he had done and cultivating the friendship of his successors.

Peace did not last. In 892 a fresh horde of Danes entered England from across the Channel. They were joined by bands of settlers from East Anglia and the north. They still held the initiative, but now Alfred was mastering the situation. He had built forts, and raised walls round centres of population, so that goods, cattle and horses could be enclosed, and the Danes could neither loot nor seize mounts for mobile warfare. They marched about aimlessly for some years, tried living off the country in Wales, and were defeated in 895 and dispersed in 896. After this — a better-known measure than his programme of fortification — Alfred created a navy. Royal ships had fought Danish ones as early as 877, when they intercepted sea-borne reinforcements approaching Exeter. The vessels which Alfred commissioned in his last years were larger and faster than anything the Danes possessed. They were of deep draught and manned by at least sixty rowers. With this fleet in being, the English could always prevent a sustained invasion. The restoration of control over the Danish settlements was a credible prospect.

Alfred died on 26 October 899. Within less than forty years the logic of his reign worked out to fulfilment. The English kingdoms other than Wessex were now no more than a memory. Alfred's successors could revive the unity once created by Mercia and revive it far more effectively, since the expansion of Wessex was generally welcome. In the territory known as the Danelaw, where the families of the Great Army lived, the English did not resist and the Danes themselves resisted only half-heartedly; their holdings and local jurisdiction were respected, and they cared more about those than they did about political sovereignty. Alfred's son Edward, and Alfred's capable daughter Aethelflaed (whose marriage had made her 'Lady of the Mercians', supreme after her husband's death), pushed the English frontier forward. Edward became king of the Mercians as well as the West Saxons when Aethelflaed died. In 918 he held the line of the Humber. His son Athelstan pressed on. The struggle for the north was harder, involving not only Norsemen but allied armies from Scotland and Ireland. Athelstan was equal to all his enemies together, and in 937 he scattered them and was king of England, with a paramountcy uncontested beyond.

4

Through every twist of fortune, the imperial singleness of Britain had survived as an idea. It passed to the Anglo-Saxons even when they were wholly barbaric, and they expressed it in the title Bretwalda, Britain-ruler. If they had conquered quickly they might have forgotten it, destroyed everything they overran, and effaced all continuity. But events in Britain took an unparalleled course. It is worth saying once more: here the people of a Roman land had become independent before the barbarians arrived, and they put up a fight. The battle of Badon virtually stopped the advance for decades, and even when it resumed it was gradual. The Anglo-Saxons did not reach the limit of their expansion until they were becoming civilized themselves. Darkness never extended from sea to sea, destruction of the old order was never general. Awareness of the country, its heritage, its earlier population, always existed. The title of Bretwalda revived and carried more and more weight until, with Offa and Egbert, it came close to standing for a genuine sovereignty which went much deeper than the supremacy of a barbaric chief.

Moreover, the formation of England as the main successor-state of the Roman Britannia had a special character. Badon and its aftermath did not affect Anglo-Saxondom socially or economically, but did affect it politically. During the pause, the small kingdoms became firmly entrenched in separateness. Each had its god-descended dynasty, each turned inwards and concerned itself with its own affairs. As they began to grow, predominance shifted from one kingdom to another. None was strong enough to impose a lasting union. When final union did come, through Wessex, it had been prepared by the imperialism of rulers like Offa but was itself more of an integration. The process of realizing the idea of a single kingdom in Britain influenced the product. Each of the units which were integrated had endured long enough to acquire a character of its own, with a bias which was not democratic but was certainly anti-authoritarian.

In a kingdom the size of Sussex or Essex, a governmental machine could not exist because there was not enough for it to do. Taxes could be paid in directly to the royal household. Grievances could be brought to the king in person. In bigger kingdoms authority was more distant, and government developed, with the beginnings of a civil service. But when a big kingdom's power extended, and especially when it took over one of the smaller ones, it had to come to terms with bodies of deeply-entrenched tradition and custom upheld by local dignitaries. Even long afterwards, countless little shire-courts and hundred-courts conserved local equity. The putting-together of England was a work of creative reconciliation.

In the early Middle Ages, the monarchies of England and France looked very much alike. But their dynamics were different. The French monarchy had been formed swiftly by one monarch, Clovis, and the feudal scheme had resulted from a weakening of its grip; the nobles had pulled away and annexed more power to themselves. In England the movement had been the other way. Small units had been gradually fitted into large ones. Regional earls were not would-be kings, they were the successors of men who had been kings long before. Their status was based on a past surrender of power and a past acceptance of responsibility. England was centripetal rather than centrifugal. It did not tear itself apart. The consequences have never ceased to be felt, in society and in politics.

Wales and Scotland followed more turbulent courses. Yet from Wales came a mystique of the monarchy which overspread Britain, the Island of the Mighty, as Cymric nostalgia dubbed it. Behind the Welshman, behind the Englishman, there was a more legendary vision of past unity and greatness. In the twelfth century, Geoffrey of Monmouth's *History* revived and expanded it. Arthur's ghost glorified the kings, Plantagenet and Tudor, who claimed to be his successors. The realm of Arthur was a fable. But the tradition of a past unity was not, and the antiquity of the royalty of England was not. The line began with Cerdic of the West Saxons. It ran through their later kings — Ceawlin the second Bretwalda, Cynegils, Cenwalh, Ine and the rest — to Egbert the tenth Bretwalda; and from him, by a well-attested hereditary descent, through Alfred the Great to Athelstan who ruled all England. The crown passed for a while to Scandinavians and Normans, but the line ran on through the wife of Henry I to his grandson Henry II and all sovereigns after him. As it extended further, the English crown became the Welsh and Scottish as well.

The House of Windsor derives from that mysterious chieftain who sailed into the waters behind the Isle of Wight towards the close of the fifth century. Where he came from, nobody knows. His chieftaincy was Saxon, his name was British. Part of his ancestry, perhaps, lay in that obscure post-Roman Britannia where the memory of Maximus lingered, and princes claimed to rule by Roman authority. If we possessed the remoter facts, they might turn out to be very strange indeed.

To explore the early history is to be conscious, despite all wars and upheavals, of a continuity which is seldom broken as sharply as it sometimes appears to be. Those who hold power are quite properly distinguished as Romans and Britons, Anglo-Saxons and Picts and Scots. Yet they cannot be rigidly kept apart. A Roman emperor is an honorary Briton. A Saxon chief is the Bretwalda, the Britain-ruler. A Pictish prince becomes part of a legend of sixth-century Cornwall. A Scottish king names his son 'Arthur'. Britain transcends their limitations, and makes all of them her own.

Chronological Table

Geoffrey of Monmouth's dates for the early monarchs are imaginary, and it would be misleading to give them here. From 55 B.C. to A.D. 440 some dates are approximate. These are indicated by *c. (circa)*. Between 440 and 500 it would usually be pretentious to give even a *'circa'* date. Except with Riothamus, who can be fixed fairly precisely, I have generally suggested five-year and ten-year intervals. After 500, most dates are given without qualification, but many are subject to a small margin of error.

B.C.

55	Julius Caesar's first British expedition.
54	Julius Caesar's second British expedition, opposed by Cassivellaunus.
c. 50-25	Commius, king of the Atrebates.

A.D.

c. 5-41	Cunobelinus (Cymbeline), king of the Catuvellauni.
43	Claudius's invasion of Britain.
51	Defeat of Caratacus.
60-61	Paullinus's conquest of Anglesey and Boudicca's revolt. Over the next few years, client monarchs are abolished in Roman Britain. End of Cartimandua's rule in the north.
287	Carausius, independent emperor of Roman Britain.
293	Allectus murders Carausius and succeeds him.
296	Reconquest of Britain by Constantius.
306	Constantine proclaimed emperor at York.
313	Edict of Milan granting toleration to Christians.
323	Constantine sole emperor.
325	Council of Nicaea.
c. 326	Helena in Jerusalem.
367-9	Barbarians overrun Britain. Reconquest by Theodosius the elder.
383	Maximus proclaimed emperor in Britain.
388	Maximus is defeated by Theodosius the younger. Legendary foundation of Brittany about this time by Conan Meriadoc.

396-8	Stilicho's reorganization of British defences (the first 'rescue' according to Gildas).
406	Proclamation of Marcus and Gratian as emperors in Britain.
407	Proclamation of Constantine III as emperor in Britain.
410	Heavy Saxon raiding. Britain becomes independent. Honorius authorizes British self-defence.
411	Death of Constantine III.
c. 425	Rise of Vortigern.
c. 428	First authorized settlement of Saxon mercenaries. Saxon raiding and squatting elsewhere.
429	St Germanus in Britain. 'Hallelujah Victory' over raiding Saxons and Picts.
432	St Patrick in Ireland.
440	Probable further Saxon settlement followed by partial loss of British control.
446	(according to Gildas) British appeal to Aëtius.
450	Further Saxon settlement.
455	General Saxon revolt under way. Widespread plundering and devastation over the next few years. Death of Vortigern. Hengist in Kent.
455-60	British refugee movement to Armorica, the historical foundation of Brittany. Coroticus, independent ruler of Clyde.
465	Round about this time, Saxon withdrawal to settlements and partial containment. Ambrosius Aurelianus in charge of counter-measures.
469-70	Riothamus, the British 'High King', in Gaul. (His campaign and departure form part of the basis of the Arthurian Legend.)
470-500	Renewed Saxon pressure and land-seizure, and invasion at new points. Political break-up of Britain. Confused warfare. Possible activity of force called 'Arthur's men'.
477	(according to *Anglo-Saxon Chronicle*) Aelle initiates South Saxon kingdom. He becomes the first Bretwalda.
495	(according to *Anglo-Saxon Chronicle*) Cerdic initiates West Saxon occupation of Hampshire.
500	Round about this time, the 'siege of Mount Badon' somewhere in southern Britain, a British victory followed by a spell of relative peace. St Illtud's school flourishing at Llantwit Major.
510-20	Increasing British migration to Armorica.
c. 519	West Saxon dynasty established in Hampshire.
531	Some Angles returning to the continent.
540-5	Gildas writing. Five British kings named by him, the most important being Maelgwn of Gwynedd.
545-50	Plague in Britain. Death of Maelgwn.

547	Beginning of kingdom of Northumbrian Angles under Ida.
c. 550	West Saxon advance from the south resumed.
563	St Columba at Iona.
577	Ceawlin of Wessex, the second Bretwalda, defeats the Britons at Dyrham and reaches the Severn.
570-90	Urbgen of Rheged leads resistance to northern Angles. Early Welsh poets including Taliesin.
c. 584	Origin of Mercia.
597	St Augustine's mission to Aethelbert of Kent, the third Bretwalda, compiler of the first code of written English laws.
c. 598	British defeat at Catterick, commemorated in Aneirin's *Gododdin*.
603	Aethelfrith of Bernicia defeats Aedan, the Britons' Scottish ally.
605	Aethelfrith occupies York. United Northumbrian kingdom.
614	Aethelfrith defeats Welsh at Chester.
616	Raedwald of East Anglia, the fourth Bretwalda.
617	Edwin, king of Northumbria.
c. 625	Death of Raedwald. Edwin becomes the fifth Bretwalda.
625	Aethelburga arrives in Northumbria with Paulinus.
627	Baptism of Edwin.
633	Cadwallon and Penda defeat and kill Edwin at Hatfield Chase. Welsh ravage Northumbria.
634	Oswald defeats and kills Cadwallon, and becomes king of Northumbria and sixth Bretwalda. Shortly afterwards he brings St Aidan to Lindisfarne.
635	Baptism of Cynegils of Wessex.
642	Oswald killed near Oswestry by Penda of Mercia with Welsh allies. Oswy becomes king of Northumbria, which is invaded several times by Penda over the next few years.
655	Defeat and death of Penda at the Winwaed. Oswy henceforth the seventh Bretwalda.
658	Cenwalh of Wessex takes Glastonbury and makes it a 'temple of reconciliation'.
663	Synod of Whitby.
664 or 684	Death of Cadwaladr.
670	Death of Oswy. End of Northumbrian Bretwaldaship.
685	Pictish victory of Nechtansmere turns back English penetration of Caledonia. Aldfrith becomes king of Northumbria and presides over a cultural 'golden age'.
686	Caedwalla of Wessex conquers and forcibly Christianizes the Isle of Wight.
689	Caedwalla dies in Rome. Ine becomes king of Wessex. Patronage of Aldhelm and other churchmen including

	Boniface, and enlargement of Glastonbury. Code of laws.
716	Aethelbald, king of Mercia. He becomes the eighth Bretwalda.
735	Death of Bede.
756	Pictish power at apex under Angus I.
757	Offa, king of Mercia. He becomes the ninth Bretwalda. Mercia absorbs smaller kingdoms.
781	Alcuin at court of Charlemagne.
793	Norse raid on Lindisfarne.
796	Death of Offa.
802	Egbert, king of Wessex.
829	Egbert becomes the tenth Bretwalda.
834	Beginning of Danish attacks on England.
838	Wessex absorbs Cornwall.
843	Kenneth MacAlpine forms united Pictish-Scottish kingdom.
865	Arrival of Danish 'Great Army'.
869	Martyrdom of Edmund, king of East Anglia.
870	Aethelred and Alfred of Wessex repulse Danes at Ashdown.
871	Alfred, king of Wessex.
872	Most of Wales ruled by Rhodri the Great.
871-7	Danish domination of England outside Wessex.
878	Danes under Guthrum in Wessex. Alfred at Athelney, from which he emerges to rout Guthrum at Edington.
884	Alfred recaptures London. Treaty with Danes. Alfred begins educational programme and brings foreign scholars to his court.
896	Alfred creates a navy.
899	Death of Alfred. England unified in ensuing four decades by his son, daughter and grandson.

Bibliographical Notes

The following list is a classified selection. Most of the books have bibliographies and references which are much fuller than this, so that a reader will find no difficulty in exploring further.

There are no individual biographies here. Britain's early rulers do not lend themselves to that treatment. They have to be evoked in their setting, whether authentic or fictitious.

British legend and historical tradition

(1) Early texts

Geoffrey of Monmouth, *The History of the Kings of Britain*, translated by Lewis Thorpe (Penguin, 1966).

Gildas, edited and translated under the title *The Ruin of Britain* by Michael Winterbottom. In *History from the Sources*, vol. 7 (Phillimore, Chichester, 1978).

Mabinogion, translated by Gwyn and Thomas Jones (Dent, 1949).

Nennius, edited and translated under the title *British History* (with *The Welsh Annals*, i.e. *Annales Cambriae*) by John Morris. In *History from the Sources*, vol. 8 (Phillimore, Chichester, 1980).

(2) Background and critical study

The introductions to the foregoing volumes. Also:

Kendrick, T. D., *British Antiquity* (Methuen, 1950).

Piggott, Stuart, *The Druids* (Penguin, 1974; Thames and Hudson, 1985).

Ross, Anne, *Pagan Celtic Britain* (Cardinal, 1974).

Tatlock, J.S.P., *The Legendary History of Britain* (University of California Press, Berkeley and Los Angeles, 1950). This is the major study of Geoffrey of Monmouth, but Tatlock's view of his role in the growth of Arthurian literature is not generally accepted.

Pre-Roman Britain and the Roman connection

Frere, Sheppard, *Britannia* (Routledge and Kegan Paul, 1967).

Jones, A.H.M., *Constantine and the Conversion of Europe* (English Universities Press, 1948).

My own book, *From Caesar to Arthur* (Collins, 1960), details the sources of information for the last phase.

Kings and Queens of Early Britain

Saints, royal and otherwise

Butler, Alban, *Lives of the Saints,* revised and edited by H. Thurston and D. Attwater, 4 vols (Burns Oates and Washbourne, 1956).

Post-Roman Britain and the Arthurian question

Alcock, Leslie, *Arthur's Britain* (Allen Lane, The Penguin Press, 1971).

Alcock, Leslie, *'By South Cadbury is that Camelot ...'* (Thames and Hudson, 1972).

Ashe, Geoffrey, *The Discovery of King Arthur* (H. Holt, 1985). Contains further developments on the theories presented here.

Chadwick, N.K., ed. *Studies in Early British History* (Cambridge University Press, 1954).

Chambers, E.K., *Arthur of Britain* (Sidgwick and Jackson, 1927). Out of date in many respects, but useful for reproductions of source-documents.

Lacy, Norris J., *The Arthurian Encyclopedia* (Garland, 1986). Now the standard reference work.

Loomis, R.S., ed. *Arthurian Literature in the Middle Ages* (Oxford, Clarendon Press, 1959). Early chapters are relevant.

Morris, John, *The Age of Arthur* (Weidenfeld and Nicolson, 1973). Also three-part revised edition in Phillimore, *History from the Sources,* vols 1, 2, 3. Valuable for material on society, politics and modes of life. Some of the historical reconstruction has been strongly criticized.

I should also mention *The Quest for Arthur's Britain* (Academy Chicago Publishers, 1987), edited by myself. As a general illustrated survey, it has not been superseded. Some of my revised ideas on the origin of the figure of Arthur are set forth with documentation in the article 'A Certain Very Ancient Book', published in the April 1981 issue of *Speculum,* the journal of the Medieval Academy of America, Cambridge, Massachusetts. *The Arthurian Handbook* (Garland, 1988), on which Norris Lacy and I collaborated, presents supplemental material as well.

Anglo-Saxon England

(1) Early texts

Anglo-Saxon Chronicle, edited by G. N. Garmonsway (Dent, 1953).

Bede, *A History of the English Church and People,* translated by Leo Sherley-Price (Penguin, 1955).

(2) General

Blair, Peter Hunter, *An Introduction to Anglo-Saxon England* (Cambridge University Press, second edn, 1977).

Duckett, Eleanor Shipley, *Anglo-Saxon Saints and Scholars* (Macmillan, 1947).

Finberg, H.P.R., *The Formation of England, 550-1042* (Hart-Davis, MacGibbon, 1974).

Hodgkin, R.H., *A History of the Anglo-Saxons*, 2 vols (Oxford, Clarendon Press, third edn, 1952).

Morris, John, *The Age of Arthur.*

Stenton, F.M., *Anglo-Saxon England* (Oxford, Clarendon Press, 1943).

Wales

Clancy, Joseph P., *The Earliest Welsh Poetry* (Macmillan, 1970).

Lloyd, John Edward, *A History of Wales*, 2 vols (Longmans, Green, 1939).

Morris, John, *The Age of Arthur.*

Parry, Thomas, *A History of Welsh Literature* (Oxford, Clarendon Press, 1955).

Scotland

Mackenzie, Donald A., *Scotland: the Ancient Kingdom* (Blackie, 1930).

Morris, John, *The Age of Arthur.*

Index

Codes: G. of M. = Geoffrey of Monmouth, k. = king,
q. = queen, Il. = illustration

255

Index